D0876312

I Love This Book!

Jack Canfield
Cocreator of the *Chicken Soup for the Soul* Series®
The Success Principles™
Featured Teacher in *The Secret*

There's nothing more important than being a great parent. But imparting life lessons and giving the gift of guidance isn't always easy. *If I Were Your Daddy, This Is What You'd Learn* allows you to stand on the shoulders of giants—those successful fathers, mentors, and friends who left their legacy. Whether you're a single parent or you just need a refresher on the important things in life, these stories from great dads are inspirational, educational, and ultimately effective ways to make informed choices and instill the best values in yourself and your kids.

Stephen M. R. Covey
Author of *New York Times* and #1 *Wall Street Journal*
Bestseller *The Speed of Trust*

In my practice as a family therapist, I often meet parents who clearly know they don't want to repeat the same mistakes their parents made. But it's often quite challenging for them to figure out what to do differently, and how to implement that difference. This book is the missing link!

Dr. Karen Ruskin, Psy.D., LMFT
Author, *The 9 Key Techniques For Raising Respectful Children
Who Make Responsible Choices,* and *Dr. Karen's Marriage
Manual—Do's and Don'ts*

This book will make a huge difference in the world ... for those who have kids or are going to have kids.

John Assaraf
Real Estate Entrepreneur & Best-Selling Author

Thank you for creating this book!

T. Harv Eker
Best-Selling Author, *Secrets of the Millionaire Mind*

If I Were Your Daddy delivers wisdom from thirty-five successful frontline dads—with parenting ideas for the modern world. As you read it, you may find yourself being parented along the way by some of these amazing men. As this fathering wisdom goes in deep, it will heal you, empower you, and enable you to pass these transforming gifts along to your own children."

Janet Matthews
Editor, Professional Speaker, and Coauthor,
Chicken Soup for the Canadian Soul

As I learned with *7 Habits*, best-selling books have important messages that resonate with readers. *If I Were Your Daddy* definitely resonates and is destined to be a very successful book.

Greg Link
CoveyLink Marketing Mastermind to
The 7 Habits of Highly Effective People
and *The Speed of Trust*

This is a magnificent book—a veritable treasure trove for any parent.

Dr. Kim A. Jobst, D.M.
Leading UK Physician & Fellow, The Prince of Wales' Foundation for
Integrated Health

Growing up in a violent home, I had no idea what true fathering could be. My father was a bully who tore the family apart with his selfishness. I had to raise myself, always working to learn more and grow beyond these circumstances. Julia—by writing *If I Were Your Daddy, This Is What You'd Learn* you have given me a greater vision and hope. These stories of fathers offering their children the benefit of their experience and wisdom have melted my heart, and opened me to the possibilities of family.

Barbara von Mettenheim, Ph.D.

Research shows that today, only about 50 percent of men feel prepared to become fathers, and more than half feel they can be easily replaced. With 24 million children living apart from their fathers, it's clear that too many men are responding to their own sense of inadequacy on how to be a father, and their absence will leave a hole in their children's souls, the exact shape of their dad. Through experienced role models, *If I Were Your Daddy* delivers to men the practical skills they need to be the kinds of dads their kids need them to be. This book is one of the most important gifts a woman can give to the fathers in her life.

Roland Warren
National Fatherhood Initiative
President and CEO

IF I WERE YOUR DADDY
THIS IS WHAT YOU'D
Learn

IF I WERE YOUR **DADDY**
THIS IS WHAT YOU'D *Learn*

Julia Espey

Foreword
By
Jack Canfield
Cocreator of
Chicken Soup for the Soul®

Courtland Publishing LLC
www.courtlandpublishing.com

Published by Courtland Publishing, Minneapolis, Minnesota.

FIRST EDITION

Courtland Publishing titles may be purchased in bulk for educational, business, fundraising, or sales promotional use. For information, please e-mail: specialmarkets@courtlandpublishing.com

Content Editing, Style, and Production Assistance by Janet Matthews
Additional Editing and Proofreading by Kenneth W. Davis
Production, Cover Art, and Book Design by Heidi Spaeth

Library of Congress Cataloging-in-Publication Data

If I Were Your Daddy, This Is What You'd Learn: inspiring parenting practices and real-life stories told by fathers who are successful in all areas. [compiled by] Julia Espey.

ISBN: 978-1-936623-00-6
   1. Self-Help. 2. Success—Psychological aspects 3. Parenting
   I. Espey, Julia.   II. Title.

Printed in the United States of America

DISCLAIMER

This book was written to assist parents everywhere in becoming better, more successful, more inspired parents. The lessons, experiences, insights, and wisdom that are related by the dads in this book are their own opinions and do not necessarily reflect the opinion of the author. This book offers no guarantee of success or of reproducing any of the results achieved by the dads interviewed for this book. In fact, one of the key concepts in the book is that people's lives and how they parent are as unique as the people themselves. Use this book and the ideas it contains to stimulate and expand your own thoughts and ideas about parenting, and what might be right for you and your family.

Every effort has been made to make this book as complete and accurate as possible. However, there may be errors both typographical and in content. The text should be used as a general guide, and not as the ultimate source for parenting or life wisdom.

The purpose of this book is to educate and inspire. The author and publisher assume no liability for any loss or damages alleged to be caused by the contents or ideas contained in the book. Please consult the appropriate professionals to obtain specific information regarding your personal family situation, and the needs of your children.

*This book is dedicated to
all the mommies who have to be daddies too,
to the daddies who want to be better daddies,*

*and to my son,
Jackson Courtland Espey,
my inspiration.*

great

One idea can change a life™

CONTENTS

WINNING STRATEGIES

UTILIZING SUPPORT

MONEY & RESPONSIBILITY

TOUGHER STUFF

REACHING HIGHER

ACKNOWLEDGMENTS

It takes a village to write a book. I've been blessed with a really amazing village. My deep thanks go . . .

. . . To all the dads in this book. Many of you didn't know me, but you trusted I'd do justice to your words and stories. Only through your generosity to me, and to this project, is this book possible. I am deeply humbled to know each of you. Thanks as well to the many dads I interviewed but—due to strict manuscript length requirements—just didn't have room for: Ray Fuqua, Dr. Gordon Ray, Chris Widener, Mike McCreesh, Ralph Metcalfe, and at least a dozen more whom I interviewed informally.

. . . to Jack Canfield, who walks his talk, and is a quintessential teacher who hasn't let his success go to his ego or cover over his heart. I will be eternally grateful for your support and enthusiasm for this book, and for caring so much for others.

. . . to my new husband, Lance, who kept me and the project alive, especially during the last few months. This includes your incredible research capacity—discovering and creating an incredible way to fund this project with committed supporters—and for taking over many duties for Jackson and our household, and for keeping me nourished and together through this long journey. Thanks also to my son, Jackson, for your incredible patience in sharing your mommy's time with the book!

. . . to my parents, Nickie and Jim Whitehead, for Mom's edits and devoted assistance, and Dad's unconditional support of whatever I do. Thanks also to the most influential professor ever, Dr. Ken Asher, for English, who saw something special in me and gave me the confidence to be a writer.

. . . to Marilyn Craigie, Judy Kudlow, Melodie and Michael Smulders, and Claudia Quill, who helped form my character, became my family, and supported me in raising Jackson solo for many years. Thanks as well to Suzy and JR Hightower, George Handley, and Lois Hornsby for your love and unconditional support for whatever I'm up to next. Thanks to Bruce

Hornsby for the rights to use your song "Fields of Gray" for the book overview video.

... to Judith Whitmore, for seeing the initial vision, for the courage to contact the first dads, and for all of your support. Thanks also to Brent Routman, Olga Graf, Cristobal Wagner, and Linda and Scott Wilkerson for your late-night discussions and friendship.

... to TUG founder Jim Bunch, whose support has been awesome; and to Phil Black and The Ultimate Game of Life (TUG) community, who opened their Rolodexes and encouraged me on for years.

... to William Watkins, for your above-and-beyond efforts to get Jonathan Reckford to be a part of this book; and to the many people who introduced me to other dads, including Jonathan Khorsandi, Stacy Steel, Bill Bindseil, Shelly Lefkoe, Barbara Duff, Andrew Flack and Jeff Smith. Thanks also to all of the dads who checked their address books and said, "Oh, this guy's got to be included," then opened a closed door for me.

... to Robert Callan, for enthusiastically championing me and this book idea early on; to Paul and Libby Scheele, who talked me off of ledges (several times), held my hand, and always encouraged me; to my "sisters," Liana Chaouli, Kimberly Joyce, and Diane Halfman; to Murray Rosenthal, for being my best "worst-case scenerio" guy and a great advisor; to Nick Nerangis, who is constantly working for the welfare of others; and to Dr. Roy Martina, Dr. Brian Alman, Dr. Kim Jobst, Dr. Shore Slocum, and Dean Kosage, Adora Sauer, Barbara von Mettenheim, and Dr. Karen Ruskin for making yourself available whenever I needed help or advice.

... to Tim Johnson, Kenny and Laurie Whitehead, Nancy Breslin, Micheal Bissonette, and Jason Gore, for your support and encouragement; to Greg and Annie Link for your expert advice over a private lunch— advice I tried to follow to the T—; to Terry Tillman, for months of pro bono mentorship; to Jack Elias, Nicole DeMario, and Jerry and Jessica Conti for your unfailing positivity.

... to the dads' associates, who tapped on shoulders and made sure everything got done on time, and who supported this book: Vincent DiCaro, Bonnie Watson, Tami Harmon, Alice Pennington, Leanne

Little, Hallina Popko, and Carole Burt from Kip Forbes' office; to Debra Orenstein for your expert literary legal support; and to dear friends Karen Sorbo and Zao, for your assistance reaching nonprofits.

… to Adrienne Sappa, for your initial cover design; to photographer Lewis Kostiner; to Kitty Shea for your early edits, professionalism, and contacts; to Michele Hodgson; and to Travis Schlaht for your willingness to make cartoons.

… to Melissa Greczy, a kindred spirit, Ajit Nawalkha and Himanshu Jakhar, who all are so brilliant. You three are Internet marketing geniuses! Thank you for being so talented, fun, and easy to work with. The best is yet to come!

… last, and especially, to my primary editorial, production, and design team: Dr. Ken Davis, Heidi Spaeth, and Janet Matthews:

… to Ken, a masterful editor and our team's "dial-a-professor"—whose accessibility, knowledge, and editing and proofreading abilities are truly awesome. What a blessing you have been.

… to Heidi, the most talented, devoted, and diverse graphic artist I've ever met! In the course of creating this book, you've not only given your all to this project, you've become one of my best friends, too.

… to Janet, an answer to a prayer at the point when this project became bigger than me. You were a true gift. Your devotion and commitment to work long hours and to allow (in your own words) "only the pure love of God to flow through me" is a big reason why this book will touch and bless so many lives. And while your professional talents are extensive and your work ethic exceptional, your most amazing gift is how clearly your purpose for living shines through your life and work. In this way, you're a beacon for others to discover their purpose, as you live so fully in yours.

Foreword by JACK CANFIELD

I first became aware of *If I Were Your Daddy* when Julia Espey introduced herself to me at my annual "Breakthrough to Success" event in Scottsdale, Arizona. She had created a mock-up cover of the title you're reading now, wrapped it around one of my own books, and courageously sent the mocked-up book to my hotel room along with a fruit plate and a bouquet of flowers. The attached note read: "Jack, congratulations! We just hit #1 on the *New York Times* best seller list! Give my love to Inga. Love, Julia." I then noticed my name listed in large print on the cover.

Who's Julia Espey? I wondered. What wisdom will this book hold once it's written? I'm a dad so I'm intrigued. What will other dads have to say? What are the most important gifts fathers can give their children? What a great idea for a book!

As parents we do pretty much anything to help our kids succeed. We give them a good education, food and clothing, a home, piano lessons, dance lessons, soccer lessons. We plop our toddlers down in front of Baby Einstein DVDs, hoping they'll emerge a bit more prepared. We schlep our kids to endless practices and competitions—whatever their sport or hobby or art. We help them with their homework. We get them through crises big and small. We do our best to teach them to be good people and we hope it sticks. Most of all, we love them no matter what. If you're reading this book, that's proof enough that you want to be the best parent you can be.

But what if we as parents actually started with the end in mind? What would being a wildly successful parent look like to you? One of the tools I teach in *The Success Principles*® is the creative power of visualization, which is exactly what Julia used to pitch her mocked-up book to me. When you visualize something you want, you use your imagination to see your goals as already complete. As Albert Einstein said, "Imagination is everything. It is the preview of life's coming attractions." In this case you can create a powerful vision around your parenting.

What image of being a dad or mom inspires you? Try this: Imagine you at your best as a parent. You're insightful, capable, and loving. You're rested, patient, and resourceful (hey, it's your vision—might as well make it good). And here's the biggie: you're just as compassionate with yourself as you are with your kids. You don't demand perfection from them or from yourself. Instead, you let go of mistakes quickly (yours and theirs) and focus on doing it better next time.

Now let's make it personal and specific, so that it's realistic like an action movie. Perhaps you see yourself responding well to the fussy baby who wants your attention at 3:00 a.m. or the toddler whose "helpfulness" just uprooted and rearranged the newly planted petunias in your garden. Maybe your vision has you successfully communicating with your teenager, the one who usually withdraws from the family and retreats to her room. Whatever form today's family challenge takes, you figure out the best way to handle it *ahead of time* in your vision—all the while remaining cool and collected. Syndicated columnist Erma Bombeck once wrote, "When my kids become wild and unruly, I use a nice, safe playpen. When they're finished, I climb out."

It pays to visualize. Harvard University researchers found that students who visualized before they performed a task had nearly 100 percent accuracy. Students who didn't visualize achieved only 55 percent accuracy. Almost all Olympic and professional athletes use visualization, including legendary golfer Jack Nicklaus, who once said, "I never hit a shot, not even in practice, without having a very sharp, in-focus picture of it in my head. It's like a color movie." So we know visualization works, and what parent doesn't need proven tools that work.

Sadly, however, you can't control your kids using visualization any more than Jack Nicklaus could have controlled how Arnold Palmer played. First, it doesn't work that way. Second, it's wrong to try. You can only influence you. Visualizing won't change your kids' behavior, but it can definitely change yours. And if you change and evolve, most likely your kids will develop for the best too.

After you've taken a few seconds to imagine yourself to be the best parent possible, you'll need inspiration and ideas to move you closer to what you want. For this there's nothing better than having the shoulders of an experienced mentor to stand on. We all need mentors. One of mine, W. Clement Stone, had such a profound effect on me that he literally changed my life. And understanding through others what works and what doesn't is one of the quickest and most effective ways to learn. In *If I Were Your Daddy, This Is What You'd Learn,* Julia Espey delivers to you thirty-five such mentors—thirty-five real dads in the trenches—each one sharing his best, most powerful and successful parenting tools, tips, and secrets.

As I discovered from publishing more than 100 million copies of *Chicken Soup for the Soul®* books, real stories from real people who've been there reach into our hearts and deliver wisdom more effectively than almost any other method. The stories in *If I Were Your Daddy, This Is What You'd Learn* instruct far more powerfully than any parenting theories or psychiatric studies you might find. Each dad has written to you—parent to parent—to share what he learned, and you will find dozens of helpful ideas, inspirational thoughts, and heart-filled anecdotes.

If you already knew how to be a better parent—how to be more effective, how to get better results with your kids, how to support them more—you'd likely do it. This is the purpose of this book, and why I think it's so fantastic. Having access to other perspectives on parenting, other approaches to parenting, is priceless. Without it, we limit what we can give our kids to the beliefs and behaviors we already know—those we brought with us from our own childhood. Sometimes our parents did a good job, and we pass that along. And sometimes they didn't do such a good job, and unless we make a conscious effort to learn something else, sadly, we pass that along too. This book offers you an opportunity to see what really works and what doesn't, and then to make different choices where you need to. After reading this book, if you find just one new idea to put into practice, it could change a child's life forever.

My own life has been dedicated to learning and teaching success principles. I've spent half my years learning and teaching how to bring self-esteem into the classroom—to kids, teachers, and educators—because children build our future. With conscious effort I repaired my own low self-esteem developed in childhood, repaired some of my relationships with my children from years of strain after a divorce, and repaired many parts of me that were underdeveloped. Then I realized I could take thousands more along for the ride by helping others teach it. In that same vein, this book is about helping parents or caregivers to teach, love, guide, mentor, show up—in short, to sharpen and develop the gifts we give our children so that we support the highest and best in them.

I appreciate psychiatrist and family therapist Frank Pittman's approach to fathering in his book *Man Enough*. I believe it applies equally to mothering. Dr. Pittman writes: "The guys who fear becoming fathers don't understand that fathering is not something perfect men do, but something that perfects the man. The end product of child-raising is not the child but the parent."

A friend said something similar: "When I realized I didn't have to be a perfect parent—only to evolve and grow and do my best—it lifted a 500-pound weight off my shoulders. It's very unlikely that I could screw up on that."

Some of the dads featured in this book happen to be good friends of mine, men whose parenting and life success I admire. Others I'd like to get to know. All have something profound and useful to offer. Read this book and try out some of the ideas found in these chapters. Dog-ear the pages when you find something inspiring and test-drive them, one at a time. And as you notice how well your child responds to the new mind-sets, values, and strategies you're implementing, let your vision and your feeling of being the greatest parent possible be a walking prayer morning, noon, and night. You just might be surprised how well it all works out.

Jack Canfield

Coauthor of the *Chicken Soup for the Soul* Series®
and author of *The Success Principles*™

INTRODUCTION

One great idea can change the life of a child. The proof is on every page of this book, a labor of love which has taken me more than three years to create. In some ways, this journey began decades ago with a fantasy about what being a mother would be like. I imagined a fairy tale of home and family, a picket fence, a wonderful husband, and smiling kids holding hands. But it just didn't turn out that way.

The reality was that once I was expecting a child, the child's father decided he didn't want to be actively involved in raising him. And that was that. My first reaction was, "Okaaay, do I get a vote?" I didn't choose it, but I had to accept it. I was now a single mom, a statistic.

While my son was still a baby, I handled things pretty well. Infants are demanding, but not complicated. But when he started growing up, and I looked at this little boy, my *one* son, emerging into being a person, it dawned on me that I had to be both mother *and father* to him. Holy cow! At that point I was just doing whatever I could to be the mother. *I had no idea how to be a father!* From the moment I knew I was pregnant, I felt hugely protective. I would have laid down my life for my child even before he was born. But now, watching this beautiful, curious little boy playing at my feet, I felt helpless. Would he have only *half* of everything he needed to be successful? Would he always be missing the fathering part—the part I didn't know how to give? My heart was heavy. I didn't have an answer.

Some years later, I attended a seminar at my son's school, Blake, in Minneapolis, Minnesota. The presenter was Marilyn Carlson Nelson, head of the hospitality empire built by her father, Curt Carlson, a Minnesota legend. The son of an immigrant, Carlson built a restaurant and hotel conglomerate that made him worth more than a billion dollars by the time he died.

That day, Marilyn told our small group an unforgettable story from her childhood. When she was in seventh grade, she was riding home from church with her parents when she began to complain about Sunday school. She didn't like it, the class was chaotic and out of control, she wasn't learning, and on and on. She boldly announced, "I'm quitting Sunday school and joining the adults."

Her father was so upset he pulled off the road, turned around to her in the back seat and said, "You're *what?*" Marilyn repeated that Sunday school was of little value. He looked at her and sternly said, "Then change it!" Her eyes flew wide open in surprise—even the adult teachers couldn't control Sunday school! But she set out to do it, rallied some others, and sure enough, they "fixed" what was wrong. Marilyn told us that her father's charge that day changed her forever. It turned her into a person who didn't complain, a person who looked for answers, found solutions, changed what was wrong, and made things grow and become better. It was the defining moment in her life.

It became a defining moment in *my* life as well. "Imagine getting that kind of solid education at such an early age," I thought. At thirteen, Marilyn had learned what personal responsibility was, *from her dad.* Then it hit me, "Oh my gosh, that's exactly the kind of influence and practical wisdom I want for my son." I wanted him to have a father who knew how to be successful, how to achieve his potential and get things done. Curt Carlson got things done in the business world, but there are other kinds of success as well. I wanted that depth and breadth of wisdom for my son in *all* areas of success, professional and personal.

That day I realized my son wasn't fated to be "less than," because he didn't have a dad around; he could actually be "more than." No longer would I live with a gnawing feeling that something essential was missing. With this new focus, I knew what he needed and I was going to go out and get it for him.

First I searched for a book that would answer the question, "What are successful dads teaching their children?" I found lots of great parenting books, and bought quite a few. But for this self-employed mom it was hard to stomach books that insisted I *should* do this or I *must* do that. They only added to my "I'm not doing enough" sense of guilt, instead of helping me through it. What I really needed were practical, real life, this-is-what-works, easy-to-implement solutions—*from dads.* I soon came to realize that the book I was searching for did not exist.

So I decided to just start interviewing dads and gathering daddy wisdom myself. I wanted advice from men who had reached their potential in their professions, but were also successful family men who had the ability to pass their insights along to their children. I created a wish list of well-rounded, capable, amazing men who were holistically successful—happy, healthy, and wealthy—who could be great influences in my child's life.

These were men I admired—physicians, business executives, athletes, best-selling authors, all tops in their fields. They didn't have to have name recognition, although some of them did. Mostly I knew *of* them, and found ways to get to them. Sometimes I simply kept asking them to help me until they finally said yes. And if being a dad was really important to them, they usually did.

I asked each of them, *"What is the most important mind-set, value, or lesson you've taught your children?"* Then "Please tell me *how* you taught them that. I need the story behind the story." Immediately their wisdom became memorable, because along with creative strategies and profound wisdom, I got funny tales, heart-warming anecdotes, and real-life examples. It was practical knowledge! At the end of each session I asked, "Who do you know?" and that led to more interviews with great dads.

The research came naturally to me. Before I got married I was a NASA engineer and researcher for ten years. I left that field, but those research skills were coming in handy now.

When I first began my research, my goal was only to pass on what I learned to my son, and close friends. Then, one day, while listening to a CD by success coach Jack Canfield, I heard him say something profound: "If there's a book you need and you can't find it, *it's because you're supposed to write it.* " Instantly, my quest became the seeds of this book.

With this new focus I continued interviewing dads. Even though many of them had done lots of media interviews about their businesses, not one of them had ever been asked about their fathering. Yet they proudly admitted it's one of the most important things they do, and they are entirely devoted fathers. Some of them bill out at thirty thousand dollars per hour when hired by a corporation for their expertise. But they gave me their time for free, saying, "If what I've done with my kids can help someone else, count me in." The result is this one-of-a-kind book. It's never been done before. (At least I can't find it.)

During the interviews I also asked questions like "Where did you learn this stuff? What was your father like? What was your childhood like?" I was surprised when so many of them said, "My father was a great *reverse* role model. He taught me exactly how not to do it." Or "I had a good dad, but he wasn't very involved in our lives." I realized there's a new generation of fathers out there, and even if they had good, loving parents, their fathers' role was very different from that of today's dad. Without a model for how to be an involved dad, they had to either figure out how to do it on their own, or find other role models. And at that point I realized that *the men of the world need this information as much as I do as a single mom!* So it turns out this book is not just for single moms; it's also for the dads who didn't have a role model, or want to evolve past the model they grew up with.

Today, one in four American children is being raised by a single parent. By some estimates that's 24 million kids with only one parent at home, equal to the combined populations of Atlanta, Chicago, Detroit, Los Angeles, and New York City! Most of these single parents are women, but there are also single dads out there, and I knew they would need this book, too.

Although the lessons I was learning were coming from men, at a certain point I realized these were simply all-around great ideas that could make anyone a better, more effective parent, teacher, or counselor. My vision for this book is that it will start a movement of parents and caregivers talking about *what works.* This way, we'll collectively all get smarter, quicker!

Once I became aware of how desperately our society needs this book, you would have thought I was drinking rocket fuel for breakfast. I poured myself passionately into it. My research uncovered frightening statistics. One survey cited that in America, 63 percent of all youth suicides occur in single-parent families. It also says that 70 percent of teenage pregnancies, 71 percent of chemical substance abusers, 80 percent of prison inmates, and 90 percent of all homeless or runaway youth come from single-parent homes, mostly single moms.

When the majority of suicides, inmates, and runaways come from homes without a father, the critical role that fathers have today in raising healthy children becomes obvious. What if we rallied behind great dads and started promoting whatever they're doing that's working? My hope is that this book will do just that, spark a flame and inspire and support the dad who doesn't know what to do or doesn't realize how important he is, or the mother who is doing both jobs, married or not, and THAT *is the mission I hold for this book.*

When my son was small, I had an underlying sense of *inadequacy* and didn't think I was a very good mother or parent. But through the process of gathering the wisdom for this book, I realized I was slowly being parented too. From these dads, I learned how to communicate better with myself, with others, and with my son. I learned how to handle my frustration and feelings of being overwhelmed, and found techniques to handle everything on my plate. One dad even called me every few months: "I've been talking to you on the *inner-net*," he would say. "I believe in you. You're doing a great job. You've got a best seller. Keep going." This was a busy man, but he somehow found the time to support me just as a caring dad would do. As I grew and learned, it was easy to give what I now possessed to my son, *and I did.*

> When the majority of suicides, inmates, and runaways come from homes without a father, the critical role that fathers have today in raising healthy children becomes obvious.

In dealing with any family challenge, instead of yelling and nagging, the pattern I knew, I now had options. Should I make it fun? Get him to cooperate? I now knew how to do both! I had new awareness and new tools, and I realized it doesn't take more time to be more effective; it actually takes less. As my son once said, "You're a lot more fun, Mommy!"

One day on this journey I experienced a profound moment: I no longer felt inadequate; I felt powerful and strong. It was as if an angel said to me, "You are a fabulous parent," and with this message, tears filled my eyes. The crushing weight of "I'm not enough" was gone. I'm not a perfect parent; none of the dads in this book are perfect. If I'd been looking for perfect, I would have found no one to interview, because we all make mistakes. But all these dads do some things well, and by harnessing what they do well, I submit that everyone can become super-capable parents too.

The vision for this book began with the hope of helping one child, my son, so it's already a success. But if the ideas in this book touch the life of just *one* other child, maybe your child—and if just one idea changes that child's life by giving her confidence or making him more effective at school or helping her cope with peer pressure or helping him deflate a bully, if it brings more harmony to your family, if it changes one child's life so she doesn't end up a statistic, then I'll have my reward for all the effort I've put into it.

I know firsthand that one great idea *can* change the life of a child. And what's the value of one life? Priceless! That's precisely the value this information has for me. I hope the wisdom, stories, lessons, and mind-sets in this book will make as profound a difference in your life, as writing it has in mine. And so from my heart to yours, I pass it along. This priceless gift now belongs to you.

Julia Espey

SHARE

Your Experiences with Us

Did You Try an Idea from This Book?
If So, We Want to Hear from You!

We would love to know how the stories in this book have impacted your life. If you have been inspired by the wisdom of our mentor dads, and put one or more of the strategies to work, we'd love to hear how it turned out for you.

Whether you're a mom or dad, a teacher or a counselor, please write and tell us which dad's ideas you tried and which ones worked. Or, if this book inspired you to create your own techniques for your children—a value, a mind-set, a life lesson—or to pass along one of your tried and true strategies, tell us about it and how you taught it to them.

Don't forget to tell us the backstory. Make sure you describe the situation before you started, and the reason why you chose a particular strategy. If it was successful, please tell us how the strategy changed the dynamics of your relationship with your child. Explain how your child succeeded, and don't forget to tell us how the dynamics in your home changed as a result.

To share your stories, just submit it to our secure website at
www.IfIWereYourDaddy.com/share

If we get enough great success stories, our plan is to publish them
in a future book in this series.

Who knows? Your success story might be the inspiration for another struggling parent to use your gift, or one of the many terrific gifts found in this book.

And thank you!

GATHERING RESOURCES

TODAY IS THE ONLY DAY YOU HAVE

If I Were Your Daddy ... I'd help you befriend fear and find courage, and realize that you make each day whatever you will. Most of all, I'd strive to be a role model worth modeling.

DAN ROONEY

F-16 "Top Gun" Fighter Pilot
& PGA Golf Professional

The night is dark in the sky over Iraq. I joke with my squadron and say, "I wish my mom was here! Guess what? She's not." We're single-seat guys, and there's no one in that jet but you. These are the moments you're most afraid of making a mistake. These are the moments you lean heavily on your faith, trusting that while you're alone, you're not really alone—it's going to work out. These are the moments you *most* appreciate being a dad—waking up four sleepy little girls, playing in the yard with them, and having them run to you and hang all over you, every time you come home.

I've chosen to be in service to my country, and I'm a dad. And I know I have an important secret to teach my daughters—a secret about fear and courage, and about making each day whatever you will.

"Daddy is going on a long trip to help people" is the way my four young daughters explain my leaving for a third tour of duty in Iraq. They ask me, "Daddy, are you afraid of flying?" I lean forward and whisper, "*Everybody* gets scared, even Daddy. Courage is not moving forward without fear; it's moving forward *despite* it." I pause and continue, "But we can't let our fear keep us from doing it anyway."

I GENTLY TEACH THEM TO BEFRIEND FEAR AND FIND COURAGE

My girls learned a small lesson about courage last summer at the pool, when they were very afraid of doing back dives. "Hey," I told them, "the only way you'll fail is to not try. I know it's scary, but I also know you're not going to get hurt. Just try, and don't be afraid to fail." When you're little, a back dive is a very big deal. You learn to trust that someone is holding you. At the pool, I was the one holding them, holding their backs until I finally let them go, and in they went, safely and victoriously. Next time, I'll help them stretch a little more, in some other way, with some other "scary" task that's just outside their comfort level. This way they'll befriend fear and find courage by progressively learning how to "feel the fear, and do it anyway"—all in the safe context, for now, of having Daddy and Mommy near. With each advancing footstep, they're building faith and courage, until someday they'll discover that it lives *inside of them*—to comfort them on dark nights, and make them bigger, bolder, and ready to do important things in life.

When we stretch the outer edges of our lives, we find our greatest moments of fulfillment and satisfaction.

My wish for my four daughters is that they become courageous, confident women who aren't afraid to take risks. When we take risks—when we stretch the outer edges of our lives—we find our greatest moments of fulfillment and satisfaction. We find our greatest faith, too. And I want my girls to find life's greatest moments.

I TEACH THEM TO SAVOR TODAY AND CHOOSE

When I'm home, one of the most special moments is when I get the girls up in the morning. Whether you're a child or an adult, morning is a wonderful time because it's the beginning of the *possibilities* of the day. Unlimited possibilities! My daughters and I have a ritual: every morning I ask them the same question, and I won't leave their rooms until they answer me. I ask, "What is today?" Their sleepy little voices come back, "It's the greatest day of my life!" I ask, "Why?" And they say, "It's the only one I have." In this little ritual, I remind my daughters that each day is theirs to create; in fact, it's the only day they have. They can make it as they *will*.

I had a college professor who, on the first day of class, wrote one word in big letters across the board: "VOLITION." He asked us, "Does anybody know what this word means?" No one said a word, so he went on to say, "It's the most powerful word in the world. Volition is the power to choose. Every day, you can get up and be happy or sad; you can choose to love or hate; you can choose to make a difference or you can choose to focus on yourself. Ultimately, this gift of choice is what defines all of us in life. That's volition."

The gift of choice is what defines all of us in life.

That class made such an impact on me that *volition* is a word I use often with my young daughters. Even at their age, they know and understand it. For them it means that their parents will guide them and love them, but ultimately, it's their choices—their volition—in life that will define them.

When Victoria knocks Tatum off the swing, she gets a time-out. But it's not her we're disappointed in; it's *the choice* she's made. That's a big distinction for my wife, Jacqy, and me, one we often talk about with the girls. In order to build confident little women, our disapproval is *always* for their inappropriate choices; our love and unconditional approval is constant. But we are clear: the power to choose is always theirs.

I GIVE THEM LOVE THROUGH UNDIVIDED ATTENTION

One of the benefits of being in the Oklahoma National Guard is that when I am home I *cherish* being home. I grab every bit of the time I'm given to interact with the kids. One of my unwritten rules is to never be on the phone when I come into the house. If I have a phone call while I'm driving home, I finish it in the driveway. When I come in the door, my phone is off and my attention is on the girls and Jacqy. This isn't as altruistic as it sounds: that moment when all four of them come running over, hang on to me, and want to play and roll around… well, those are some of the most special moments of the day. Sometimes I even dash home, even briefly, just to have them run to me and throw their arms around me, one more time. (And I give Jacqy a kiss, too!)

We're away from cell phones, we're away from TV, we're not sedentary—all of the things that are eroding the family.

After that, spending time with my daughters can be as simple as taking one or all of them with me to the grocery store, playing golf together as a family, or playing "Freeze Monster" with them. Let me tell you about "Freeze Monster." Because we don't watch much TV, we all head outside, and I become a kind of neighborhood toy. Eleven girls live in our cul-de-sac, and they all come out to join us. My role as the Freeze Monster is to hit them with a Nerf ball, and the one I hit is frozen until somebody goes through her legs. But the truth is that it doesn't matter what we're doing because we're together. We're away from cell phones, away from TV, we're not sedentary—all of the things that I think are eroding the human family. This way, four active girls have the whole of me.

I LOVE THEM BY BEING A ROLE MODEL
WORTH MODELING

Unlike some of my friends—dads who learned parenting by doing the *opposite* of what their parents did—my parents were superb role models. From them I learned courage. My dad has always pushed the envelope of life. He's not a fighter pilot, but he's been a risk-taker as an entrepreneur.

He's written seven books, and as a professor he's mentored a whole lot of kids. He's a man who has always led by example, and he set things in motion for me.

In Stillwater, Oklahoma, where I grew up, my dad and I were often together on a golf course as the sun was setting. More than once, he told me to never get a job in order to accumulate wealth. Rather, he told me, wealth is truly found in doing what you love. "Hey," he said, "I want you to figure out your *absolute favorite* things to do in life, and then do those things each and every day. You never go to work if you love what you do." My dream was to become an F-16 fighter pilot and a PGA golf professional who owned a golf course. That was my ultimate job description, and I give credit to my dad for planting that seed in me. By giving me the permission to find and pursue what I love, he made my life an act of volition. It's a gift I will pass forward to my children.

> *Wealth is truly found in doing what you love.*

My mother gave me some sage advice too. She said, "Your daughters will marry a person *just like you*. They'll find someone who treats them like you've treated their mother, and respects them like you've respected their mother." It was humbling and inspiring to think that I was demonstrating and forming their expectations for a lifetime mate. And their volition to choose a husband will be colored by the one they see in me.

I SHOW, RATHER THAN TELL THEM, HOW TO SERVE

You see, children have the innate ability to sniff out hypocrisy. If you want them to live their lives and behave a certain way, you have to walk that walk. That's why my job as the founder of Folds of Honor, a foundation that provides post-secondary educational scholarships for children and spouses of military men and women killed or disabled in service to the United States, is so *instrumental* in the girls' development. Because I've dedicated the majority of my life to helping other people, I'm able to share that with my daughters. Now, when they've earned money or received it as a gift, they voluntarily donate some of it to the foundation. They meet the children who are scholarship recipients—the ones without daddies or mommies now. For them to see that "Daddy is helping people" is to see how to find fulfillment.

For them to see that "Daddy is helping people" is to see how to find fulfillment.

I believe that at the end of our lives, we're not going to be asked how much money we made or what accomplishments we had, but rather, how we used our time and talents in the service of others. I know that if I live these values and lead by example as a parent, there's a great probability that my children will end up embracing those values as well. My hope is that someday I'll hear them saying, "You know, Dad, we would love to take the lead at the foundation, and dedicate our lives to helping other people as well." But, again, this won't happen by my volition. They will be the ones who decide.

I'LL STRETCH TO LEAVE THEM A LEGACY

A friend once gave me the coolest advice. He said, "When your child is born, after the doctor sucks the amniotic fluid out of her mouth and nose, you'll be in a position to see her take her first breath. Notice it." I did. Breathing is the first great act of volition. And with her first gasp, I felt a responsibility and a divinity in my life that changed me forever. It changed my focus... it changed everything. Up until that point, my life had been pretty much all about myself and achieving my goals. Now I had to stretch my limits and adopt new ones, because now my actions could have consequences that reverberated for generations. Actions speak much louder than words, which people say all the time. But to truly live it—to not just expound a virtue, but to silently embody it—is, I believe, one of the most profound things imaginable. It is to be a model worth modeling.

The only way my daughters could ever disappoint me is by being afraid to venture out and take risks. So the legacy I strive to give them is to be a father who inspires and leads the way—a father like the one I had. Being present, doing small and large acts of courage, choosing a life that serves others—these are decisions that define the quality of our lives. Being confident and courageous, and having a positive impact on the world, I hope this will be their and my volition today. After all, today is the only, and greatest, day we have.

My squadron and I have finished another night over the mountains and deserts of Iraq. I think again about my daughters. They, and I, are blessed to live in a country that I'm proud to defend, a country where we all have the right to choose—where we all have *volition*. And I'm blessed to be a dad.

"A leader is one who knows the way, goes the way, and shows the way."

John C. Maxwell, American author, speaker, and pastor, who has written more than fifty books, primarily focused on leadership.

WHO IS MAJOR DAN ROONEY?

Dan with (wife) Jacqy, (children) Victoria, Tatum, Mia, and Reese

Major Dan Rooney flies—and so does the organization he founded, the Folds of Honor Foundation. Folds of Honor, a nonprofit organization, provides scholarships to the spouses and children of military service members disabled or killed in service. More than twelve hundred scholarships have been awarded to date.

Besides founding, and serving as CEO of Folds of Honor, Rooney is an F-16 pilot in the Oklahoma Air National Guard, a golf course owner, a residential developer, and a PGA professional golfer. He has served three combat tours in Iraq and is a two-time recipient of the coveted "Top Gun" award.

For his work with Folds of Honor, Rooney has received the White House's Presidential Volunteer Service Award, the Air National Guard's Distinguished Service Medal, the Ellis Island Medal of Honor, and the PGA's first-ever Patriot Award. He has been recognized as one of *People* magazine's 2008 Heroes of the Year, and one of ABC World News Tonight's Persons of the Year for 2008.

Rooney's golf course, The Patriot, opened May 31, 2010, in Tulsa, Oklahoma. A percentage of all profits, guest play, and member contributions from The Patriot directly benefit the Folds of Honor Foundation. Their mantra: "Great Golf for the Greater Good."

Rooney and his wife, Jacqy, live in Broken Arrow, Oklahoma, with their four daughters, Victoria, Tatum, Mia, and Reese.

www.foldsofhonor.org

TRUSTING THE COMPASS WITHIN

If I Were Your Daddy ... I would help you learn how to access and trust your inner guidance by asking you a simple question and facilitating your own discovery. You'd learn that the right answer to every decision and every choice can be found within you.

T. **HARV EKER**

Entrepreneur & Best-Selling Author

The very nanosecond I saw my first child's face, I was overwhelmed by a feeling of a love I'd never known before: blinding in its acceptance and numbing in its sweep. It was, without question, the most profound moment of my life, and I knew then that being a father was going to be the greatest gift of my life. And so it has been.

The seminars I present center on helping people improve themselves and live up to their peak potential—not just financially, but in all areas of their lives. Having studied and tested many principles, I've discovered which ones work and which don't and used them in parenting my own two children. My strongest desire is for them to grow up to be strong, discerning individuals capable of making wise choices.

There is one truth that applies to all of us, regardless of our age: at the end of the day, the only person you have to live with is the one looking back at you from the mirror. If you're not happy with yourself, then nothing in your life will be in its right place. I believe that helping children to be happy with who they are is the foundation for equipping them to forge happy, fulfilling lives.

I also want my children to be skilled in the practice of holding themselves accountable, and when they don't know how to proceed, to always look within for the proper direction. Kids must learn to confidently make their own choices rather than look to others—their parents, friends, or society at large—to direct their decisions. We each have to assume responsibility for our own choices, and own the consequences of each choice. This process needs to begin in childhood—so that kids learn that good, bad, or indifferent, the outcome is theirs.

When I explicitly tell my children what to do or not to do, I stand in the way of their learning that every choice they make has an effect. I want them to totally grasp that their choices are based on their own thoughts and decisions—and that these occur inside them. Only when they really recognize this can they come to control the process that ultimately shapes their lives. My task as a parent is to introduce them to the tremendous power residing within them.

The question I often ask my children is "If you do that, how will you feel about yourself?"

As my daughter and son were growing up, I consciously used every possible opportunity—from day-in-and-day-out interaction to major events—to help them grasp the power of their own choices. There's one question I used to ask them, and it's one I still like to ask. It gets to the heart of, and serves as a great guide to, making any decision. I ask, *"If you do that, how will you feel about yourself?"*

When my daughter was in college, one night she called me. "Dad, I need some advice," she began. "Should I go out with this guy who's really good looking and popular? Or," she continued, "should I see this other guy I have more in common with, but who isn't nearly as good looking and doesn't fit in as well with my friends?"

Now, this may not seem like an earth-shattering decision, but each of us, every day, makes hundreds of decisions that shape the course of our future. This was a perfect opportunity to guide her through heart-directed decision-making. So I listened to her tangled ball of possibilities, and then I asked her The Question:

"Honey, if you go out with the popular, good-looking guy, how will you feel about yourself tomorrow?"

Silence. "Hmmm," she paused and thought. "Maybe a little superficial, like I can't really be myself ... maybe not so good, I suppose. But with the other one, I think I could be just me. You know, it really doesn't matter what anyone else thinks about him... I'll probably have a great time. Thanks, Dad." Problem solved.

Notice that while she called and asked for advice, I actually didn't give her any! I was there for her and simply posed the question that encouraged her to seek the solution within herself, one that was authentic to her. This is my fundamental approach to life and parenting: make decisions so that you like the person in the mirror!

When you feel good about yourself, you're probably doing the right thing. Being honest feels better than being dishonest. Excellence feels better than mediocrity. Keeping confidences feels better than gossiping. Loving feels better than hating. Doing what you agreed to do—even if it's inconvenient—feels better than breaking your word.

> When you feel good about yourself, you're probably doing the right thing.

Doing what's "right"—honoring a deep internal sense of "right" and not what others say you "should" do—means aligning yourself with your higher consciousness. Making positive, life-affirming choices lifts your energy and connects you with your own divinity. When you truly feel good about yourself, your choices, and the world you subsequently create, you vibrate at a higher frequency. Even young children know and feel this; it's an innate ability we all have. There are few lessons more important in life than learning to check in with and trust your own heart, and then set your course accordingly.

My son is a year younger than my daughter and attends the same college. Unlike his sister, who loves to achieve academically for her own self-satisfaction, he finds his self-esteem and identity in social settings. He's a highly social leader-type and belongs to a fraternity. He's also very smart and had been getting by on studying an hour here and there while his peers invested considerably more effort. He had no inner motivation to put more focus on academics, and he'd been content making grades that were just OK.

One day he and I were talking about what he might do after college. He told me he was interested in business and had decided he'd like to be a business major. But he also realized his grades might be an issue when it came to getting accepted into that program. So I asked The Question:

"How do you feel about not having the grades to get into the program you want?

"Not very good," came the reply.

"What will it take for you to feel good about yourself?" I returned.

He was quiet for a bit and then said, "I'll have to get better grades. And I guess that means spending less time at the frat house and not going to every party, like I usually do."

Now, some parents might have bulldozed in at this point with the "I'm paying your tuition, therefore I expect you to …" conversation. Certainly launching into something like this would have relieved my own frustration, but my son would have missed the connection as well as the chance to find his own motivation. I knew it needed to originate with him, so the focus and commitment would also be his to own and pursue. Had I approached it differently, this crossroads could have devolved into a source of contention between us. More importantly, it would have had a seriously negative impact on his ability to empower and manage himself.

It had to originate with him …

So I asked him to consider another question, to ensure the answer would not come as a parental opinion or dictate:

"Son, if you don't think something is working, or you aren't happy with the results, could this be telling you that you need to change something? Why not try a different approach and see what happens? What if you make a really good attempt at getting a better grade, just to see if it's worth the effort? Hey, maybe it's not. But the only way you'll know is to try it and find out for yourself."

"Well," he replied, considering my words, "I can't study at the fraternity. There are just too many distractions."

"So go to the library or find another quiet place," I suggested. "Just see what happens, and how the results make you feel about yourself."

A few days later, I got an enthusiastic phone call. He'd decided to try it, and as a direct result had just aced the latest exam!

"How do you feel?" I asked him.

"Great!"

"How does this feeling compare to partying?"

"Well Dad," he said, "I love to party, but getting this good grade makes me feel even better about myself."

A really important thing had just happened. In his brain he'd now linked feeling good with getting good grades. This new link stuck, and two years later he was still earning straight A's. By parenting through questions, and keeping quiet about my own opinions and judgments, I allowed my son to learn something very powerful: When you connect a good feeling with something you want to accomplish, your subconscious mind will help you to succeed. Success suddenly becomes much easier and way more fun. It did for him.

Connect a good feeling with something you want and your mind will help you to succeed.

SELF-CORRECTING VERSUS PUNISHMENT

I don't believe in "punishing" my children. Don't we all really just want to help them learn to make better choices? When you make a wrong decision, there's usually an unpleasant consequence naturally. If the experience is painful enough, you remember the decision and its effect, you're not likely to repeat it. This is simple self-preservation, and I believe the same holds true for my children. I thus avoid playing "the enforcer," a role that would divert their attention from their own learning while they focus instead on locking horns with the authority figure: me!

One day before my son was old enough to drive, he decided to use our family car to pick up a friend and go somewhere. His mother and I were out of town. He reasoned that he wasn't going very far and that he'd never get caught, so it'd be okay. As it turned out, a neighbor saw him and told us. And he got caught.

Now, I could have come down heavily on him, made a lot of noise, grounded him for life, and so on. But instead I asked him The Question: "How do you feel about yourself?" In this case, he said he felt fine. He really didn't think he'd done anything that bad, since nothing had happened to the car and he was about to get his driver's license anyway. He'd checked his own moral barometer, and nothing registered.

So I pointed out a few additional facts. If the police had caught him, he wouldn't have been able to get a driver's license for another two years. Moreover, he hadn't asked permission to use something that didn't belong to him—a car, no less. In effect, he'd broken our trust—a serious result. So I asked him, "Does this mean we can't trust you to do what's legal, or trust you to make choices that keep in mind the safety of others?"

Enroll your children in self-correction: "What would you do if you were the parent?"

This was one of the few times when he wasn't able to see a perspective beyond his own, even when encouraged to do so. His reasoning was shallow, so I had to step in and help him realize the importance of his behavior. And *how* I "stepped in" was really important!

This was an opportunity for me to employ one of the practices I teach: enroll your children in the process of self-correction by asking them to think from another perspective, perhaps as a parent. I asked him to think deeper and help me resolve an issue that he was dismissing as "no big deal." I turned the tables, and asked for his opinion.

"What would you do if you were the parent and I was the son?" I began. "If you wanted your son to be trustworthy and responsible, how would you help him learn the difference between building trust and destroying it?"

He quickly replied, "I'd give him a warning."

"Well," I said, "a warning is good, but with only a warning it could still happen a second or even a third time. So warnings might not work. What else might you do to correct the situation, and make sure the message got through so it didn't happen again?"

He ended up coming up with a list of "reminders," as we call them in our family, so the lesson would be remembered. This can be a loss of privileges, such as having an early curfew or having to earn money to pay for something damaged. It's something uncomfortable and unpleasant that motivates them to remember that whatever they did, it's not a good idea to do it again.

Being the authority figure imposing a punishment distracts them from taking full responsibility for their choices.

By asking for his help in this way I kept myself from being the authority figure imposing a punishment. If I had become the bad guy, it would have distracted him from taking full responsibility for his choice. Since he decided on a consequence of his own making, rather than my doing it, there was no resistance or anger from him. He owned the entire experience, generated his own list of reminders, and changed his views about what had transpired.

He never repeated the incident, and his ability to think beyond his own viewpoint and understand the importance of trust seemed to crystallize.

In my seminars I teach that there are three ways of learning: verbal, modeling, and through high-impact events. The last way, a high-impact event, is the most powerful and fastest way to change a behavior. My son's self-imposed laundry list of reminders needed to be uncomfortable enough for him so that he'd absorb the lesson; they had to become a high-impact event for him. He decided that if he were the dad, he would ground the kid for two weeks, plus have him do a list of additional chores. It seemed fair, and we agreed.

The ability to make mindful decisions is a learned skill. By asking simple, defining questions that keep us on track and alert to our feelings, we empower ourselves and teach our children to create road maps for their own success in life. Most importantly, they end up loving and being happy with that very special person in the mirror. They feel good about themselves, and that's the most important gift we can nurture in our children.

"If you are guided by an internal compass that represents your character and the values that guide your decisions, you're going to be fine."

Brenda Barnes, Sara Lee CEO, who left Pepsi Co. in the 1990s as the highest-ranking female executive, in order to care for her family.

WHO IS T. HARV EKER?

T. Harv with (children) Jesse and Madison

T. Harv Eker is the son of European immigrants who came to North America with little more than thirty dollars to their names. Though raised in Toronto, Canada, Eker has spent most of his adult life in the United States. He opened one of the first retail fitness stores in North America and grew the business quickly, in time selling a portion of it to a *Fortune* 500 company and becoming a millionaire. He couldn't sustain his financial fortune, however, and the money was gone within two years. This experience led Eker to develop his theories about people's mental and emotional relationships to money. Realizing that his—everyone's, really— "inner money thermostat" is set for a specific amount of financial success, he researched and wrote the book *Secrets of the Millionaire Mind,* which rose instantly to best seller status. Using the principles and practices he'd learned, Eker redrew his own money blueprint and, this time, kept and grew his millions.

During Eker's years of struggle, he vowed that if he again became rich, he would help others do the same—not just financially, but in all areas of their lives. Today, he is president of Peak Potentials Training, one of the largest and fastest-growing seminar companies in the world, helping thousands to reach financial freedom.

Eker is the father of two grown children, Madison and Jesse.

www.harveker.com, www.peakpotentials.com

THINKING WITH YOUR HEART

If I Were Your Daddy ... I'd teach you to be independent thinkers whose actions inspire others. I'd show you by example how to make every day matter, by "thinking" with your heart.

TOM CONIGLIARO

Goldman Sachs Managing Director

I wonder how many Americans would say that September 11, 2001, changed the direction of their lives entirely? It certainly did for me.

On that morning, I was supposed to attend a conference at the World Trade Center, but the confirmation letter got buried on my desk. Somehow the event never made my appointment book. And so I wasn't there. *I wasn't there.*

I work one block away from the center, and I was among the thousands who ran for safety amid falling debris, smoke, and sirens. I arrived home that evening shaken but safe, and I walked through the front door into the arms of my waiting family. I was grateful to be alive, but my heart carried the weight of those who would not be returning home.

When you survive something like that, everything changes. As time passed and the shock and sorrow softened, I came to realize I was looking at a different image in the mirror. It was as if the old one was wiped away, and a new man took his place. A better man. A better person. A better father.

How many parents stop to think about what we model, day after day, to our children? Do our actions in life truly match our words? I found myself asking these questions.

After the events of September 11, my life suddenly seemed remarkably short and precious. My thoughts were marked with challenge: *I'm forty years old. What kind of example have I been to those around me? Have I really thought about what I am doing and why? What am I trading my life for?*

Up to that point, I probably had been inadvertently teaching my kids to care too much about the opinions of others. I come from a long line of people-pleasers, and I had become one too. The irony was that wanting to please my parents, my professors, and my coaches motivated many of my successes, but it also left a huge part of me undiscovered and unfulfilled. Rather than blazing my own trail, I had followed the well-worn paths of others. I was modeling to my kids the status quo: *Just follow the path commonly trod* and leave the call of your heart on the floor in the closet, unexamined.

How many parents stop to think about what we model, day after day, to our children? Do our actions in life truly match our words?

Now, I'd found a new voice inside: *I'm not concerned with what people think anymore. I want to examine what I'm doing and make sure it feels right to me, rather than trying to satisfy someone else's view.* I felt as if I'd crawled out from an invisible web of familial expectations and societal do's and don'ts. I found fresh air! The more I embraced this thinking, the more I started to do things outside my normal reflexes.

I found that I wanted to inspire my children to do the same. I wanted to help them find the courage to chart their own course and be heart-led, independent thinkers whose actions inspired others.

Our hearts were suddenly wide open to the needs of others, not just within our familiar community.

As I set the example, our young daughters also began to follow similar paths of authenticity, making choices different from teenage norms. As a family, we all seemed to step out of one box into a new world. Our hearts were suddenly wide open to the needs of others, not just within our familiar community, but everywhere.

FIRST STEPS: VOLUNTEERING AS A FAMILY

One of our first changes was to volunteer to do mission work in Mexico. We didn't know anyone else who had done this, but we heard about the Amor Ministries, an organization out of San Diego that every year takes literally thousands of people into the slums of Tijuana to help build homes. It's very organized and very safe. My wife, Lisa, and I decided to volunteer our family (including our nine- and twelve-year-old daughters) to work one week a year for three consecutive years.

Up to that point, my family knew only the comforts of elite suburbia. Our daughters' friends and their families were upper middle class by America's socioeconomic standards. Beyond pictures and television images, poverty wasn't something we understood or felt. That was another world, someone else's world.

We rented a van, and off we went to Tijuana, where we joined about 140 other volunteers, including a lot of other kids with their families. We never felt as if we were in a dangerous area; it was certainly economically depressed, but there wasn't a lot of crime.

Our girls ran and laughed with the local children. In playing, it was as if the universal language of love broke down any communication barriers. We spent a week in the mud, building homes alongside seemingly poor families, who we discovered were in fact truly wealthy. Their lives were rich in spirit.

Great happiness came from their reliance on each other. *They* became *our* models, and we experienced a family awakening. Our original intent— "Here we are! We're going to do something really 'good' for you"—was turned upside down. We received much more than we were giving.

Back home, people thought I was crazy to do this and said things like "Why would you go to Mexico in the summer, in the desert, to live in a tent, work in the dirt for a week, and build a house for people you don't know?" But unless you do it, you just can't understand.

The experience for me was life-changing, and over the next three years these trips changed our daughters' lives too. Into their teenage forms were born humanitarian and courageous spirits. Living amid poverty challenged their fears of the unknown. They were stepping into places that were truly unfamiliar, but had something more to offer. Things, people, and experiences once foreign became approachable.

PERSONAL ACCOUNTABILITY: BE THE EXAMPLE

The tragedy of September 11 inspired another major change in me, and my choices again helped me to become a role model for my children. Though I'm not an alcoholic or anything close, I decided to stop drinking. This may not seem like a big step, but I *am* half Irish! I initially gave up alcohol for Lent, which isn't uncommon, but after Lent, my inner voice challenged me to keep going. I reasoned that if I wanted to lead by example, then I needed to do this in all areas of my life, both personal and professional.

That decision made a dramatic impact on my kids. I'd never

> The tragedy of September 11 inspired another major change. I decided to stop drinking.

had a problem with alcohol, but I felt I wanted to do this. Many of my colleagues didn't understand when I stopped drinking completely, because my profession requires constant socializing. In the corporate business world, drinking is the norm when entertaining clients. Unless addiction is an issue, you're expected to drink. However, my new convictions were stronger than the social expectations of the world around me. *I'm a successful person, a competent person. I don't need to drink to gain anyone's approval or to move my business forward.*

It was not lost on me that my teenagers would need similar strength when they faced peer pressure. I wanted them to have the inner resolve to know they were well liked and OK just the way they were. They didn't need to drink to fit in or be fun. I wanted to give them, by example, the perspective and the strength to say no.

Within a very short time, Lisa and I witnessed our girls making different choices. We overheard their telephone conversations concerning parties and the drinking escapades all too common to this age group. They began to *repeat my words* to their friends. The parties that "everyone goes to" took on far less allure, and instead they began to spend weekend nights in small groups with friends who were interested in natural fun.

> *Instead of "parents know best" and "adults are fully developed," I modeled the process of "becoming" and growing.*

Encouraged by their choices, I was spurred on. Instead of subscribing to the old paradigm that says "parents know best" and "adults are fully developed," I modeled the process of "becoming" and growing. My daughters moved alongside in their parallel universe. Our focus on "peer norm" was being replaced by the still, quiet voice within each of us.

THE GREATEST CHANGE AND REWARD: EXPANDING OUR FAMILY

All of these personal transformations led our family to make the greatest decision of our lives: we adopted twin boys from a high-needs background whose ethnic origin differs from our own. The person who inhabited this body before September 11 might not have chosen this path and thus missed one of the greatest joys of his life: being a father to two amazing boys whose spirits shine through a skin color different from mine.

Knowing that so many kids from disadvantaged backgrounds need good homes, Lisa and I had started to think about adopting. We began by looking into foreign adoption but never got comfortable with that process. Then Lisa met someone through church who knew of an organization that worked with the state, and ultimately we worked through them.

We said, "Look, we're basically open to sibling groups of any race." Because we were that open, within a week or so of getting certified we got a call that twin baby boys were available. Would we like to come and meet them? So we and our daughters went to see them, and it turned out they were born on my oldest daughter's birthday! We took that as a sign from heaven, and the deal was pretty much sealed at that point.

After that, we were truly a different family. The way we thought, lived, and embraced opportunities and experiences definitely changed. When new opportunities came along (like adoption), instead of thinking "Why should we do this?" we asked, "Why not?"

SAY "YES" TO PERSONAL DEVELOPMENT

Our older daughter learned to say yes on her own when meaningful opportunities to help others came her way. The summer after her junior year of high school, she came home one day and announced that she was volunteering at an orphanage in Costa Rica. The trip revealed a rising independent spirit, effusive and free,

Our daughters did things that were once beyond their comfort zone.

expanding to embrace a world in need. Just like me, she is now reaching for places that were once beyond her comfort zone.

As I look back on the transformation of my life since 9/11, I realize I'm a living testament that developing yourself isn't self-centered; it's a priceless gift to your children. As parents we model self-development by sharing our journey, and life becomes a continuous evolution rather than a fixed point.

Developing yourself isn't self-centered; it's a priceless gift to your children.

We equip our kids with an essential tool for happiness and success: the ability to embrace personal growth with their *own* hearts as the driver.

I didn't start out knowing there was another way to live. Life brought me an experience that awakened me with a jolt. I wasn't trying to be a better father, but I became one. I learned to let my heart lead the way, and now I completely trust that its guidance is true above all else. As a result, I'm watching my children do the same.

"The greatest lesson of my life has been to recognize that I am solely responsible for my life—not living to please other people, but doing what my heart says."

Oprah Winfrey, American television host, actress, producer, and philanthropist. She is widely regarded as one of the most influential woman in the world.

WHO IS TOM CONIGLIARO?

Tom with (wife) Lisa, and (children) Christine, Elizabeth, Mark, and James

Tom Conigliaro has climbed high on the Wall Street ladder. A top managing director for Goldman Sachs since 2003, Conigliaro heads up the Hudson Street Division, which provides third-party research to Goldman Sachs clients and invests in alternative investment research firms.

Before joining Sachs, Conigliaro spent sixteen years at Merrill Lunch, where he worked in derivative sales and equity sales trading. Most recently Conigliaro headed the global soft dollar and directed commission businesses. In addition, he had responsibility for running sales across the company's institutional clearing division.

But Conigliaro also gives back. As chair of the advisory board for Liberty LEADS, he plays a vital role in that organization's mission of helping more than three hundred high-risk fifth- through twelfth-graders stay on track for admission to highly selective colleges and universities.

Conigliaro earned his undergraduate degree from Widener University in 1985 and an MBA from the University of South Florida in 1986. In 1994, he was designated with the Chartered Financial Award (CFA).

Conigliaro lives with his wife and their four children in Summit, New Jersey. He has taught his children the value of hard work and solid relationships, helping them achieve their dreams. Using his networking skills, Conigliaro has helped his younger daughter, Christine, move toward an acting career, and his older daughter, Elizabeth, get a start in television production. Says Conigliaro, "I just did what I believe any dad would do."

When I was a young man,
I wanted to change the world.
I found it was difficult to change the world, so I
tried to change my nation.
When I found I couldn't change the nation, I
began to focus on my town.
I couldn't change the town, and as an older man,
I tried to change my family.

Now as an old man,
I realize the only thing I can change is myself,
and suddenly I realize that if long ago I had
changed myself, I could have made
an impact on my family.
My family and I could have made
an impact on our town.

Their impact could have changed the nation
and I could indeed have changed the world.

Unknown Monk, AD 1100

"Place the oxygen mask on your own face
before assisting your child."

Airline Regulations

FINDING THE GOOD
AND MAKING LIFE FUN!

If I Were Your Daddy ... I'd help you find fun in whatever you are doing. I'd teach you to follow a healthy lifestyle, find your own self-worth, and always focus on the positive.

ROY MARTINA, M.D.
Holistic Physician and Educator

Even as a boy, I knew I wasn't going to father the way I'd been fathered. A lot of us are like that; we say we don't want to be like our parents but then years later we have a sudden, unpleasant realization that we've become just like them. Being a parent is an enormous undertaking, and the instruction manual we're handed down, the "watch and be like me" invisible guide we all get, may not be the one we would have chosen. That was certainly the case with me. A boy's first role model is always his father, and my dad provided me with a fantastic *reverse* role model, someone who teaches how *not* to be. When I was still pretty young it became crystal clear that I wanted another way to live my life.

Home was the Caribbean Island of Aruba. My dad was a police officer—a stern and joyless man who was all macho cliché. He never showed any affection toward my mother, nor tenderness toward me.

As a boy I learned early that to earn his pride and attention I needed to do something "worthy." It felt to me like he linked love to results, and this tied my self-esteem to doing things to make him proud. Because I craved his love and approval more than anything, I worked hard to perform well in sports and school.

But at school I was easily distracted and had difficulty paying attention, so winning his approval for good grades meant staying up late to do the work I hadn't finished in class. With only six hours of sleep a night, I went to school with bags and dark circles under my eyes, and so I came to associate achievement with stress. I also suffered from asthmatic bronchitis, and the medicine I was given caused hyperactivity as a side effect.

Fortunately I was diagnosed with what today is called attention deficit disorder, or ADD/ADHD. A psychologist suggested that my parents sign me up for judo as a physical outlet, and a means of corralling my focus. I took to it naturally and ended up winning more than two hundred trophies and championships, including two world records, in judo, karate, kickboxing, and other martial art, in my lifetime.

My karate teacher, Sensei Nicolas, was a wise, kind, and loving man who became like a second father to me. He gave me a perspective and beliefs far more constructive than what I was getting at home. He taught me my first empowering mindset: to believe in myself and not take things so personally. Under the guise of martial arts, he taught me empowering habits, such as meditating and visualizing my goals, and believing that anything is possible. With his guidance I could imagine and see the life I actually wanted - and I learned I could create it. So with that strong vision and awareness driving me, I left home when I was sixteen and went to Holland to study medicine.

I broke out of my parents' paradigm.

I emerged with a medical degree in hand, and a whole new life in front of me. With Sensei Nicholas's teachings, coupled with the discipline and philosophy of the martial arts, I broke out of my parents' paradigm. Who I started out as by default and who I become through deliberate choice were worlds apart. By consciously expanding my world far beyond the one I was born into, I was able to create what I envisioned: a fulfilling, happy, vibrantly healthy, and decidedly *fun* life.

In my early twenties I met and married Erica. When our two sons were born, I wanted to pass on the perspectives of true health and emotional well-being that I had learned. And now I could create the father-son relationship I'd always wanted with my own dad.

IT'S GOTTA BE FUN

One day when my older boy was still a toddler, we were doing number and word flashcards when his focus began to drift. So to grab and hold his attention I started to make the activity lively and fun. I found that when I playfully rolled through the deck, he was more willing to participate, and caught on more quickly. When I saw the direct correlation between fun and optimal learning and performance, fun became the objective, not the by-product. As both boys grew, I applied to all their activities this idea of having fun as the goal. This was a real generational shift. Where my father had motivated by withholding love and approval, I encouraged my sons to explore what motivated them, *what they considered fun,* and joyfully move through life.

> *When* I saw the direct correlation between fun and optimal learning, fun became the objective, not the by-product.

As they grew, it was exciting for me see them both take to the martial arts on their own. Besides providing superb physical conditioning, self-defense sports teach respect, focus, humility, mindfulness, and care of the weaker party. I knew these activities would tone my sons' characters as well as their athleticism, just as they had mine.

Once again, my focus around sports and competing was to make it fun. How the boys approached an activity mattered more to me than their scores or winning. I always asked, "What about this is fun?" When

I zeroed in on what was enjoyable, it directed their attention there. For the things they didn't like doing, the question became "What *could* be fun about this?" We found ways to make seemingly boring things enjoyable by turning them into games. For instance, when the boys had to run and train to build stamina for championship matches, we chased each other and held mock competitions. It was still strenuous, but this made it fun, which translated into staying more engaged, faster learning, less stress, and superior results. Time after time I saw this approach working its magic.

Once at the national tae kwon do championship, while my youngest awaited his turn he was engrossed in his Nintendo. When his name was called, he nonchalantly looked up and said, "Oh, my turn." Pressing the pause button, he handed me the device and said, "Watch this for me, Dad. I'll be right back." He went, competed, returned, and matter-of-factly resumed playing his game. He hadn't stressed over his match whatsoever.

"Was it fun?" I inquired.

"Yeah, it was fun," he said with a big grin. He'd just won nationals!

Both my boys became black belts and won many competitions and championships. But win or lose, the first words out of my mouth afterward were always *"Did you have fun?"* I wasn't your typical sideline sports dad/coach, and I definitely wasn't my father's son. I made sure my boys never felt any pressure to perform or win *for me*.

Making something fun, however, doesn't mean doing "whatever whenever" and expecting trophies. My sons' tae kwon do activities required endless hours, enormous dedication, and exhaustive training. Their natural gifts and enthusiasm certainly helped, but commitment and personal investment were still required for them to excel.

Instead of studying harder, try to make your classes entertaining.

This fun formula (fun = better results) applied to many things, including their schoolwork. At my urging, the boys found whatever fun they could in their studies. But like many kids, my youngest considered most of what he was learning in high school to be "useless," so he allowed himself to get bored, and consequently struggled. He did just enough to stay afloat, and getting him to do even that took considerable effort. I pointed out that when he liked a subject, he did well. So to help keep him get engaged, I reminded him of the "fun formula." Instead of encouraging him to study harder, I encouraged him to be creative and find a way to see the class more as entertainment than as obligation. It worked.

Parents have a pivotal role. If fun is your goal for your children, it'll be their focus too, and their brains will go there without prompting. They'll get great results with much less stress and strain.

TEACH THEM TO BE PROUD OF THEMSELVES

Early on I began asking my children what they liked about themselves, and I repeated variations of that question over time: "What do you really like about yourself? What are the things you like about being you?" Bringing their focus to what they *liked about themselves* in this way strengthened their self-esteem. It made them aware of all the positive things about themselves they *should* feel good about.

It was important to me to teach my sons to savor their successes as their own instead of having their positive feelings dependent upon the approval of others, even Mom's and Dad's. Like many parents, my mother and father had made the honest mistake of wanting to be proud of their children. When my father said, "I'm proud of you for winning that competition," for instance, my own self esteem became directly connected to his praise of me, which required me to achieve specific results. Outer measurements like this don't increase a child's intrinsic sense of self-worth, and I was no exception.

When they did well at something, we asked, "How does that make you feel?" as opposed to saying, "We're so proud of you."

By contrast, Erica and I encouraged our boys to accomplish things for the purpose of feeling good about themselves, versus impressing us. When they did well at something, we asked, "How does that make you feel?" as opposed to saying, *"We're* so proud of you." This subtle shift conditioned them to own their feelings, and not to tirelessly pursue outer acclaim, which is fickle at best. They had fun and felt good about themselves. They also realized that their parents' love didn't rise or fall because they earned a medal or lost a match, brought home good grades or fumbled a class. Knowing how to be proud of themselves and make themselves happy empowered them with a critical life skill.

FINDING FUN WHERE THERE APPEARS TO BE NONE

Having kids buy into the need for it makes them willing participants.

My father ruled with an iron hand. Whatever cooperation existed among my siblings and me arose out of fear of consequences. I felt there had to be a better way to accomplish things. To be engaged in anything, children—just like adults—must buy into the need for it. So when my sons resisted doing their chores, I sat them down and asked, "Does this chore really need to be done?" As part of that discussion, I posed some worst-case scenarios: "What would happen if we didn't take the garbage out? How long would we be able to live in a house that smelled of decaying food? What if worms and other insects start living in the garbage and infesting the house?" With this greater perspective my boys' grumbling protests quieted, and they eventually agreed that yes, doing such and such was necessary.

So then I asked, "How can we make this fun?" They offered several answers: playing music, doing the task together, rewarding themselves upon its completion. My youngest volunteered, "It would be way more fun to wash the car, Dad, if you promised to play paintball with us this weekend." That sounded like fun to me too, so I agreed. Suddenly, they were willing participants with an entirely different attitude—and we had a blast playing paintball. They were acquiring a powerful life skill: make it fun, or link it to a self-designed reward, so you can wholly commit rather than doing the task halfheartedly or resentfully.

BEING EMOTIONALLY HONEST AND FINDING THE GOOD

My father never told me he loved me, even when I was really young. He also never seemed interested in what his children were thinking or feeling. Parent-child conversation didn't exist. From the time I was small I was expected to be a "real" man and deal with challenges on my own. With my own boys, early on I decided to do all this differently. I wanted to show my sons that a real man understands that true strength comes from being vulnerable, emotive, and affectionate. Keeping emotions pent up has nothing to do with being a man. Whenever my boys came through the door, I hugged them and said, "I love you." And they would say, "Yes, we know, Daddy. You tell us a million times. We know it by now." They are grown men now, but I still hug them and say, "I love you," and I have no plans to ever stop.

When the boys were five and seven, Erica and I divorced. We shared custody, and for the first year I encouraged them to talk about their feelings regarding this new arrangement. I began by sharing a thought, memory, or wish, and sometimes we ended up crying together. In this area there's a fine line between appropriate sharing and harmful dumping. But my father had never showed any emotion, and from him I learned that you can't equip your children to be emotionally intelligent by hiding your feelings from them.

You can't equip your children to be emotionally intelligent by hiding your feelings from them.

In the early months following the divorce, the boys tried to talk me into coming home. At a certain point, I realized they were stuck. To redirect their focus I asked, "Hey, guys, tell me what's fun about this new arrangement." At first they were startled, but because they were in the habit of doing this, they managed to come up with a few advantages. They got to spend more time alone with me. My rules differed somewhat from their mom's. We played soccer, paintball, and lots of games every visit. We got to eat out a lot, and so on. So even though the divorce was something none of us liked, I started to guide them toward the benefits of having two homes.

After a few months they began focusing more on those benefits, instead of what was missing. After about six months, they seemed completely fine. I hadn't invalidated their feelings, or shut down from hearing how they felt. But by helping redirect their focus to find the *positive way forward,* I kept them from staying stuck in the negative.

REINFORCING THE POSITIVE VERSUS PUNISHING THE WRONG

*B*eing overly occupied with what's wrong can actually reinforce the problem—*what we focus on expands and grows in our life.*

My father was judge, jury, and executioner all in one. Whenever we kids did something wrong, he asked if we understood we'd broken whichever rule and would be punished. He then issued his verdict, which was usually that we were to be hit repeatedly with his hard rubber police baton. I didn't for a minute believe the stock line he spoke as he struck: "This hurts me more than it does you." Bent over, my pants around my ankles, all I knew was that I was dirt.

Children being reprimanded for a certain behavior often interpret the punishment as a statement that *they* are wrong; *they* are bad. They miss the message that what's at issue is their *behavior.* Being overly occupied with what's wrong can actually lead to reinforcing the problem, because *that which we focus on expands and grows in our life.* And I didn't want to expand unwanted behavior or a "problem" by giving it all of my attention—I wanted to minimize it.

Children love pleasing their parents, and they will quickly repeat rewarded behaviors, so I chose to acknowledge and celebrate their good and positive behaviors. I focused on those things I wanted my kids to keep doing, and I ignored (as much as possible) their negative or weak behaviors. And, of course, I always affirmed that the child was loved.

I focused on those things I wanted my kids to keep doing, and I ignored (as much as possible) their negative or weak behaviors.

To do this, I used something called "sandwich feedback." In the first part of this feedback, no matter what behavior needed to be addressed, I began by finding something good to acknowledge. The second part—the middle of the sandwich—involved going over what could be improved, in the form of a constructive suggestion or request. The last involved always letting them know I have faith in them, I see their greatness, and I love them.

To use sandwich feedback effectively I first had to get myself to a place where I was neutral. If I was not neutral, if I was still angry or upset, I could not do it. To do this I really had to work on my own stuff first, so from the time they were young, although I was teaching them, they were teaching me as well. It was always a very humbling experience.

For example, like me, my youngest son was hyperactive and struggled with ADD. In his hyperactive mode he ran around the house and accidentally broke things. Vases, chairs—it was always something. And just like my father, I initially reacted negatively to these crashes. But as soon as I realized what I was doing, I quickly switched gears, let go of my anger, and got myself into that neutral place. This required facing some of my own stuff. Then I began focusing not on my son's hyperactivity, but on his energy and excitement as positive, desirable components of his behavior. While we cleaned up the vase, or whatever was broken, I would tell him that I admired him for his energy—that he had so much passion in what he was doing. The only problem was *the way* he was using this energy and passion. He needed to watch out a bit more because the vase cost money and we could not keep replacing the stuff that got broken. Then I would finish up with something like, "I really love you and care about you. No matter how many vases you break, I will always love you." I sandwiched the correction in a way he could hear it, between two affirmations.

I sandwiched a correction in a way he could hear it, between two affirmations.

As I continued to focus on his energy and enthusiasm, he did become more careful. I could see that in the throes of an ADD attack, he was trying hard not to break things, even though applying that kind of restraint was a bit stressful for him. In the end, his ADD proved an advantage for him, as had mine. As he became able to channel excess energy into physical activity for many hours a day, he became a standout athlete. Having excelled at the martial arts myself, I couldn't help but notice that the "how" of our respective rises differed markedly. Because the boys always had fun and every activity made them happy, their successes happened for the right reasons.

Now, no matter what life throws at my sons, they reflexively know how to air their feelings, embrace the positive, and to whatever degree, find the fun. Such a formula, if you can call it that, was planted in their beings throughout their upbringing. It's all they know.

WE TEACH AND THEY TEACH

I always thought it was me teaching my children, equipping them with empowering mindsets and attitudes. Then one day my older son set me straight. He was in my office when I received a phone call that really upset me. Only about seven at the time, my son looked at me and said, "Daddy, it's a good time to breathe. Do you want me to help you to breathe?" He had just attended one of my workshops, but I was so upset it took a while for me to realize that he was echoing right back to me exactly what I was teaching others. I was instantly humbled. It was such a huge "aha" to realize that as adults we can go out and preach and teach whatever we want, but if we give children a chance to express themselves, they can be wise beyond words. He was *my* teacher. Children are a divine spirit in a child's body, and this kind of clarity gives you a whole new level of respect for the magnificence of a child. It certainly did for me.

For a complete description of Dr. Martina's successful ADD approach with his son, visit:
www.ifiwereyourdaddy.com/roymartina

"*You must take personal responsibility. You cannot change the circumstances, the seasons, or the wind, but you can change yourself.*"

Jim Rohn, American entrepreneur, author, and speaker. A self-made multi millionaire, Rohn is commonly regarded as a legendary icon in the personal development industry.

$\mathcal{W}$HO IS ROY MARTINA, M.D.?

Roy with (children) Roy Enrique Sunray and Joey Erick Sky

Dr. Roy Martina isn't your garden-variety GP. This dedicated complementary medicine practitioner is also a master of the martial arts—a sixth-degree black belt and a seven-time undefeated European champion in free-fight full-contact karate. He's turned his personal triumphs into his professional mission: to help others change their self-defeating habits.

After seeing how conventional and alternative medicine failed to restore full health to his patients, Martina began researching solutions that help bodies and minds heal. His breakthrough natural, self-healing remedies are at the heart of his Omega health coaching and training workshops. He's taught with the likes of Deepak Chopra, Masaru Emoto, Eric Pearl, and Debbie Ford. His list of who's who clients includes tennis star Nadia Petrova, British actor Kate Beckinsale, and nine-time world champion Muay Thai kickboxer Robbie Kaman.

A native of Curacao who grew up in Aruba, Martina knows a thing or two about winning. He holds the 1977 record for the fastest knockout (four seconds) in free fight full-contact karate and the 1979 record for seven consecutive knockouts in a single day. Martina is also a prolific writer. His fifty-plus self-help books include the international best seller *Emotional Balance.* His transformational audio and video programs include guided meditations on stress relief, mental resilience, and weight loss.

Martina lives in Florida. Preventing cancer and slowing the aging process are his current research passions.

www.roymartina.com

INSPIRING COOPERATION

If I Were Your Daddy ... I'd help you learn the art of cooperation and give you the freedom to express yourself.

JOHN GRAY, Ph.D.
Best-Selling Author
& Relationships Expert

I was coming home from a long trip, another book tour with back-to-back radio and television interviews. A year into my marriage, I was a new father of a baby girl and two beautiful stepdaughters, ages eight and twelve. As I entered the house, I heard raised voices coming from the kitchen. I listened, aghast at the way my daughter was speaking to her mother. Entering the kitchen I quickly dominated the situation, shouting, *"Don't you dare talk to your mother that way ever again!"*

Shocked into silence, my daughter tried to process what had just happened. As she held in her hurt and resentment, I watched her self-esteem plummet. By raising my voice that way I had intimidated and frightened her, and in that moment, I realized this was exactly what my father had done with me and my brothers when he needed to control the situation—*because he didn't know what else to do.*

FEAR AND INTIMIDATION ARE NEVER THE BEST CHOICE

There's nothing wrong with telling children that their behavior is inappropriate, and doing what is necessary to correct that behavior. However the way I had just done it was not something I ever wanted to do. I never wanted to be like my father, yet look what I had just done. I must have picked up that negative behavior subconsciously, and despite my distaste for it, it came out because I had nothing to replace it with. What a wake-up call! Less than thirty minutes later I was at my daughter's bedroom door saying, "You didn't deserve to be spoken to that way. No one does. Can you forgive me?"

This was a turning point. The event had such a profound impact on me that from that day forward I never yelled at my kids again. Instead I sought more effective and loving ways to communicate and support them in growing up. Once I learned those ways, I could choose them—so much so that twenty-some years later, I wrote a book, *Children Are from Heaven*, about the many ways to manage and support your children without resorting to fear, intimidation, punishment, and shame.

FREEDOM TO EXPRESS NEGATIVE EMOTIONS

I grew up in a family of six boys. My mother created a very safe environment for us with her unconditional love and acceptance. I knew I could always go to her and express my thoughts and feelings, without fear of judgment, disapproval, or invalidation. She was always interested in what I had to say, and I always felt heard. She didn't demand that my ideas be perfect, nor did she point out to me how much more she knew as a result of about thirty more years of living.

Dad, on the other hand, was her opposite in such matters. If I was upset about something, he would explain to me exactly why I shouldn't be upset. If I came up short or deficient, he focused on how I could be "better" or "different." As a result, I experienced him as resisting who I was, and I didn't feel safe sharing myself freely.

On top of this, my father assumed the role of the family "heavy." When we six boys were out of control, my mother would just defer to him to take charge. Although she certainly had some boundaries, when any of us began pushing against them, it was up to Dad to come in and restore order. My parents' roles became polarized. She became the "yes" person, and he became the "no" person—a division of labor that prevented him from exploring how he might also be a "yes" person. As the enforcer, he raised his voice to gain control, which made him the bad guy, while my mother got to remain the saint. And that's just how it was. Of course, I later realized that both my parents were doing the best they could in raising six sons. As parents, we can't expect perfection of ourselves; instead we need to keep striving to do the best we can.

FINDING A BETTER WAY: COOPERATION VERSUS RESISTANCE

When I talked to one of my brothers about being a father, he said, "I know what *not* to do; I don't want to control my children the way we were controlled as kids. But I don't know what *to do* instead!" He was right. It's not enough to recognize that what you're doing *doesn't* work; you have to find something better to take its place. It's a common problem. When parents find that what they are doing is not working, their only recourse is to revert back to what their parents did when *they* didn't know what to do. When children are out of control, frustrated parents can easily slip into out-of-control behavior themselves, yelling and threatening. However, that behavior just intimidates and scares children. After a while kids learn to correct themselves out of fear rather than out of respect, and their needs never get heard.

It's not enough to recognize that what you're doing doesn't work; you have to find something better to take its place.

I began to wonder: was it was possible to encourage my children's highest potential, but still maintain harmony and structure in our home?

It turned out the answer was a resounding "yes." I learned I could manage my children without having to yell at them, and this gave them tremendous permission to express themselves. My goal was to support my daughters in developing a strong sense of self, because therein lies the gift of their greatness. Every great thinker, artist, scientist, and leader in history had a strong sense of self-identity that enabled him or her to forge through opposition and resistance, say no to past conventions, and think creatively. Thinking of my three daughters, I realized that three future leaders slept under our roof. The way Bonnie and I expressed love, and helped them grow, would make all the difference in how their lives unfolded.

Cooperation rather than coercion became the family approach.

I knew if the girls were going to develop a positive sense of self and stand apart from to the *status quo,* they needed the freedom to question and even resist authority. They needed to be able to push back against us, yet still understand and stay within the boundaries of acceptable behavior. Just as my mother had done, we let our children know that their feelings were valid, respected, and heard. That didn't mean our children always got their way, because in the end Bonnie and I were still in charge. The difference was that cooperation rather than coercion became the family approach.

FREEDOM TO CHOOSE AND COOPERATE:
USING BENEFITS AND REWARDS
INSTEAD OF PUNISHMENT AND THREATS

All parents want two things: they want to motivate their kids, and they want to control or manage them. On the surface, fear usually works to create obedience, and for this reason it's been used by parents for centuries—because they've had no better ideas. However, fear will never awaken a child's natural motivation to cooperate, nor can it support his or her spirit. Obedience means they are simply subordinating their own will to their parents' will. Cooperation, on the other hand, means *joining* their will to their parents' will, and those two strategies are simply miles apart.

Deep inside, children are basically programmed to one prime directive:

they want to please their parents, because their survival depends on it. In a parenting class I learned that cooperation is their preferred, even natural, state. It turned out my job as a parent wasn't to

ℱear will never awaken a child's natural motivation to cooperate, nor support her spirit.

control, enforce, or punish, but to minimize resistance and redirect them into their natural state of cooperation. What great news! This job could be done by using a more positive approach that motivated by rewards rather than threats. I decided to try it out.

One sunny Saturday morning, my daughter and I agreed we would go to the park. I repeatedly asked her to get ready, but she basically ignored me. So I had several choices. I could get irritated and start using threats and penalties like "If you don't put on your jacket *right now,* we won't be able to go to the park." I could slip into an outburst, "You *never* listen, you're not paying attention," using angry negative statements that expressed my frustration, made her "bad," and possibly injured her self image.

Instead I chose to motivate her through benefits and rewards. Looking her in the eyes I lovingly suggested, "If you put on your jacket right now, we'll have plenty of time, and we'll be able to go to the park." The difference was that I had to change the consequence from negative to positive. With a positive consequence, *my request* quickly became *her desire,* and she got ready. Soliciting her cooperation honored her, because it gave her freedom to choose a benefit rather than be overpowered or penalized. The promise of *more* inspires everyone, young or old, to cooperate.

THE IMPORTANCE OF BOUNDARIES

When you truly allow children to express themselves when they're upset, there should be boundaries around how—and how much—they're allowed to express themselves. Although the parent must learn not to dominate the child, the child also has to learn to express his or her truth respectfully.

For such learning to occur, home has to be a *safe* place. Managing negative emotions is a necessary part of creating a successful fulfilling life, and home is where children learn how to do that safely. Being able to feel and express their negative emotions safely would allow them to develop a strong sense of self and gradually discover their inner wealth: creativity, intuition, love, confidence, joy, compassion, conscience, and the ability to self-correct after making a mistake.

> *Being able to feel and express their negative emotions safely would allow them to develop a strong sense of self.*

As a result, whenever the kids came and talked something over with me, I always considered their point of view. Occasionally I'd even change my mind because my kids had a better idea. Still, once negotiations were over, sometimes they just needed to honor my request. For these occasions, I used what I termed the "commander voice."

CALM, COOL, AND COLLECTED: USING THE NEUTRAL, AUTHORITATIVE COMMANDER VOICE

One of my daughters repeatedly left her bicycle out. I'd explained to her many times the importance of putting it away in the garage. "I might run over it with the car, someone could trip over it, or it might get stolen." She'd understood. "Do you agree it's important to put it away?" "Yes," she'd said. And yet the bike would be left out again.

To solve this problem, I could have threatened to take away privileges or raised my voice and intimidated her— and either of those tactics would likely have worked, but not without some hurt too. So instead I used what I called the "commander voice." I would remain in control of myself, staying cool, calm, and collected. My voice would be strong, firm but neutral, repeating the request until it is done.

So using my commander voice I said, "I want you to put your bicycle in the garage." She said, "Why do I have to do it now?" I just listened and said again, "Right now, I want you to put the bicycle in the garage." Again, "Dad, I'm busy. I don't want to. I might use it later." It felt like she was baiting me to drag out the threat, and part of me wanted to give in and say, "Do it now, or I will take it away," but I resisted. Still using the commander tone, I simply repeated the request again, and then again, until she complied. I didn't have to say, "We're not going anywhere until the bicycle is in the garage," because my steadfast, certain tone said it for me. At a certain point she realized this was not a negotiation, and I wasn't going to budge from my position. She put the bike away.

$\mathcal{T}$he "commander voice" is strong, firm but neutral, and repeats the request until it is done.

I've found this to be a very simple yet powerful technique. The first time you use it your children will be surprised when you don't escalate your voice and instead just keep repeating the command. You may have to say it twenty times. However, the next time they hear that voice they will comply after fewer repeats. After the third time they quickly learn that this tone of voice means, "This is not a negotiation. I'm not budging." After that, you don't have to repeat it often before they comply.

This works because children are hardwired to win your approval, and they realize you're not giving up and they're not getting out of it. The more successful children can be in winning your approval, the healthier they will be.

EVERYTHING WE NEED IS ALWAYS AVAILABLE

One of the positive key messages I received from both of my parents is that we are all totally responsible for the world we live in, the situations we end up in, and the people we are with. We create it all through our choices. If we can learn our lessons, we can make better choices and take better actions, and thus create the life we want. In the process of creating this life we want, *everything we need is always available.* That's a level of trust in life I grew up with and I see in all my kids—that they will have what they need.

So how did my daughters turn out after all this? Well, one of them is a therapist and works with children. She's committed to helping the community, and helping children with their body image and the resulting self-esteem.

Another daughter is an event planner, currently at home raising her family. She's an incredibly nurturing parent, and one thing she is passing along to her kids is the gift of remaining calm when things are upsetting. For example, recently her daughter was stung by a bee. Rather than getting all upset and frightened and mad at the bee, my daughter caught the bee, then talked about how frightened it probably was. "Now, let's let the bee go and be free." She just maintained a sense of calmness and helped her daughter understand the situation in a positive way, unlike the path many people take when they're in pain or danger. They let fear or upset take over. They become agitated, worried, and scared, and that's the message they give their children. However, when we stay calm, and take positive action to solve a problem, then our kids receive the message "Right now we may not know what the answer is, but we'll find it." And so we always have what we need to take the next step towards solving problems in our lives—and achieving our goals.

> She maintained a sense of calmness and helped her daughter understand the situation in a positive way.

My third daughter is an actress and singer. Because she grew up with the freedom to safely express herself, she has a powerful personal charisma on stage.

It's up to each parent to identify what we liked and didn't like from our own upbringing. We must take what works, and replace what doesn't with something better. No parent needs to be polarized into being the enforcer parent or the "yes" parent—as I discovered. For me this involved learning and then adopting skills with my daughters that were positive and nurturing rather than damaging to a child's will. The result is three confident, cooperative, and compassionate young women, each with a strong, healthy, and independent sense of self.

Of all the intangible gifts I've given my children, I consider my mother's gift—the feeling of always being heard and validated—one of the most important. I've given it to them and trust they will pass this gift along to their own children. From what I've seen, that process has already begun.

"Feelings of worth can flourish only in an atmosphere where individual differences are appreciated, mistakes are tolerated, communication is open, and rules are flexible—the kind of atmosphere that is found in a nurturing family."

Virginia Satir (1916 - 1988), noted American author and psychotherapist, known especially for her approach to family therapy.

WHO IS JOHN GRAY, Ph.D.?

John with (wife) Bonnie, who have three children and three grandchildren

John Gray, Ph.D., is the best-selling relationship author of all time. His groundbreaking 1992 book, *Men Are from Mars, Women Are from Venus,* was, according to *USA Today,* "the number one bestselling book of the last decade." In the past fifteen years, more than forty million "Mars-Venus" books have been sold in more than forty-five languages.

An internationally recognized expert in the fields of communication and relationship, Gray focuses uniquely on helping men and women understand, respect, and appreciate their differences. For more than thirty years, he has conducted public and private seminars for thousands of participants.

John Gray received his doctorate in psychology and human sexuality from Columbia Pacific University in 1982. He has served as consulting editor of *The Family Journal* and as a member of the Distinguished Advisory Board of the International Association of Marriage and Family Counselors. He is a recipient of the Smart Marriages Impact Award.

John Gray has appeared on almost every talk and news program—including *Oprah, Larry King Live, Good Morning America, The Today Show,* and the *CBS Morning Show*—and his nationally syndicated column reaches thirty million readers.

John Gray, an avid follower of his own health, fitness, and relationship advice, lives in northern California with Bonnie, his wife of twenty-three years. They have three grown daughters and three grandchildren.

www.marsvenus.com

SELF-DISCOVERY

FINDING & FIRING YOUR SPARK OF BRILLIANCE

If I Were Your Daddy ... I would applaud your originality, however wacky, and cheer your jumps into the unknown. Thinking big and acting boldly would be your normal, and I'd promise to help you find and ignite your native fires of brilliance.

MALOUF ABRAHAM JR., M.D.

Allergy Specialist & Art Collector

My wife of nearly fifty years, Therese, and I recently attended a wedding in our little Texas town of Canadian, where about 450 people were packed into the pews of this little Protestant church. In the front was a small pool where people are immersed during baptism. On the altar was a flower arrangement with candles and fake plastic greenery, all stuck into a Styrofoam base. We were sitting about halfway back while the organizers continued setting up folding chairs in the aisles, packing even more people in. Sitting there in the windowless church, I felt like a sardine stuffed into an airtight can. I thought to myself, "If there were a fire, people would have to climb over all these extra chairs and Grandma's crutches and Grandpa's walker and everything to get to the doors." It was a funny thought, actually; I wasn't being serious. But then I saw it: the plastic flower arrangement was, in fact, on fire at the front of the church!

I watched in amazement. Nobody moved! Nobody did *anything!* Am I the only one who sees this, I wondered? I mean, the college football players standing there in their tuxedos and chewing gum (which I think makes a person look like an idiot) were just feet away from the blaze and they weren't moving. And there I was, this geriatric person, who took off like a shot, winding my way through all these extra chairs and people and walkers and crutches to get to the burning altar. Luckily, there was water in the baptistery, so I started scooping it with my hands onto the fire. Still, not another person moved. I and I alone threw water on that fire and put it out. There I was, standing in this layer of smoke, beside the now smoldering altar, and looking out at all these people, including those gorilla football players who never did move. I made the sign of the cross and chuckled inside; now that the fire was out, it was a funny scene. I said to myself, "Bless you, my children. Today is *not* the day you get written up in *Time* magazine or broadcast on CNN as one of 450 people who perished in a fire of Styrofoam and fake flowers in this tiny, windowless church *because no one took action!*"

When you act boldly, when you're bold in life, you may be the most qualified person around simply because of your willingness to act. I've observed human inertia of this type my whole life. Most people are followers; they want to be led or to have someone else solve their problems. I've never been a follower. Instead of waiting around for things to happen—for life to work out or for someone else to put out the fire—I act and I act boldly. I raised three kids to live the same way. Today, my grown sons are men of action. I intentionally instilled and encouraged that mind-set in all three of them.

When you act boldly, you may be the most qualified person around simply because of your willingness to act.

WHAT EARNS A GOLD STAR?

I was raised in Canadian, Texas, and one of the reasons I came back to my home town was to pick up where I'd left off and try to impress my dad. If he'd been a jerk I wouldn't have cared because he was so impressive. In fact, he was brilliant. My dad, Malouf Abraham Sr., graduated from high school at fourteen and became legendary. He was generous, smart, and honest, and everybody in local politics and the oil and gas industry who knew him was impressed with him. But I wanted *him* to be impressed with *me*.

However, growing up in this little Texas town, if you weren't a football hero, you were nothing, and nothing else I might do mattered. Although I tried, I didn't fit in. Oh, I was included. I was a good student, a good this, that, and the other, but I knew I wasn't what people were looking for. They were looking for me to be *like my dad.* And I wasn't.

Your mother can tell you every day how wonderful you are (and mine did), but I needed to hear it from my dad. A son never wants to disappoint his father. He always wants to impress him, wants him to be proud. If you never get that experience, your dad can up and die on you, still unimpressed, and you're left hanging. Which is what happened to me.

Your mother can tell you every day how wonderful you are, but every child needs to hear it from his dad too.

I never wanted my sons to be left hanging, feeling they had never been able to impress me or hadn't lived up to my expectations. So I looked for things to be impressed by, and I told them. I made sure I gave credit where credit was due. One quality that most impressed me was the trait that saved us all that day in the packed little Protestant church. It's something my father definitely had; I valued it in myself and I wanted it for my boys. It was to be creative, bold, and willing to act.

I've known many people with a high IQ, and people with a lot of money or land or something else, but I've known very *few* people with a terrific imagination and the courage of their convictions. I'm talking about people who decide to do something even though others around them might say, "You can't do that, that won't work." It's the people who say, "Just watch me," and then go do it anyway. I value that kind of defiance—

an "I'll show you" attitude—and it's great that life made me pretty much that way. I always tried to foster it in my boys. When they stood up and did something bold or different or creative, I made a big deal of it. If I'd been handing out gold stars, like mommies do to kids who poop in the potty instead of a diaper, my gold stars would be for thinking outside the box and then having the guts to give those ideas a whirl. I think accolades need to be earned.

And that's just what my sons did. They were always coming up with innovative ideas. "Boys," I'd say, "I don't know if this is going to work or not, but I so admire you, and I'm thrilled you've even come up with an idea like this. I sure hope it works, and I think it will! And even if it doesn't, I'm just thrilled you've even wanted to try it." When their ideas didn't work out, it wasn't a big deal. Success was in the trying, and the greater the creative stretch, the bolder the approach, the better!

Success was in trying, and the greater the creative stretch, the bolder the approach, the better!

In our family, success meant being original, not winning a prize, and I applauded the approach more than the result. Had our family written history books, they'd have said that Thomas Edison *succeeded* (not failed) ten thousand times before changing the world with a working incandescent light bulb, because he kept trying new things. He kept innovating until the light (literally) came on. Likewise, in his own way, each of my sons thought of new ways to be resourceful, talented, and creative in his own right.

I should mention here that our sons had an unorthodox breeding ground with Therese and me. If you surveyed our neighbors, they might have said our family was likable but kind of nuts, something folks probably still say about me. We lived by the values we espoused. We weren't afraid to try things no one had thought about doing. Nothing was impossible, no idea too crazy, for the Abrahams. We were the family who bought the old Baptist church in town for fifteen thousand dollars An abandoned architectural landmark with beautiful features hidden by a decade of grime and neglect, it was slated for demolition. Sure, it was a nontraditional family home, but heck—once we fixed it up, we had the best housing deal in town! People thought we were crazy. My wife finally hammered a sign in the front yard that read, "We think you're crazy too!" With this—us—as their model, the boys grew up knowing that every idea had potential rather than worrying about what others thought. What freedom!

These were the convictions I wanted embedded in his consciousness: "Dad believes in me. Anything's possible."

I wanted our boys to know that their every vision was possible. Once, when our oldest, Eddie, had gone to bed, I was sitting on his bedroom floor as we talked in the dark. I said, "Eddie, when you grow up, you'll be president of the United States and live in that big white house and I'll come see you and stay in one of those fancy bedrooms." From the headboard came the retort, "I'm not going to be the president of the United States." I answered back, "Somebody's got to do the job, Eddie, and you'd be good at it." These were the convictions I wanted embedded in his consciousness, in his dreams, as he drifted off: "Dad believes in me. I can do whatever I want. Anything's possible."

WISDOM IN FAMILY MEALS

Innovation wasn't just about big-deal stuff in our family; we welcomed new approaches to the everyday. In my medical practice I was always impressing upon people the importance of family meals, and I learned about some studies that were done to determine what all goes into somebody becoming a National Merit Scholar. It turns out that the biggest common denominator was they all grew up in a home where there was a family meal. So I'm a big advocate.

Even as the boys got older, our family gathered around dinner every night. They could miss it with two hours notice and a good reason, but otherwise we expected everyone seated with hands washed by 6:30. Sometimes they would bring last-minute guests, but we always had enough food for everyone. Therese would fix these wonderful home-cooked meals, and *no TV blared while we ate.* When we sat down, the plates were stacked in front of me. We would hold hands and have the blessing, then I would serve each plate and send it around. It just seemed more civilized to me. The last plate was mine, and then we'd all pick up our forks and start eating at the same time.

My middle son, Salem, always challenged everything. He once asked, "Why can't we just put the food in the middle of the table?" I said, "Let's try it." The next night we gave it a try. It was every dog for himself and the boardinghouse reach. It was the funniest scene ever and it's good no one got seriously injured. Even Salem noted, "I think it was better the way we did it before." I said fine.

That's how decisions in our family were made. If the kids came up with better ideas, we championed their creativity and gave it a try. Nothing was too unorthodox. When trying something new, we weren't the least concerned with doing it poorly at first or even flat-out failing. When you remove the fear, who isn't up for trying new things? This mind-set, I believe, accounts for a fair share of our sons' later professional successes.

When trying something new, we didn't care if they flat-out failed.

NOT SO BOLD AS TO BE BLIND

Although I had some great successes as a dad, I also had one big parenting blind spot, the long, hard revelation of which turned my hair prematurely white.

When our youngest son, Jason, was little, he was such an energetic little guy and cute as can be. We saw him as being kind of like Fonzie on the *Happy Days* television series—a boy the other kids seemed to look to and wanted to be like. But when he was about eight years old, he seemed to quit growing. We also noticed that he wasn't learning to read, so we became concerned about those two issues. We had his growth hormones checked and all that. They seemed okay, so we decided to give him time. But by the time he was twelve, he still hadn't learned to read. We worked with him and the school worked with him, and all they could focus on was "Jason can't read."

For years we grasped at every straw we could find to uncover the roots of his reading problem until someone suggested he might be dyslexic, which at that time wasn't a common diagnosis. When we heard about the Kildonan School in Amenia, New York, that offered a six-week program for kids with dyslexia, we sent Jason there for the summer.

We naively thought that the problem would be cured, that everything would be fine and he'd come home a reader. Instead, we heard, "Here's the situation. Jason is severely dyslexic, and he's bluffed his way along up until now. Reading is like a foreign language to him. But puberty's going to be kicking in any time now, along with other issues, and you're likely to start seeing serious behavior problems. We recommend you enroll him here for the next school term." We were all kind of stunned but we said, "OK."

So Therese and I returned to Texas, and Jason stayed and went to school in New York for the next two school sessions. The Kildonan School was out in the country and had a lot of outdoor programs, like skiing and horseback riding. The boys had to clean out the horse barn and do a lot of other physical labor as well. They were learning through *experience* rather than by sitting in a classroom.

Constantly focusing on what's wrong erodes confidence in even the strongest of children.

Best of all, the Kildonan teachers helped Jason discover what he really needed: self-awareness and self-confidence. Constantly focusing on what's wrong erodes confidence in even the strongest of children. Instead, these teachers looked for and found his *aptitudes* and encouraged him to do more in these areas. Of course, they tried to improve his reading, but mostly they helped him and the other boys realize that there were other routes to learning beyond reading, and that following alternative paths wasn't a big deal. They listed inventors and historical figures who'd had dyslexia—Walt Disney, Thomas Edison, Leonardo da Vinci, Henry Ford—a list that helped both Jason and me to see there wasn't anything wrong with him. He just needed to learn differently. Back here in Texas, along with the teachers at our local school, we'd been focusing on *what he could not do*. But those wonderful teachers paid attention to what he could do, and he was good at so many things!

So what aptitudes did the Kildonan educators find? *Something that had been there all along.* Having been raised in a Texas rodeo town, Jason had spent his childhood riding and roping horses at the Junior Rodeo. Down at the arena people would tell me, "That Jason, he has such balance, and he is so good with horses." I'd smile and nod but it sailed right by me, and I'd think, What's that? Who needs that? They could see he had a knack for it, but I didn't value those skills. The only reason I sat on a hard bench eating a disgusting hotdog in the dusty arena was because my kid was out there doing his thing. In my zeal to push him and his brothers toward big thinking and doing, I overlooked the arena in which Jason's excellence came *easily*.

All of which taught me a huge lesson: kids' abilities and understandings are theirs alone. Because Jason's talents and gifts weren't mine, they slipped past me. Life had strangely repeated itself; it was much the same as when my talents and gifts weren't recognized *I'd been so focused on solving a "problem" that I saw only the problem!* or acknowledged—by my dad and by those looking for a football star, that is. And because I'd been so focused on solving a "problem," I saw *only* the problem! I missed seeing *all* of Jason. Everyone's brain has its own boons and blocks; everyone's heart, its own fire. I had three "men of action" indeed, but they were individual beings with their unique way of expressing their boldness.

AND THEY'RE OFF!

So what happened to Jason? After two years at Kildonan, he came back to Canadian, graduated from high school, then attended a nearby junior college, taking a two-year course called ranch and feedlot management. It was all about the animals and the land and the plants—everything he was interested and excelled in. And he blossomed! He married a darling girl and they have two gifted and talented kids. At the age of twenty-two he acquired land of his own, and now he keeps more than 2,200 horses that are so mentally healthy that people call Jason a "horse whisperer." He's not shy on ingenuity in the area of his strength. He does things no one said was possible. He became nationally acclaimed for breeding racehorses via embryo mare transplants with an unmatched 100 percent success rate. He later became a celebrity in the Texas horse world. He learned to fly a helicopter to work his ranch, then created and now stars in his own television show, *The Helicopter Horseman.*

Jason is not alone in being impressive. Each of my boys had gifts in different areas. Jason's older brother Salem spends his days trading up to one percent of the volume of the Chicago Mercantile Exchange from our little hometown. And Eddie, our oldest, is brilliant at managing a huge and complex ranch organization.

We enouraged them to be boys of action, so they naturally became men of action.

As each son discovered his area of excellence, he also recognized how perfectly his skills complemented the others', and the three went into business together. Encouraged to be bold boys of action, they naturally became men of action. Now they cook up ideas and do deals that leave their father—and often the county commissioner—shaking his head. The little brother who couldn't read comes up with things no one's ever done, and with the support of his brothers they figure out how to do and profit from them. They're not only creative, they get results too.

I spent my whole life trying to impress my dad, and because of that I always let my boys know I was impressed. I made sure they never had to wonder or struggle with that issue; this gave them a foundation, an emotional security, that's necessary in kids. They're happy, and while others sometimes call them crazy because they are so creative and bold, they've figured out where they excel, and their dad is still around to acknowledge it.

What I've learned, and the message I would give people who have a child who maybe can't read or whose schoolwork isn't going well, or who battles about something, is this: you must ask, "What can we focus on that is the child's strength?" Maybe he has a mechanical aptitude or he's good with his hands, or maybe he has a terrific personality and makes other people laugh. Or he has organizational skills, or he's good with animals and the land like Jason. But it's important to focus on what children *can* do, not what they *cannot* do.

It's important to focus on what children can do, not what they cannot do.

Because of Jason, I finally learned that each of my children had bright, powerful sparks within him. The greatest gift parents can give their children is to help them identify that thread in them that's unique, because from that flows everything needed for whatever that person is supposed to do to create a happy and, yes, a bold-crazy-wildly successful life!

"*When one door closes another door opens; but we so often look so long and so regretfully upon the closed door, that we do not see the ones which open for us.*"

Alexander Graham Bell, scientist, inventor, and engineer who invented the first practical telephone.

WHO IS MALOUF ABRAHAM JR., M.D.?

Malouf with (wife) Therese, and (children) Eddie, Salem, and Jason

Dr. Malouf Abraham Jr. is that rare person who has achieved prominence in two fields—in his case, medicine and architecture—and has developed a true passion for a third, fine art.

Abraham earned his medical degree at Southwestern Medical School in Dallas. He served as a doctor during the Vietnam War, earning an Air Force Commendation Medal for his work treating military personnel returning from Vietnam with allergies.

Later, Abraham's allergy clinic became one of Texas's largest, due in part to his allergy vaccine inventions, which have been called "magic potions."

But Abraham has also had a lifelong commitment to art and beauty, and designed his own studies in architecture and landscape design that took him to New York, Arizona, England, and France. He did all the designs for his large Texas estate, "The Citadelle," which *Texas Homes* magazine called "the Panhandle's most talked about home.

Texas governor George W. Bush appointed Abraham as a state art commissioner, and he has served on many boards and commissions involved with art and historic preservation. His tree planting projects have been recognized by the Urban Forestry Commission, and he serves as president of the Abraham Art Foundation. Abraham's extensive art collection is his pride and joy, a treasure he plans to donate, along with The Citadelle, for the public's enjoyment.

Abraham and his wife, Therese, have three sons and thirteen grandchildren. They live in Canadian, Texas.

www.thecitadelle.org

THE UNIQUE YOU

If I Were Your Daddy ... I'd teach you that everyone has a unique talent and life purpose. I'd resist the temptation to mold you into somebody and instead, I'd encourage and support the individual you are.

HENRY DAVID ABRAHAM, M.D.

Harvard Psychiatrist & Nobel Peace Prize Co-Recipient

Fatherhood, to me, is defined by my belief that hardwired into every person is a complete and perfect inner architecture of talent and purpose. But helping children discover theirs can be like solving a puzzle: it requires a vigilant watch for clues as the young person before you grows. It is the Greatest Treasure Hunt Ever. My three kids had strengths very different from my own, so I paid close attention to what each naturally liked doing or was good at. I paid special attention to what they were doing when they seemed happiest. As they became teenagers, I watched for those occasions when time seemed to disappear and their activities became childlike, engrossing them in the moment. I viewed these moments as telltale indicators of their gifts, inclinations, and talents.

In my experience as a psychiatrist and parent, I've found it equally true that children are often born with certain shortcomings—handicaps or challenges. These challenges may initially seem disheartening, but they can become part of a child's unique qualifications to be, to do, and to see things like no one else. While it might be tempting to view a challenge as unfortunate, a genetic burden, it can actually become part of the very fiber that drives a person toward greatness and uncommon success.

Challenges can actually become part of the very fiber that drives a person toward greatness.

Our second child, Jon, came into this world an extremely anxious little boy. One day when he was about four years old, I heard terrified screams. Running into his room I found him pressed against the wall in horror. A mosquito was buzzing around. It wasn't really threatening him or even physically near him, it was just *there*. After I killed the mosquito, I tried to calm Jon down, but when the standard approaches failed, I took a different tack.

I said, "Hey, Jon, let's use our minds to see what we're really afraid of. Let's study bugs and things and find out all about them." Still quivering, he helped me dig out the encyclopedia. We looked up and read about several kinds of bloodsuckers, including mosquitoes. "Oh, look! A leech!" My son was simultaneously captivated and horrified. With his little face twisted up in a painful grimace, he could barely look at the page. "It says here that leeches are used for medicine to help people," I read, "and that they live only in South America, which is very far away."

So began the process of learning how to deal with his anxiety through the intellect: gathering facts to determine whether his feelings, particularly the unsettling and fearful ones, had merit.

Another time when Jon was a little older he was getting ready to go to overnight camp for the first time, and predictably his anxiety was running high. He had a hundred tension-filled "What if …?" questions and kept asking them repeatedly. My wife, Carol, and I knew it was important for him to go—to stretch beyond his comfort zone and conquer his fears. Steadily reassuring him, we managed to get him in the car and get on our way. As we drove, we continued to talk him through his worries, but that didn't seem to help. As we got close to the camp, we were suddenly passed by a motorcycle gang—none other than Hell's Angels. Without warning my own sense of humor emerged and I said, "Son, see those guys?"

"Yes," he said.

"Those are your camp counselors." And I waited.

After a moment of stunned silence (while he figured out that I was joking) we broke through and he laughed, and it detoxified the whole experience. Happily, he went on to have a great summer.

Jon's strong tendency toward anxiety required Carol and me to help him develop tools to combat it. He learned to apply his intellect and think things through before reacting, and he learned that humor was a powerful medicinal tool. Throughout his successful career he has used both these tools, and learning them came as the direct result of being born an anxious kid. He had to master his early challenges or they would have mastered him. His own journey revealed his personal inner architecture, composed as it always is of both challenges and strengths, all perfectly designed. Through them emerged his unique perspectives and accomplishments, and today he's tremendously successful in television, film, and other media. Watching how he contributes to the world, I see him using qualities once perceived as shortcomings but now transformed into advantages.

> *Qualities once perceived as shortcomings can be transformed into advantages.*

STRENGTHS TO THE FOREGROUND

Jon's older brother's story is also uniquely his own but equally telling. At the age of thirteen, Peter seemed like a lost teenager. He had few friends and his grades had been falling steadily at the prep school he attended. We did all the typical concerned-parents things, helping him with his homework and going to his school to check in with his teachers. We still didn't know what was going on, so we began pulling in reinforcements.

We had Peter tested physically, neurologically, and emotionally by one psychologist after another. Some of them specialized in education, while others focused on other aspects of life. We didn't know about his specific learning style at the time, but we did discover that Peter had an auditory processing problem. Identifying the problem was one thing; solving it proved to be another thing altogether. No matter how many experts poked, prodded, and pontificated, there wasn't a clear solution to his challenges and his unconventional style of learning.

When each of Peter's grades became a D, it was time to consider switching schools, and we found ourselves looking at the local public school. I called the principal and explained my son's situation and asked if we could come in for a tour. The principal agreed, but suggested that I not accompany my son. "Just drop him off at the door," he said, "and we'll take it from there. By the way, what's his favorite subject?"

"Hmm," I responded, because there wasn't a good one. "Wrestling," I came up with. "He's undefeated."

While I knew my son needed a new environment, this experienced educator knew even more: Peter needed a fresh school experience anchored on an interest and a strength. When we arrived at the school the next day, Peter was met at the front door for his tour by the captain of the wrestling team. This young man took him to his classes and pointed him out to all the other wrestlers. This was just what Peter needed to hear. Then at lunchtime he met the whole team, and by the time he was done with that day of school he had a whole group of friends who were on the wrestling team. They took him to the gym, suited him up, and he got to wrestle a senior, the high point of his junior high career.

He blossomed because he had something tangible to feel good about.

Peter came back totally empowered by his gift for athletics. He was not a great scholar, but he was a personable kid who was a great athlete. He blossomed in this new setting because his peers valued his strengths and because he had something tangible to feel good about. His learning handicap seemed to fade into the background. He—we—just dealt with it as part of the stream of his life, instead of it being our whole focus as it had been before. Because the new environment actually supported his talents, he became happy, relaxed, and fulfilled. Freeing all that emotional and physical energy allowed him to concentrate on working with and strengthening his natural skills and talents. These skills—the strategic thinking, discipline, and focus learned through sports—became his strongest qualities as an adult. Going from zero to the hero emboldened him to believe he could accomplish whatever he wanted, and gave him the knowledge that he could tackle challenges that people said he couldn't. It gave him chops and provided the platform for extraordinary self-confidence as an adult. Today he boldly and successfully maneuvers as an international businessman, outearning me in the process!

THINKING OUTSIDE THE "BASICS" BOX

Generally speaking, if you struggle with the three R's (reading, writing, arithmetic) in the conventional U.S. education system, you're discounted at best and punished at worst. Understandably, those who are not three-R-gifted often suffer self-esteem issues. This is what I saw developing in our daughter, Rose, whose high school performance was less than noteworthy.

I decided that a good way to boost her self-esteem was to find tangible ways for her to operate from her strengths, even in the midst of a three-R world.

So I said to her, "Rosie, let's follow your strengths. Just fill in the blank in this sentence: "I am happiest when I am _____."

Let's follow your strengths. Just fill in the blank: "I am happiest when I am _____."

At first she answered, "Hanging out with my friends," but as I kept repeating the question, she soon articulated real interests, which of course were her aptitudes: the visual arts, performance, music, voice. From that day forward, we consciously set about reinforcing those areas.

One day I asked her to come to my office, where I pulled from the back of my shelf a dusty but prized object. "I'm giving you this camera," I said. "This is my camera, but it's not just any old camera. This camera marched with Martin Luther King. I want you to understand that this is a historic camera."

My daughter stood motionless, listening curiously. I slid the camera across to her as if it were an offering. "I'll pay for all your film and developing. Just go and shoot." Picking it up she looked it over.

"Thanks, Dad," she said with a smile.

That camera was, I think, a breath of life for her. The artistic, creative, and genius part of her that lay partially dormant was about to be awakened. Indeed, that camera rarely left her person. As I requested, she went out and shot pictures. She became her high school photographer and won awards for her work. It was as if I had opened a door and the sun rushed through it, and she could see for the first time what she was good at and what people liked her for doing. Born along with this were her confidence and personal power.

She might have reacted by using drugs and other destructive behavior, and certainly, her self-worth would have plunged!

If I had demanded that her every grade be an A and positioned her to get into Barnard or Vassar or what have you, I'd have done her a great disservice. Hers was a visual gift. What might have happened if I'd made her focus on linguistic or numeric outlets? I'd have pushed her into certain mediocrity at best, and she'd have been frustrated and confused. At worst, she might have moved into reactive mode through drugs or other destructive behavior, and her self-worth would have plunged. This is the scenario I see in at least half of the teenage drug abuse cases I treat in my psychiatric practice.

I didn't just give my daughter the camera and then disappear. I wanted to see what she was doing. I wanted to see her work. While art isn't an aptitude of mine, working diligently and doing well are, so I helped her apply herself and excel in her gifted area. We discussed her art and I gave her honest feedback. I wouldn't issue undue praise when it wasn't deserved, yet I was *highly* sensitive to *never* send the message "It's not good enough." Instead, I asked questions to propel her forward: "What was your intent in this piece?" "What could you have done differently?" "What did you learn?" "What part did you like the best?" By challenging her to think critically to find a solution rather than feeling bad about herself when it didn't turn out so well, she learned to separate results from self-worth, and to not invest negative emotion into failed attempts—failures that might make her timid. I helped her understand that temporary "failure" is a ticket to learning. When her art pieces were interesting, as most of them were, my strongest message was always, "Great! Let's see what else you can do."

I shared with her something I learned from one of my sports heroes, Larry Byrd. Before every game, he would go out and shoot 300 foul shots. Now, this may seem like a lot of work, but as a result he was the best foul shooter in the NBA. Embedded in that story was this message: no matter who you are, no one is naturally excellent. People who excel get there by doing it a lot, even if it's an area where they have a lot of natural talent. So with your kids, if they love something, you want to encourage them to do it a lot.

Of they love something, you want to encourage them to do it a lot.

The message I consistently and clearly conveyed to Rose was that I expected her to work hard and shine. It's a value I model in my own life, and I expected the same from her. But because I placed my expectations in areas that were completely in sync with who she is—her authentic self—she did excel. She learned to push against the edges of her own capabilities as opposed to pushing against me. It would have been simply a crime to pressure her to succeed in a direction that did not fit her. Instead, I assisted her to develop her own commitment to excellence, one that was internally based rather externally motivated by the wish to please me or anyone else.

Rose went on to study art full-time at an acclaimed visual arts program. Her poignant photographs often move people to tears. She's won award after award and is exceedingly happy. I marvel that the once-frustrated student, confused about herself and unaware of her gifts, has developed into the fully engaged and thriving young woman I see today.

What I've learned from all three of my children is the importance of letting each person choose his or her own destination, so that person believes in where he or she is going. Any goal can be a destination, but one fueled by a heartfelt belief that emanates from within has the power to turn a destination into a destiny. As children grow and develop, they'll own the whole of the experience when they pick their path and then walk it—navigating the obstacles and absorbing the accolades en route. When they discover and pursue their inner architecture of talent and purpose, they learn early that they are capable of great things. And this frees them to truly enjoy the journey of life.

"A successful life is one that is lived through understanding and pursuing one's own path, not chasing after the dreams of others."

Chin-Ning Chu, strategist, author, speaker, and descendant of Chu Yuan-Zhang, the pauper who became the first emperor of the Ming Dynasty

WHO IS HENRY DAVID ABRAHAM, M.D.?

Henry with (wife) Carol, and (children) Peter, Jon, and Rose

Dr. Henry David Abraham, a retired Harvard Medical School faculty member and a Distinguished Life Fellow of the American Psychiatric Association, has contributed significantly to the wider medical and academic communities in the areas of psychiatric medicine and substance abuse. His book, *What's a Parent To Do? Straight Talk About Drugs and Alcohol,* draws from his twenty-five-plus years as a specialist in drug abuse.

His interests run far and wide. They include the prevention of nuclear war, his efforts for which resulted in Abraham being named co-recipient of the 1985 Nobel Peace Prize for the International Physicians for the Prevention of Nuclear War created by the Physicians for Social Responsibility. Ensuring that society's underdogs have access to medical care is another of his causes.

In a different professional vein, Abraham writes plays, situational comedies, documentaries, and works of fiction. His latest novel, *Nanokill,* was critically acclaimed, and he has won an Emmy and two Peabody awards for his television work.

Abraham credits myriad sources for not only his success but his survival: his many public school teachers, the scholars at Muhlenberg College in Pennsylvania and the scientists at the Johns Hopkins University School of Medicine. Serving as ballast for his professional pursuits has been the steady love of his wife of more than thirty years, Carol, and their three children.

www.drabraham.com

NURTURING GENIUS

If I Were Your Daddy ... I'd guide you through your life's early passages, and help you gain awareness, develop resilience, learn how to access inner wisdom. You'd grow up knowing that you are brilliant beyond your imagination!

PAUL SCHEELE
Transformational Thought
Leader & Educator

I first became a daddy amid soft lighting, music, and massage. Our first child, Ben, was experiencing the first of many passages in his life—being born. We knew the event was sacred, and we welcomed him to this world by placing him on his mother's abdomen. We knew we had brought a genius into being, a genius like every child who has ever entered life on this planet.

That fact has been the foundation for everything my wife, Libby, and I have done as parents. We didn't approach parenting with the mindset that we need to *teach* our children. Instead, we felt that our real job as parents of "genius learners" was to provide a safe container that would allow them to find their fullest expression, while exploring their own world. We knew if we could do that, the world around them would teach them everything else they need to know.

Although Libby and I were very average students ourselves, our three sons—Ben, Scott, and John—each tested into the gifted and talented programs at our local public schools. I think this is because, right from the beginning, we talked to them and treated them as if they were geniuses. We guided them in learning four essential qualities: *knowingness, awareness, self-esteem,* and *resilience.*

KNOWINGNESS: THE CHERRY ON THE CAKE

One day when Ben was about five years old, we were at my parents' house for an event that involved a cake. On the top of the cake was a bright red, very tempting maraschino cherry. "Can I eat the cherry, Daddy?" Ben asked, looking up at me. "Well," I said, "it's OK with me, and it's probably OK with your grandma, but let's see what your body has to say. Let's do some muscle testing. Your body will give us the answer."

Muscle testing is a form of applied kinesiology, where you can test to see if a food or substance is good for the body. While Ben held the cherry close to his body I asked the question: "Is this a good food for Ben?" When I pressed down lightly on his other arm, it went weak, indicating a negative response. "Oh look, your body doesn't like it," I commented. "But the decision is yours, Ben. Do you still want to eat the cherry?" "No I don't want it," he said, and put the cherry down.

The power to decide is ours. Trust your own knowingness.

The power to decide how life is going to go belongs to each of us. One thing Libby and I wanted our sons to learn was to *trust their own knowingness.* With such trust, they would value their knowing, instead of giving up their authority and adopting a powerless attitude, one that says, "I'm a victim here; I don't know; I'm stupid, you're smart; what do you think?"

For example, when a son came up with creative ideas, we rarely said, "No, you can't do that." Instead, we tried to say as often as possible, "Yes, and..." Such as "Yes and if you do that, here's what might happen. Is that what you want? What is it that you want to create?" Or "Yes, and here are additional choices you might consider."

AWARENESS: AROUND THE DINNER TABLE

The Barksdale Institute of Self-Esteem teaches that we're always doing the best our current awareness permits. In our family, Libby and I tried to make life always about learning and growing. We knew that our sons came into this life with a certain state of awareness, and our job was to constantly facilitate its expansion. In our family, the yardstick of growth and success was not the *immediate result* of their efforts, but whether or not they had *learned* something. We knew that when they did something that turned out badly, they were doing the best their current awareness permitted. By constantly increasing their awareness, they could constantly improve their results. So we always encouraged them to reflect upon, "Have I increased my awareness? If I did, then I'm growing."

By constantly increasing awareness, you can constantly improve results.

This concept of constantly expanding awareness permeates all areas of our lives, and Libby and I always tried to model the behaviors we expected or wanted to instill in our sons. So at the dinner table, we regularly took turns reviewing our day with each other. We knew that one key to having success in life, relationships, and business is to form a habit of doing this. As Dr. Buckminster Fuller said, this practice lets you "live in day-tight compartments" in which you can gauge what happened against what you desired to create, thus increasing your awareness, and allowing you to improve your results the following day. So at dinner every day we asked each other, and then each of the boys

1. What was something that went really well today?

2. What didn't go as well as you would have wanted it to?

3. What is something you are looking forward to tomorrow?

The five of us would talk things through, try on different options and solutions, and then ask the final question: *"Have you increased your awareness today?"* If the answer was "yes," then there was growth, and that's all we could ask of ourselves, or our sons.

Our boys came to understand that whatever their result, it was always a by-product of their state of awareness. Our dinner discussions honored each child's genius, because we encouraged them to look *within,* pause, evaluate, and increase their awareness. This exercise always placed them as the creator of the events in their own life. They came to learn that they were neither a bystander nor a victim.

By my reviewing *my* day in front of them, I was also demonstrating that I didn't do things perfectly either. That awareness can be a serious relief to a growing child. With this kind of dinner dialogue, our boys naturally adopted this self-awareness process. When they were still quite young, they were already learning a powerful internal strategy for life-long achievement: how to self-evaluate and self-correct.

> Whatever their result, we encouraged them to look within, pause, evaluate, and increase their awareness.

RESILIENCE: "YOU'RE PULLING MY LEG!"

Back in the 1980s a respected colleague of mine in the field of human development said, "The most important task any business manager has is to raise the self-esteem of his employees." When I heard this I thought, if it's important for employees it must be *very* important for children. I immediately knew one of the most important tasks I had as a father was to reinforce and build the self-esteem of my kids.

After giving it some thought, I determined that an important pillar in developing strong self-esteem is the ability to bounce back from defeat, or "resilience." Resilience means you're not afraid to keep trying something until you get it right, no matter how long it takes, because "missing the mark" is not linked to your self-esteem.

As an educator and specialist in the field of human development, I've observed that one of the main reasons why many people are so miserable

A pillar in developing strong self-esteem is the ability to bounce back from defeat, or "resilience." is they've never forgiven themselves for their screw-ups or bad decisions. They perceive that they've "failed" in some way, and their self-esteem plummets. This is just a behavior—a conditioned response they learned when they were growing up, without finding a way to heal and rise above.

So I began to consciously foster our sons' resilience through games, laughter, imagination, and play. While these were absolutely fun times, I created them so they were also instructional on many levels.

(1) The first key to being resilient is the ability to *be receptive,* and have tolerance for ambiguity. If something is worth doing, it's worth doing badly at first. To encourage this mindset in my kids I made up silly games, similar to those used by actors training for improvisational comedy, and we all played. This allowed them to see that in order to do something, they don't have to know exactly how to do it. We played in free form, just going with it, as children naturally do. No matter what happened, I always gave the boys lots of "high fives" for trying.

(2) The second key to resilience is the ability to *be generative*—to embrace paradox by knowing there is no one right answer, and by being willing to generate ideas with minimal judgment. For this the boys really enjoyed "Mad Libs" (found on the internet), along with car games and bedtime stories. "Mad Libs" are fun word games that encourage creative thinking, and demonstrate that all answers are valid, and equally as funny. Another car game we played to encourage creativity was to tell the most outrageous fib to each other—the most fantastic story. In response, the others would say, "You're pulling my leg!" and then take their turn. This spurred all of us on to think outside the norm and create fanciful, expansive tales. I would also tell outrageous bedtime stories, and let the boys fill in the twists and turns, which allowed them to be part of the creative process.

(3) The third key to being resilient is the ability to *be persistent.* If at

first you don't succeed, join the club! It takes "time on task" to develop any new skill, and if you give up too soon, you'll end up missing out on the best things in life. So together we would tackle difficult problems for which there were no clear solutions, or go for adventure hikes in nature, all of which modeled the attitude of persistence. By watching me build my own business and create many innovative products, the kids saw that if you're willing to persist, you can achieve whatever you set your mind upon.

BEDTIME STORIES: BECOMING HEROES

We found three tools in particular that helped our boys learn awareness, self-esteem, and resilience. One was bedtime stories. Every night that I was at home I read to the kids, and we always chose stories with deeper messages. After reading two children's books, I would then tell them a story built from significant events or learning experiences they'd had during the day. These stories were actually "therapeutic metaphors" and involved the kids as central characters. Bedtime stories always involved a breakthrough learning experience that made the kids heroes. For example, they were able to save their mom and dad, or help the world overcome a crisis. These metaphors were designed to instill in my kids an appreciation of virtuous characteristics, and find the heroic capacities within themselves.

The ritual of being read to and told original stories not only helped develop their habits as readers, it also developed their imaginative thinking. The therapeutic nature of the ritual also contributed to our goal of raising kids with high self-worth and self-esteem. Besides expanding their awareness of the world, it gave me the opportunity to help them visualize themselves moving from the dependency of childhood, to the expanding independence of adolescence, to the responsibilities and interdependence of adulthood.

DIALOGUE: EIGHT-HUNDRED-POUND GORILLAS

An important part of honoring genius children—*all* children, remember—is helping them become aware that they are not islands: they are in an interdependent, cocreative relationship with everyone around them. There is never a victim. So if something happens that you don't like, you need a method to air it that gets to the root of the whole matter. As a family we discovered and regularly used a second tool—a communication exercise based on Gestalt therapy.

You need a method to air out difference that gets to the root of matters.

The exercise rests on three issues that you communicate back and forth in dialogue: I'm *upset*—I *want*—I *appreciate*. It goes like this:

Upset: "I'm going to say something I'm upset about, or resent about, your behavior." For every upset or resentment that you have, there's really a hidden demand about how you think the other person "should be" instead. Otherwise you wouldn't be upset.

Want: "I'm going to tell you what I want, what I think "should be," by saying exactly what I want or demand from you or for you."

Appreciate: "Then I'm going to finish off by sharing what I appreciate about you."

One person begins and goes through the exercise while the other person listens *without interrupting them.* Then you switch. You take turns going back and forth until there are no more upsets or demands to be expressed. For every one person's *upset-want-appreciate,* the other person must match it with another. If one person thinks he has run out of upsets, he can still say, "I'm **upset** that you have more upsets toward me than I have toward you. I **want** you to quit already, but I **appreciate** that you can converse in a way that will get things cleared up."

It's important to note that at no time during this exercise is the other person compelled to *agree* with you, or do what you are asking. This exercise is not about changing the other person. It *is* about uncovering what's really going on. It short-circuits the upset by exposing its hidden, and usually unreasonable, demands.

Truthfully, upsets are a result of unmet needs. One person feels a need, and when it's not being met she can become upset or resentful towards the other person, as if the other person should know, or is somehow obligated to meet her need or expectation. Every unexpressed want or demand has a hidden, twisted "should" being imposed on another person. If we hope to get what we want in our relationships with others, we must make our requests explicit. They can then choose to agree or disagree, but at least our expectations are clear to ourselves and others.

This exercise is masterful because it constantly reaffirms what we appreciate about each other, and the many ways the relationship is important to us. We don't get upset with someone we just pass on the street, because we have no relationship with them. It's only because we appreciate another person enough to stay in relationship with him, that these issues come up.

> *This exercise gets us directly to our feelings, wants, and demands, and reafirms why we love each other.*

Libby and I found this exercise gave us a way to effectively and honestly address our personal issues with each other, and with our sons. It gets directly into our feelings, wants, and demands—while at the same time affirming why we love each other. We use this exercise for significant emotional upsets, as well as much less "weighty" ones. It's a good idea to practice it ahead of time on minor things, so if at some point in the future a large "eight-hundred-pound gorilla" problem enters the house, the family has a tool to communicate that each person has agreed upon, and is comfortable with. We found it to be a beautiful centerpiece for being in relationship and communicating truthfully.

When Ben was about twenty-eight he was living at home temporarily. I noticed I was becoming increasingly unhappy because I felt he wasn't contributing to the family workload. So I approached him one evening and asked if we could talk using the upset-want-appreciate approach. He agreed, so I began:

Me: "Ben, I am *upset* that you think that because you worked all week, you don't have to do any work around the house. (pause) I *want* you to carry an equal load of chores as long as you're living in this house as an adult. (pause) I *appreciate* that you are working hard outside the home, and you have a need to take care of yourself."

Ben: "Dad, I am *upset* that you want housework done on your schedule, not on my schedule. (pause) I *want* you to let me sleep when I'm exhausted, and trust that I will get to it when I can. (pause) I *appreciate* that you've created a home in which I can live, and that you care for the cleanliness and appearance of the house."

We kept this going for about three or four rounds, which was typical. By using this wonderful technique, Ben and I got out all our unexpressed feelings about this one issue.

I wasn't trying to change my son, nor make him yield to my demands. That's not what this exercise is about. Certainly just being able to express what was beginning to bottle up inside made me feel better immediately. But the magic of this exercise is that it short-circuits resentment. One person gets to see how she is expecting something of someone else that may not be appropriate. That person may not even be aware of the hidden demand reflecting the hidden unmet need in herself. Now fully aware of the upset and want, the other person can adjust or shift as he choose. Because the exercise always ends with appreciation, it provides a context of great mutual respect, which facilitates deep significant emotional conversation. In this case, Ben chose to become more conscious of contributing around the house, and I became less uptight about it. It proved once again to be a masterful, simple way to communicate differences and air feelings—out in the open.

> *The magic of this exercise is that it short-circuits resentment.*

RITES OF PASSAGE: HUNTERS AND WARRIORS

A third tool we've found helpful is the celebration of important passages, or transitions, in our sons' lives. The first celebration occurred when our first child, Ben, was born. We recognized the importance of making that moment sacred, and as time passed, our awareness continued to expand.

After our second child was born, I became involved in "men's work," which paid attention to the ritual initiation of men into a society of men. We still see a form of this today in Judaism, when at age thirteen a boy takes his bar mitzvah. He leaves childhood behind, and accepts new responsibilities. And in the bat mitzvah, the girl becomes a woman. In Native American traditions, the adolescent boy undertakes a vision quest alone into the wilderness. When he returns, he takes his place with the men as a hunter and warrior, and leaves the things of childhood behind. Children know about and look forward to these rites of passage, and the changes they bring, from a very young age.

Today our culture has lost touch with rites of passage into adulthood.

Today our culture has lost touch with rites of passage into adulthood. As a result, both parents and children often miss the various points of transition out of childhood, at which certain behaviors and attitudes must be left behind and new ones embraced. Without some kind of ritual around these transitions, parents have a harder time shifting their kids into accepting the changes and growth necessary to become responsible adults in society.

Applying the principles of "men's work," as my three boys grew, I began to conceptualize a series of ritual initiation experiences. I gathered ideas from certain indigenous traditions and combined them with my own understanding of the neuro-cognitive realm, meditation, and male archetypes. I designed a series of father-son retreats for my kids. The first one occurred when the boys turned ten—when they turn to double digits. The second occurred when they turned fifteen, which might be called the age of discrimination. At this age they are confirmed by the church and invited to become a contributing member of the church community. They also obtain their driver's permit, which our society recognizes as an indication of accepting a certain level of responsibility. The third retreat was at age eighteen, when they graduated from high school and began moving from dependence to independence to inter-dependence. The initiation process I created was as much an evolution of my fathering as it was an initiation for my child into the wisdom of elder men in society.

These retreats were modern-day rites of passage. They gave us an opportunity to delve deeper into the parent-child relationship, and expanded awareness of the changes required from all of us. My sons knew about these rites of passage and the growth they brought from the time they were quite young, and they looked forward to them. For them, it was about letting go of childhood and moving into a zone of greater accountability and responsibility. For me, it was about making a transition from father/daddy to father-mentor. And there were also changes required from their mother.

Libby and I have now been married more than thirty years, and all three of our boys have grown into very successful young men—each very different. From aerospace engineering and industrial designing, to business franchising and working with people, to mountaineering and international business, each is pursuing his passion. They are sponges for new ideas, each one immensely creative and resilient.

By treating our children as the "genius learners" they were, and taking them through rites of passages into their adulthood, we successfully guided them to accept responsibilities and to grow their own awareness. Through the years, what needed to emerge within them did emerge, just as we expected it would. Today I stand in awe and wonder at three men, who with total awareness, have stepped into the fullest expression of who they are. I could have asked for nothing more.

For a fuller description of the three "rite of passage" retreats Paul Scheele created for his sons, please go to:

www.ifiwereyourdaddy.com/paulscheele

"All children are born geniuses. 9999 out of every 10,000 are swiftly, inadvertently, 'de-geniused' by grown-ups ... Motivated entirely by love, but also by fear for the futures of the children they love, parents act as though they know all the answers and curtail the spontaneous exploratory acts of their children, lest the children make 'mistakes'. But genius does its own thinking; it has confidence in its own exploratory findings, in its own intuitions, in the knowledge gained from its own mistakes."

Dr. Buckminster Fuller, American architect, author of thirty books, designer, inventor, and futurist. One of his best known architectural designs is the geodesic dome.

$\mathcal{W}$HO IS PAUL SCHEELE?

Paul with (wife) Libby, (children) John, Scott, and Ben

Paul Scheele activates resources within organizations and individuals around the world, transforming the ordinary into the extraordinary. He believes everyone is brilliant and dedicates his life to facilitating the genius potential within. His success as a founding partner of Learning Strategies Corporation, scholar, thought-leader, author, speaker, trainer, husband, and father demonstrates the credibility and value of his work.

Scheele Learning Systems focuses on leading-edge programs to create economic and environmental sustainability, increase social justice, and allow spiritual fulfillment to be realized. Paul is a dynamic presenter who entertains as he educates, allowing audiences to quickly learn with ease.

Paul Scheele provides expertise in transformational leadership, whole-brain accelerated learning, communication skills, and accessing the genius mind through keynotes, trainings, consulting, and self-study products. He is a visionary practitioner of human development who guides people to succeed in life. Paul is highly regarded for his breakthrough work and endorsed by other peak performance celebrities such as Jack Canfield, Tony Robbins, Ken Blanchard, Brian Tracy, plus many others.

Paul Scheele has authored and co-authored dozens of self-study programs including PhotoReading©, Natural Brilliance©, Genius Code, Abundance for Life, and developed Paraliminal© technology, now available in over 50 audio titles. His best-selling books, *PhotoReading©* and *Natural Brilliance©* are available in fifteen languages and his eBook *Drop Into Genius* has been enjoyed by his worldwide audience. Scheele holds degrees in biology, learning, and human development. He is doctoral candidate for a Ph.D. in Leadership and Change at Antioch University.

Paul attributes much of his success to the loving support of his wife Libby. They have three brilliant adult sons.

www.ScheeleLearning.com, www.LearningStrategies.com

MAKING THE TEENAGE YEARS EASY AND FUN

If I Were Your Daddy ... from an early age I'd treat you as an adult, teach you about the power of choice, and always accept you for who you are. I'd scout the way first and be your example of how to create an authentic and happy life.

TERRY TILLMAN
International Leadership Trainer & Educator

I may be one of the few parents who loved my kids' teenage years, because we glided through them when many people hit turbulence. From my perspective, those years were wonderful, and I don't believe it was an accident. I'm not a "normal" father by any measure of normal, and my girls, Kim and Wendy, definitely had far from a normal childhood. Still, I'm happy to say we had outstanding results together. They went through so much and are now so wise and successful, and sometimes I think they are wiser than me!

Their mother is an alcoholic, and I divorced her when they were just six and three. This was Eugene, Oregon, circa 1968, and back then fathers were not allowed to have custody of their children under any circumstances. The court sent Kim and Wendy to live under the watch of their maternal grandparents in Minnesota, and the separation was difficult for all three of us.

Several times a year they would visit me in Eugene for extended periods of time. They never wanted to leave, and saying goodbye was one of the most emotionally difficult things I've ever done. As the older sister, Kim would assume a responsible and maternal role as she led Wendy by the hand down the ramp and away from me. Watching them vanish onto the plane felt like a punch to the gut. Only when they were safely aboard and out of sight did I allow my tears to show. After one wonderful visit, they were saying, "Good-bye, Dad," and telling me they didn't want to leave. They started walking down the ramp, but turned around suddenly for a last look and caught me crying. This was probably the first time they had seen me cry, and they ran back to care for me and give me a hug.

Not only was it OK for a male, a father, to show vulnerability, it was important.

The lesson was huge: it taught me that not only was it OK for a male, a father, to show vulnerability, it was important. Being real and emotionally honest brought us closer together. I'd unknowingly been following the playbook of my father's generation, the one that insisted men be strong and withhold their emotions, even with their kids. I had put up a wall and didn't even know it. That wall was an illusion of protection against feared pain, and it walled me in. But on that day, I discovered it was better to take it down. Being truthful and authentic like this allowed me to connect to my daughters more deeply than ever.

A few years later another visit was coming to an end. The girls were about twelve and fifteen, and the "Dad, we don't want to go" chorus was in full crescendo. Finally wising up I said, "Then don't. Why don't you just stay here?" So they did. They moved in with me and I became Mr. Mom. We figured we would let their mother take the initiative if she wanted to, but she didn't. Not a normal circumstance for sure, but there was a lot of love and respect expressed between us, and that's the main reason it worked. I got them through their teenage years when most parents struggle. We had no trouble at all, and I loved it.

WHEN YOU NEED TO DO IT DIFFERENTLY

It was important for me to be a different kind of father than mine had been. I had good parents, but if I were designing them, I certainly would've changed a lot of the ways they parented. My dad was stern, and he rarely smiled or seemed to have a good time. Successful in business, he was a community leader and basically a decent man, but not a lot of fun and extremely critical. Nothing I did was ever good enough. I was an A student, president of the honor society, quarterback of my high school football team, accepted into Stanford University—a kind of all-American kid—but he gave me little or no acknowledgment, not even one *"attaboy!"* So I just kept trying to gain his approval and affection by doing better and better.

Some good things came out of all that, mainly learning the importance of showing love. I certainly didn't get much loving from my father. In our house no one ever expressed affection, verbally or physically. Everything I missed out on I wanted to make sure my kids got. I had to learn to create new habits of hugging, purposely encouraging and accepting them for who they were, not what I wanted them to be. There's no manual for parenting, but luckily we can learn from, and improve on, the past. My dad was a great example of what didn't work for me, and I was inspired to be a better father. Unconditional love, support, and approval were the most important gifts I wanted to give to my girls. They didn't have to do, have, or be something to win my approval. I let go of hiding my feelings and trying to be the perfect, strong dad that I'd tried to be at the airport. I wanted them to see my wounds and

I let go trying to be the perfect, the strong dad, and we became honest and open instead.

scars and warts, to see how I dealt with and moved past my hurts and issues. I wanted them to know we could be "real" with each other—honest and open. As a result, we became connected instead of separated. In my mind, instead of "me and you," it was "us."

COCREATE AGREEMENTS WITH KIDS

We had few teen-to-parent struggles, and from my perspective these years were both easy and fun. They were great kids and we always found a way to work together so they didn't need to pull away from me to assert their independence. Starting when they were very young, I talked to them like they were adults capable of reasoning. Mostly I let them live by their own choices because I wanted them to learn the power of choosing, and that choices have consequences, some desirable, some not. Some parents disagree with this approach and believe their kids need tighter boundaries, but I've seen it work so well that I remain an advocate.

We didn't have rules in our family. We had agreements.

For example, we didn't have rules in our family. We had agreements that we reached through open discussion. If one daughter wanted to stay out until 2:00 a.m. on a date, and I wanted her home at 10:00, we'd sit down and debate why 10:00 was my position and 2:00 was hers. We'd negotiate and come to an agreement. This way it wasn't just me telling her what to do; she gave me her word. Once an agreement was reached I expected the girls to live up to it, and they usually did. I wasn't into punishment, so if one of them broke her agreement, we would discuss consequences and decide on those together too. I matter-of-factly upheld any of those consequences—there wasn't any wiggle room out—because they had made an agreement. As a result my girls didn't act out, and I never had to become a controlling dad to make sure they were safe.

In some of my seminars I work with teenagers and parents, and I see this problem of controlling parents and rebellious teens over and over. By not demanding that my children live within my limiting boundaries, I managed to avoid that issue. And sure, their choices weren't always my preferences, yet I mostly went along with them so long as they weren't illegal or harmful to anyone. This meant not *doing* things for them, but rather *being there* to catch them if they fell too far.

I was big on letting them experience the consequences of their choices, and afterward, we'd discuss it. That's how they learned. If it didn't work out the way they hoped, the energy was not, "Bad girl, shame on you." I never once shamed them. My intention was always "I see you and how beautiful you are, and let's build on that. I don't have to punish you, because the results of your choices themselves, if they are bad ones, will punish you, and you will learn."

I don't have to punish you—the results of your choices themselves will be your punishment.

Learning personal responsibility through actions and consequences leads to greater self-esteem, stronger decision making, and a can-do attitude, as opposed to having a parent be the judge, ruler, and enforcer. For example, when the girls first moved in, Wendy was very messy, and I was always cleaning up after her. I'm a pretty orderly guy. So we had a little talk. I explained that this was my house, I was paying the bills, and here was how I wanted things done. I said, "I see you're not doing them that way, so how can we work this out?" When she got defensive I said, "This is not about blame. We just need to come to an agreement we can both live with." So I offered, "You can keep your room any way you want, but in the areas we share, here's how I want it. Does this work for you?" It did, and so we agreed.

Eventually she would say, "Hey, Dad, I can't find my other sock. Have you seen it?" or "Hey, Dad, I don't have any clean jeans to wear tonight." "Check in your room," was my standard reply. Gradually she started taking better care of her stuff. The key was I never swooped in to fix the "I can't find this" problem, nor did I nag about her room. Her choice of being messy brought its own consequences, and these were her teacher. Today, as a mother with a child of her own, she runs her house with impressive organization.

Here's one of my favorite examples. When Wendy went out on her first date, we discussed what time she needed to be home. I met the boy and all that stuff, and I liked him. I think she was fifteen and he was seventeen, with a car. Off they went.

The phone call came at midnight. "Dad, I'm at the police station. I'm in trouble."

"What happened?" I asked.

"Well, we were in the car, and there was some beer in the car, and a policeman came, and now here I am."

I drove down to the police station. She was terrified. She asked, "What's going to happen to me?"

"We'll find out," I said.

"What *could* happen?" she implored.

"You'll have to go to court tomorrow and talk to a judge," I answered.

"Then what?"

I paused and said, "Hold on, let me show you something."

I took her to the jail and led her to the drunk tank. Ever seen a drunk tank? Trust me, it's horrible. A bunch of drunks were crowded in a cell with rancid air and barf on the floor. Some had passed out and others were making lewd comments. It's just not a nice place. I turned to Wendy and said, "If you keep making these kinds of choices, the consequences can lead to this. Is this what you want?"

I didn't have to do much more. I never had a problem with her drinking or doing drugs, and I'm sure that's part of why. I never had to punish her, but if I had, I know she just would've pushed back and resisted. Instead of building a wall between us, that moment at the jail built a bridge to her own common sense, maybe the best part of the experience. And our communication and connection remained stronger than ever.

TOLERANCE AND ACCEPTANCE BUILDS BRIDGES

Undeniably the teen years can be tricky. Teenagers are no longer children but not yet adults. They're individuating and trying to figure out who they are and how they can do things. When they challenge a parent's perceptions, judgments, and beliefs about what's right, it's stressing for both. But I discovered that tolerance and acceptance form the most effective bridge to reaching other people, including my teenage daughters. I didn't experience much acceptance from my own father, which made it even more important to me.

When I recently asked Kim what she learned most from me, she responded, "Among the biggest things you taught us were tolerance and acceptance. There's definitely more than one way to do things, more than one way to be. It's OK if I'm different or someone's not 'normal.'"

Here's a great example the girls learned from. Every summer I do wilderness training, taking sixteen people into Idaho's backcountry for personal growth and learning through mountaineering and whitewater rafting. Almost every year I get a call from a parent, saying, "I have this problem teenager. Do you think it would do any good to send him on your trip?" I usually say, "Yeah, send him and we'll see." Almost 100 percent of the time the teenager is terrific.

The problem is the parent demands that the teenager be somebody other than who the teenager is experimenting at being.

There was one kid who showed up dressed all in black—black shoes, black fingernails, black clothes, black spiked hair, black eye makeup. My first thought was a judgment: "This kid's going to be a case." Quickly catching my judgment, I simply welcomed him. Okay, I thought, he wants to wear all black, so he'll cook in the sun, his makeup will run in the water, but that's fine if this is what he wants to do. He'll experience those consequences, and eventually he'll figure out he can be more comfortable making different choices.

Once he saw that I wasn't trying to change him, but was instead looking for the best in him, he relaxed. He pulled his own weight, helped with chores without complaining, participated in all the activities, and made friends with older participants. I've seen this happen over and over. In every instance the problem isn't the teenager; the problem is the parent demanding that the teenager be somebody other than the person the teenager is experimenting at being.

My dad was critical of almost everything I did; he judged many of my choices, showed little interest in my activities, and seldom offered approval. From his example I learned how damaging this can be, so I determined that I would to purposely at suspend judgment, develop acceptance, and allow others to be who they were. I consciously worked on celebrating the best in everyone around me, including teenagers who sometimes seem to make odd (but not illegal) choices. If we consider that there are 6.5 billion people on this planet who all think, believe, and behave differently, it only makes sense to become more tolerant and open to different ways of doing things. The other choice is to live with judgment, frustration, and negativity.

> *Seeing the part of me that was like him made it easier to accept him as he was.*

This accepting position is the one I tried to adopt with my kids. If I had a problem with one of them, I first looked to myself, not the child, and asked, "What's my part here that's keeping us from relating?" I've come to learn that what I see in others is a reflection of something in me, like a mirror. As for the kid in black, in him I recognized the part of me that wants to be my own person. Seeing this made it easier to change my attitude about him. First I accepted that part of me, which made it easier to accept him, as he was, and this put him on the receiving end of acceptance.

ARE YOU LIVING IN YOUR AUTHENTIC SELF?

Both my father and his father were successful businessmen, and I grew up with all my relatives assuming I would go into business too. So as a young man I started and grew six businesses, mostly because on some level I was still seeking my dad's approval. As a result, by the time I was in my early thirties, I had all the trappings of success: nice house, nice cars, good football tickets, local recognition, and all that stuff. But it turned out that what I was doing wasn't authentic to my true Self. Outside I maintained the image of success. Inside I felt bankrupt, like a failure. I was unhappy and knew I had to do something about it. What if I passed this forward to my girls? It was a frightening thought. By example I was teaching them to suffer for the safety of material success, and this stirred me into action.

I needed some advice, but I had no inspiring role models close to me, nor any wise adult I felt safe speaking to. So I went looking for answers and an older mentor, and I ended up spending a day in a retirement home. I talked with people ages seventy to ninety and asked them about life: "What's the most important thing you learned? What's the wisest thing you could tell a youngster like me?" To my surprise no one revealed a profound secret, but every last one of them talked about *regrets:* "I always wanted to play the piano. But look at my arthritic hands. I can't do it now." Or "I was so busy I missed my daughter's ballet recitals and son's baseball games." Over and over I heard regrets: "If only… ," "Why didn't I… ," "Sonny, before it's too late don't you forget to…" They had taken care of their physical, material, and financial responsibilities, but never made time to follow their inner longings and do what was in their hearts. They now talked about the importance of people and relationships.

I showed my girls they could choose inner security over the illusion of certainty.

I realized if I didn't make a change I would be one of those ninety-year-olds looking back saying, "Why didn't I? It's too late now." I figured the only way I could fail now was to not take action, so I did an about-face and followed my heart into another career and lifestyle. By doing so, I showed my girls they could choose happiness, personal satisfaction, and inner security over outer security—the illusion of certainty or the status quo. This put me in a great position to help them, when the time came, to make authentic, courageous decisions about their own lives.

Today I can gratefully say I'm a recovered businessman who replaced the bankruptcy inside with a subjective wealth and richness that can never be taken from me. Because I'm doing what I love, the financial success follows. Yes, it required boldness and short-term sacrifice, but it set a great new family precedent—to follow your heart. As the educator Joseph Campbell famously wrote, "Follow your bliss and the universe will open doors for you where there were only walls."

HELPING YOUR CHILDREN BE FREE AND HAPPY

A few years ago Wendy's husband, Adam, wanted to make a bold move and start his own chiropractic practice. They had financial concerns—it seemed risky. Wendy ended up encouraging her husband to go for it, asking: "What did he have to lose? He wasn't happy." Both girls weren't afraid of trying new, different, "scary" things. They've seen Dad do it! And so, Wendy completely supported her husband to pursue his goals and dreams, and helped him find the courage to do it.

They weren't afraid to try new, different, "scary" things. After all, they've seen Dad do it!

My older daughter, Kim, is also no stranger to taking risks for the sake of happiness. She works in the entertainment industry where it's always feast or famine. But if Kim feels she won't get along with a director or producer, she turns the job down, while most of her contemporaries are afraid to do that. They accept jobs they don't like and work with people they don't enjoy, leaving them stressed out and unhappy. Kim avoids all of that, and she gets plenty of work and loves it. I believe this is because she knows who she is, and she's not afraid to remain true to it.

Although at times I may have fallen short, my intention while raising my daughters was to support them in discovering who they were, and then support them in being true to that self in all they do, and *never* push them to be something they're not. I believe that's why their teen years were such a joy, and felt easy to me.

When your kids are still children, it's *easy* to see them as divine: their true spiritual Self is not yet hidden or protected by personality, or by limiting beliefs and behaviors. The pure, beautiful essence I saw in my two girls as babies was something I've never forgotten. Their majesty, purpose, and completeness was so clear. I just knew it was who they really were, and that divine identity was what I wanted to support them to live from.

Some of our most enduring Truths about life proffer wisdom like "To thine own Self be true" and "Follow your heart" and "Be true to your Soul." I take these Truths to be parenting directives as well—there is no greater gift than giving our children the freedom to follow their hearts and to know themselves. This is a certain recipe for success. And when children are recognized and honored for who they are, all the ages and stages of life, including the teen years, are decidedly easier and more fun. When we take the path of authenticity ourselves, we are a scout for our children to follow.

An ancient Chinese proverb says, "If we all sweep in front of our own door, soon the whole street will be clean." I started with me; I listened to my daughters; we compromised all the way through. We became "real" with ourselves and each other, and that's the most beautiful way to be.

Terry Tillman shares more ... how he taught his daughters to "mine for gold" to approach life's unexpected twists and turns. Go to:
www.ifiwereyourdaddy.com/terrytillman

"I was once afraid of people saying, "Who does she think she is?" Now I have the courage to stand and say, "This is who I am."

Oprah Winfrey, American television host, actress, producer, and philanthropist. She is widely regarded as one of the most influential women in the world.

WHO IS TERRY TILLMAN?

Terry with (children) Kim and Wendy

Terry Tillman calls himself "a recovering businessman." His business career began at age fifteen, when he manufactured track hurdles with internationally famous track coach Bill Bowerman, founder of Nike. After earning a Stanford University degree in economics and finance, he went on to a series of successful ventures, including ownership in TV stations, a satellite cable business, a video production company, and real estate sales, where he became a member of the Million Dollar Real Estate Sales Club.

After thirty years of business success, Tillman exchanged his type A behavior for a life of service, spiritual development, coaching, and facilitating personal and organizational growth. He grew his facilitation skills as training director for Insight Seminars, then founded his own company, 22/7, through which he conducts seminars and speaks internationally, designs and facilitates leadership training for organizations and the public, and coaches executives.

A licensed pilot, white water rafting guide, ski instructor, and marathon runner, Tillman spends much of his time climbing mountains, the ones you can see and the ones you can't see: "the mountains inside your soul." In between treks, he teaches other people how to climb and how to know "the majesty of the territory within."

Tillman has two grown daughters, whom he says are among his best friends.

www.227company.com

IT'S YOUR RIDE

If I Were Your Daddy ... I'd use the quietly instructive power of stories to guide you to self-discovery—to face fears, to maintain balance, and to keep on pedaling.

*M*URRAY ROSENTHAL, D.O. FAPA

Psychiatrist & Chief Medical Officer

"Mastering life is rather like a learning to ride a bicycle," a wise man named Surya once told me. He then told me a story, and I never forgot it.

There's so much we want our children to know, so many lessons we want to impart. Yet raising a child isn't the same as teaching a class; there are no curricula, no textbook chapters to assign. Parents' well-intended stabs at formal instruction, "Will you listen? This is important," often feel forced and meet with rolled eyes and feigned appreciation: "OK, Dad, sure. Can I go now?"

The secret is to enter through the heart, not the brain, and one of the best ways to do this is by telling a story. A well told story magically merges a timeworn message with the currency of your voice. It's a gift that once given, forever connects the giver and receiver—something whose full use and meaning lie ahead. Oral traditions are cornerstones of many cultures. But today, 24/7 media chatter often drowns out the sweet, simple act of teaching by telling. A tired parent, too, will often just go silent. But if you have a good story that delivers life wisdom, it just means being on the alert for an opening, and them gracefully allowing the story to melt into the conversation.

I was fortunate enough to be blessed with a story whose layers and impact carried me—over life's daily rises in the road as well as its periodic mountain passes. That story came to me through a magical encounter I had in India with a man named Surya, a psychiatrist turned philosopher.

Upon completing my medical residency, I celebrated by grabbing my backpack and heading to the Far East. For six months I met amazing people in every country I visited. While I was visiting the Bay of Bengal, my guide called to me over her shoulder, "You must meet a man and I will arrange it; after all, you are a doctor." There's no way she could have known that. "Sure, OK" I said, even though I had no clue what she was talking about. She led me to the nearest taxi and said something to the driver in Hindi. To me she announced, "I will call Surya so he will be expecting you." This Jewish kid from the suburbs of Philly didn't have the slightest idea what was going on as I traveled to this stranger's house on the outskirts of town.

Surya's warmth immediately put me at ease. We talked of many things. My travels were soon to end and I would be resuming my life in psychiatry. The road ahead was a challenging one, and I think he sensed it. I listened intently, and at one point, Surya paused and looked at me with parental tenderness. "Now I will tell you a story that you will share hundreds of times with your patients. It is a metaphor about life, fear, and achieving balance." I sat transfixed.

The fears we face are necessary if we are to discover who we are.

Now, three decades later, not only have I told the story as he predicted, influencing hundreds of patients, but I have also used it as a pillar of my parenting. My two children and I still visit it from time to time as we did during their childhoods and teen years. Without fail, the story reminds us all that the fears we face are necessary if we are to discover who we are.

"Mastering life is rather like a learning to ride a bicycle," Surya began.

"When you were a child and saw a bicycle, what prevented you from jumping on and riding it?"

"Fear that I'd fall and get hurt," I replied.

"Yes, this is true for everyone," he said. "So how is it that a child who is afraid of falling will eventually get on the bicycle and try to ride it?"

"Well, having a parent or older friend there certainly helps, but I guess you develop a sense that what you will experience if you can learn to ride is worth the chance of falling."

"Yes, yes," Surya answered, and continued: "The child wants the freedom and experience of riding with other children. Of course there are some children who, paralyzed by fear, never learn. But most do; most find a way."

"So," he went on, "when you overcame the fear enough and got on the bicycle, did you ride it smoothly?"

"No," I said. "I went down straightaway."

"Ah," he said. "And what did you learn from that first fall?"

"Well, I survived."

"Yes, but still you struggled as you learned to ride. A bicycle is a precarious experience for a child. You're half riding, half falling. The fear of falling and getting hurt makes you overcorrect each move, which only worsens matters."

Better to show the child how the others are really doing.

Surya continued, "Everybody struggles with the bicycle of life. At times you believe you'll never master it. You look around and it appears everyone is riding smoothly but you. But are they really?" he asked, not waiting for my reply. "If newcomers measure themselves against those who appear to have mastered the task, they may feel they could never equal that competency. Better to show the child how the others are really doing."

And so he did. "If we make a movie of the best riders in the world and slow it down, are they really riding smoothly?"

"No," I responded. "They're simply making smaller corrections."

"Indeed, yes," Surya responded. "And they make them so quickly it appears there is no movement at all. They are falling but there is no perception of such. Having shown the child that professionals are imperfect, we now need to point out what the best riders are wearing."

"A helmet and gloves," I answered confidently.

"Why would a professional who knows how to ride a bicycle 'perfectly' need a helmet?"

"Because everyone falls at some time," I replied.

"Of course. Everyone falls from the bicycle of life," Surya repeated. "You don't ride it expecting not to fall. Instead, you *prepare* for the fall."

"So now," he continued, "here is the child. The child has overcome his or her initial fear, gotten on the bicycle, and like everyone else accepted that there will be struggles and possible falls. There remains one critical component that cannot be taught through logic. It's a singular experience each person must discover for himself. What's the one thing that can't be conveyed by words alone? The final key to mastering the bicycle?"

> *Balance comes not from struggling, but from accepting that struggle is part of the journey.*

"Balance."

"That's it! Yes! Balance comes not from struggling, but from accepting that struggle is part of the journey. You must discover for yourself what balance is. You may forget facts and details about a bicycle, but you cannot unlearn balance. Once mastered, it is a transformation. The discovery of balance puts you in a different state. It becomes part of you."

Surya was about to close the circle. "But the struggle, falls, lessons, and attainment of balance were not the reasons the child first decided to face his fears and get on the bicycle. Never lose sight of that of which you dreamt—the freedom and exploring. Balance is but a passage that moves you toward the real experience: that which led you to discover something about *yourself.*"

I released one of those deep breaths when everything shifts around you. "I see it."

Throughout our conversation I'd had many recollections of my childhood: challenges, fears, and more than my share of falls. I saw it then, *When we face our fears we experience the most important ascension available to humans: self-discovery.*

and even now I see it clearly. When we face our fears we experience the most important ascension available to humans: self-discovery.

RIDING LESSONS 101: OVERCOMING FEAR

The bicycle story found its way into discussions with my patients years before I became a father. I never knew when it would be useful, and never once in my twenty-six years of practice did my patients fail to understand the story. Often, in fact, they referred back to it years later. Now, kids… they're an altogether different story, particularly when they're yours.

When our children were too young to understand the story, I nonetheless used it to guide my interactions with them. Jonathan, our eldest, zoomed as soon as he could walk. His stocking-footed scooting around on hardwood floors usually ended with a collision into walls or other solid objects, followed by yelps that swelled into blood-curdling screams. Initially, every episode earned him the panicked parents' reaction to their firstborn. Once I noticed the little guy ramping up to yelp while looking around to see who was there to react. And I remembered Surya's bicycle story.

"I heard you, sweetheart. Are you hurt?" I called out with love and concern, *without* rushing over to help as I usually did. "Do you need me to pick you up or are you OK doing it yourself?" I waited. Jonathan had a curious reaction. Instead of having me automatically make everything OK, he had to decide for himself. There was a lengthy pause before he said, "Guess I'm OK," rather tenuously.

"It looks like the fall scared you, huh?" I pointed out.

He rubbed his shoulder. "Hurt too." He moved into position for an examination. I put on my best doctor's face and together we examined his "injury," concluding that he would survive.

After that, his self-induced crashes took on a different quality. I waited for the inevitable yelp and then called out, "Need help?" On the rare occasion when I had real concern, I stepped in. Mostly he got up and dealt with it himself or came to Dad for a second opinion. He was never helpless. Jonathan was learning that he could fall and take care of himself, or turn to me if needed. *He was beginning to ride.*

He was learning that he could fall and take care of himself.

For our daughter, Sammi, the first defining moment came when she was seven. I'd arrived home and she was there at the door, as was our ritual, the first to greet Daddy. This evening, she looked serious. I don't recall her request, but I responded that I'd happily oblige if she reminded me later. Bursting into tears, she declared, "I can't, Daddy! You know I have a bad memory!"

I was dumbstruck. Falling to my knees so we were at eye level, I said, "Sweetheart, what do you mean?"

"I just don't remember things," she explained, tearfully. "I had a list to remember in school and couldn't do it."

I told her to sit tight. I changed out of my suit and was back at her side in a flash. "Get your jacket, darlin', we're going for a walk on the beach." I was about to see if I could teach my frightened child how to master a bicycle she'd become fearful to ride.

As we walked, I listened as she rattled off her perceived failings at remembering things. "Daddy works with Alzheimer's patients, and I promise you, Sammi, I've never seen it start at age seven."

"I have an idea," I continued. "You love to draw with Mommy, right?" (My artist wife had drawn with our kids as soon as they could lift crayons.)

"Well, right now, I want you to make a picture in your mind. Can you picture a lamb?"

"Sure, Daddy."

"Instead of its wooly coat, imagine it covered in rice. Can you picture it?"

"Sure," she grinned. "I can see it."

"OK, keep seeing that lamb and let's have some fun with it. Give it carrot ears, a tomato nose…," and on and on I went. Sammi giggled as I directed her to make the imaginary lamb sillier and sillier.

"Now, you have made a most amazing imaginary lamb. Tell me all about it."

Sammi launched into a detailed explanation, recounting every last detail of her silly lamb, a task far more exacting than the list that had thwarted her an hour earlier.

"Honey, the list of everything on your lamb is twice as long as the lists you've forgotten before." Her mouth fell open. "You have your mom's mind—the mind of an artist. It's a very special gift. You remember pictures. All you need to do is make a picture in your mind."

I'm not sure how to describe such a transformational moment, the blink in time during which another human being, right in front of your eyes, *shifts, regains balance, and rides off straight and sure.* My daughter did it that evening. For several years after (with decreasing frequency, sadly), she caught me off guard by whispering, "I still remember that silly lamb." So do I, my sweetness, so do I.

In a blink, another human being can transform right in front of you.

At seven she was still too young for the whole bicycle story. So my job was to reframe her fear of falling and let her discover her own balance. I don't know if this episode led to Sammi's confidence, particularly during her midteens. I do know that after that magical walk, I never again heard her express fear about her inability to tackle a problem. Sammi went on to become a wonderfully independent, internationally minded young

My job was to reframe her fear of falling and let her discover her own balance.

woman. She initiated her own transfer to a boarding school in England at age sixteen, found a summer job in Paris at seventeen, and attended college in Paris thereafter. She has fearlessly pursued a life vision that's clearly pictured in her mind, one that's hers and hers alone to dream.

DISCOVERING YOUR INNER GEAR

Having learned early to pick himself up, Jonathan's war cry became, "I don't need any help. I can do it myself." By the time he went off to college, his figurative bicycle wobbled to the side of overconfidence. Nevertheless, I let him go, even though college was in Australia.

Before leaving him in his dorm on Australia's Gold Coast, I put my hands on my son's shoulders and looked into his eyes. By now he was a foot taller than me so I had to look straight up! "I want you to know that you can't fail me Jonathan," I said. "You're pushing your comfort zone here, trying something new, and I'm very proud of you whatever the outcome. Remember, I'm here for you."

"I know, Dad, I know."

I recognized the "Please, no lecture" voice. He was happy I'd helped him get established, and equally happy to have me go so he could get on with it. I kissed him on the cheek and took one long look at my boy, now a man. *He wanted to ride this one on his own,* as he should.

Two years later, while driving alone at night on a sparsely traveled road, one of his front tires blew. His car went into a skid and, as he told it, hurtled sideways for an eternity before stopping. All was black and silent around him when he opened the door and stepped out onto a bush that promised firm ground underneath. The bush was actually on the side of a steep embankment, down which Jonathan promptly fell, stopped only by barbed wire at its bottom.

Alone in the dark and scared, he reached for his cell phone, only to discover he'd let it run out of juice. For the first time in his nineteen years he was terrified. He was bleeding, in pain, and fearful that this was the end of his life. No one was going to help him. Perhaps recalling the body checks he'd done after colliding with walls at home, he made sure no bones were broken, then slowly climbed back up the embankment. By his telling, he then walked an hour in both directions and saw no lights or passing cars. He wasn't sure if he was injured or how badly. He'd never felt so frightened and alone.

For the first time in his nineteen years he was terrified.

Eventually he decided staying with his car was safest. Just then lights appeared, and lumbering down the road came the most beautiful tow truck he'd ever seen. Hours later, his car was in a lot and he was safely home and in need of his dad.

If you think you feel helpless when your sick baby can't articulate what hurts, imagine being ten thousand miles away when you're scared, hurting, bleeding teenager calls. My wife was in Europe with our daughter when Jonathan's call came in the middle of the night.

"Dad, I had a blowout. I'm home and scared and don't know what to do."

"OK, son, you did the right thing to call. We'll get through this together."

The next twenty-four hours were tense. We considered my jumping on a plane or his coming home. But neither were options. He hadn't yet been checked medically and was an emotional wreck. I told him what to do and in what order, and I steeled him to take control. A physical evaluation revealed cuts and abrasions that required simple treatment and a tetanus shot. He'd be fine physically.

Emotionally, he couldn't concentrate in school and often cried spontaneously. We talked twice a day. I was on pins and needles deciding whether to go rescue him or help him from afar. I couldn't hear his yelp or peer around the corner to check on him. My own bicycle was wobbling.

During one of our discussions he opened up about fearing death out there on that embankment. "Jonathan, you've gone through an ancient ritual of which most youth today are deprived," I said. "In early days, males went into the woods to hunt alone and face their demons; it was part of growing up. Today, we're insulated from these experiences. But now you've had one of them and, look, you *survived*. You never again have to worry about feeling overwhelmed by that feeling. Unlike most kids your age, you've faced it and you took action. If you were still in a tribe, you'd be honored as a man." I waited and then offered, "Still, if you need me, I can fly out tomorrow. Two days and I'll be at your side. Think about it and call me back."

It took him less than an hour. "Dad, I do need to talk to someone about this, but if it's okay with you, I made an appointment to see a school psychologist here." I swelled with pride. He was quiet and then said, "As long as I have your words in my ears, I'll get through this. You don't need to come. I'll be okay." Though bruised and shaken, *he remounted his bike himself and started riding again.*

In ancient times, before there were written works, parents taught their children and they taught theirs through the rite of storytelling.

Surya's story had transformed me, transformed each of my children, and this is the power of a good story. In ancient times, before there were written words, parents taught their children and they taught theirs through the rite of storytelling. Ancient Vedic and Tibetan medical wisdom was sung to anchor the words in ear and mind. Stories remain a charmed way of passing on truisms and pieces of our lives. They masquerade lessons as entertainment, big philosophies as lullaby-like pocket tales.

We're duty-bound as parents to teach our children these important lessons, and stories present the goods in the *most* alluring and lasting packages. Through all the potholes, over all the loose gravel, stories stick.

I'm ever grateful to have been given the gift of Surya's grand metaphor and to have used it to equip my children on their respective rides. They mounted their bikes. *I gave them a push and I let go.* The story and all its tributaries absorbed into their beings, they found their balance and sped away, powered not by their parent but by words echoing from corners deep within.

"Everyone wants to live on top of the mountain, but all the happiness and growth occurs while you're climbing it."

Andy Rooney, *60 Minutes* commentator and great storyteller

WHO IS MURRAY ROSENTHAL, D.O. FAPA?

Murray with (wife) Janet,
(children) Jonathan and Samantha

Dr. Murray Rosenthal life's work is dedicated to providing hope for those in pain. Overcoming chronic pain himself, he went on to help build one of the most successful privately held clinical research groups in the country, California Clinical Trials. As its CEO and medical director, he managed more than 450 clinical trials and published dozens of articles on a wide range of psychiatric topics, including sleep, pain, anxiety, depression, and the medical implications of underrecognizing and undertreating emotional disorders.

Rosenthal did graduate work in biochemistry and experimental pathology and developed an assay for the melanin content of cells that is still used today. He went on to medical school and a psychiatric residency at University of California San Diego.

Rosenthal has served as consultant to the state attorney general and to the San Diego City School District. He has been medical director of an inpatient eating disorders program and consultant to the neurologic units and heart rehabilitation and transplantation programs at Sharp Memorial Hospital.

After the sale of California Clinical Trials, Rosenthal rejected retirement, choosing instead to assist in the development of Millennium Laboratories, a clinical laboratory that serves the chronic pain specialist. He became its chief medical officer and currently devotes his time to developing liaisons with leading pain specialists, assisting in the publication of research from the lab, and lecturing on the bio-psycho-social implications of chronic pain.

When not working, Rosenthal enjoys travel with friends and family, photography, and sailing.

WINNING STRATEGIES

LISTENING TO YOUR INSPIRATION

If I Were Your Daddy ... I'd find out what inspires you. Then I'd help you build a successful life around it so you live in your genius.

JOHN DEMARTINI, D.C.
Human Behavior Specialist and Educator

Once when I was in Brisbane, Australia, a lovely woman attended one of my presentations and afterward asked if I could do a consult with her son.

"Certainly," I said.

"Let me give you a little preface," she began. "I'm a single mom. He's sixteen years old, and he's lazy. I want him to work, but all he does is sit in front of his computer playing video games. He's not doing any sports, he's not working, and he's just a lazy slouch. Can you fix him?"

I smiled and said, "Well, I'm not going to fix him, but I will certainly chat with him." So I went and sat down with him and said, "What's up?"

He went, "Oh, nothin'."

"Your mom asked me to chat with you."

He said, "Yeah, she's on my case."

I asked, "What do you love doing? What are you up to?"

"Well, I'm just doing video games," he responded, with his head still buried in one.

"What video games do you love the most?"

He said, "Well, I love doing animation and stuff."

I asked, "Do you love computer video games?"

"Yeah."

"Are you pretty good at them?" I asked.

"Yeah."

"Do you love actually developing your own games and being creative like that?" I asked.

"Yeah," he said.

"Do you know a lot about computers?" I asked.

"Yeah."

So then I asked him, "What kind of creative activities can you do on your computer?"

"All kinds of creative programming."

And we kept chatting, and after an hour of hearing about all that he could do I asked him to help me develop part of my website.

When I came out of the room, his mother said, "Well, did you straighten him out?"

"No, I *hired* him."

"What?" cried the astonished woman. "You hired him?"

"Yeah," I said, "he's quite gifted when it comes to computers."

"You're joking!" was all she could come out with.

You see, this woman knew almost nothing about computers, so she was projecting something from her generation onto her son, expecting him to go out and play sports and get a job at a hamburger joint or something. I said, "Your son, right now, is a little genius with computer software programming, and very shortly he will probably have his own software development company and make more money than you could have ever imagined, and then you might just be eating some of your words."

I continued, "Right now, we're living in a computer era. It's something you've repressed, so he's specializing in it. My advice is to go and find out what your son is doing and see if he can't put it into action, doing projects related to what he loves."

He did the website work and a software project for me, and he was brilliant at it. He's now twenty-three and making more money than his mom. Her values were that he should be working and making money, and once her values were being met, she was fine. But originally she was projecting an expectation onto him that didn't match *his* values, so she experienced nothing but resistance. He wasn't really lazy; he was only seemingly "lazy" according to her values. *He was inspired within his own values.* Children are always inspired doing what they value most. As a parent, you have to find out what that is, capitalize on it, and let your child excel at it. He and his mother get along differently now because she's recognizing his genius.

Children are always inspired doing what they value most. As a parent, you have to find out what that is and let your child excel at it.

I have three beautiful adult children: two daughters, Alana and Breccia, and a son, Dan. Two of them work for me, and one does research for me while he's in college, so we've remained close. One of my main guiding principles in parenting was not to impose my values onto my children. Instead, I encouraged them to be congruent and authentic to themselves. I firmly believe that all human beings, starting right from childhood, have their own natural genius. Whenever they are living congruently with their own highest values, they awaken that genius.

When I wanted to communicate something to one of my children, I *first* found out what was important to him or her. After asking some simple questions, I then communicated my message in terms of whatever that was. For instance, when my son, Dan, was little, he went through a phase when he was very into Pokémon. If I took him to a Pokémon movie, he just loved it. If I asked him about Pokémon, like what was his newest Pokémon card, he loved it. But if I talked to him about something else, he didn't relate to it. If I asked him how he was doing in school, he'd go, "Uhh . . . " But if I asked him what he learned in school *relative to Pokémon,* he'd open up! When I communicated to him in the *context of his interest* and bridged out from there, he was engaged.

From Pokémon my son moved on to music, and during that period I had to listen to his music (a bit) to know how to relate to him, just like my parents had to listen to mine. During this period I asked him questions like, "What lyrics are you enjoying the most? What do you get from it?" By asking him about what was important to him, he would open up with me.

A child's values are going to evolve, so as parents we are wise to be observant and adapt. Just like adults, children are always demonstrating what's important to them through what I call "twelve value determinates." I look at how they *fill their space, spend their time, spend their energy.* What *energizes them?* How do they *spend their money* when they get it? Where are they *most organized, most disciplined?* What do they *think about* and *talk about* most, *dream about* most, *converse about with their friends* most? What are their *long-term goals* and *what inspires them?*

> *Just like adults, children are always demonstrating what's improtant to them through "twelve value determinates."*

If I tried to impose something on one of my children that wasn't in his or her value system, it would basically bounce right back to me, and I'd get a "Huh?" and a blank look. Instead, I paid close attention to their values, and as long as I related new ideas and concepts to the things that were important to them, they'd listen. Just like in sales, if you communicate your message in other people's highest values, they are more apt to buy.

At one point one of my daughters was struggling a bit in school, so I asked her what classes she was having the most difficulties with. I then helped her to think about how those subjects related to her own interests (her values at the time), because if she could make that connection, she could turn things around and likely be more inspired by the process. If not, she was going to bomb that class. It's that simple.

Whether they're aware of it or not, human beings live and make decisions according to their higher priorities and values. And whenever they are living congruently, their genius emerges. They are inspired. They can't wait to get up and do it. When my son loved video games and wild music, I didn't negate it; I just went with it and whenever possible expanded on it. "Let's go look at the video store and explore all the video games," I said. "Who are the heroes and icons in your games? Tell me a few ways they're similar to the ones in history or literature class."

In his Pokémon era, we went to the Pokémon store and I said, "Learn everything you can. Master Pokémon so you know everything about it, and you'll gain confidence with your knowledge." Well, he was so inspired he threw himself into this task and eagerly learned everything he could. This wasn't work; it was an inspiration, because we want to learn about what's most inspiring to us, and our confidence grows when we're able to do what's most meaningful to us.

> *Our genius emerges and our confidence grows when we to do what's most meaningful to us.*

Marilyn Wilhelm is an extraordinary teacher I had the great privilege to study with. By the time her students are nine, they are learning multiple languages, religions, sciences, and philosophy. By age twelve or thirteen, some of them have become professors at universities. These are initially ordinary children. Critics didn't believe she was able to do this, so they gave her random children from Harlem in New York City, some of them troubled crack children. Within five years she produced the same kind of results.

She did this by first finding out what each child's genius was and what was inspiring to that child. She memorized the top five values of each child and let the children excel at everything they did. She would say, "Okay, Joey, you're interested in music. In 1927, what was the number-one music at the time? I want you to find that out for me. And Shaquille, you're into finance, you want to be a wealthy guy. What was the banking system doing in 1927 and who started that banking system?" She'd get them all involved in whatever they were interested in. She then had them teach the others what they learned, so everybody was listening to everybody else. Each child was the hero and the leader in the class.

LOVE WHAT YOU DO AND YOUR CHILDREN WILL LEAD AN INSPIRED LIFE

Historian Jacques Barzun said, "A successful education whets the appetite of a person to learn, so for that human being's entire life there's a constant desire to learn more about everything." This was what I wanted for my children, and for all children. If children are inspired by what they do, they'll not only excel at it, they'll be training themselves to always do what they love. One day they'll wake up and find themselves living an inspired life—doing what they love in life. Unfortunately, 99 percent of the population doesn't do that. They don't live true to their own lives and subordinate themselves to the authorities around them. They have Monday morning blues, Wednesday hump days, and thank-God-it's-Fridays. The way to prevent this is for children to discover early what's inspiring to them *and then go out and live that,* whatever it is. I may not agree with it at times, but that's not my job. My job as a parent is to understand that it's *their* path, not to try to fix them or change them, but to observe *their* values,

My job is not to try to fix them, but to observe their values, love them, and communicate within their value system.

love them for who *they* are, and communicate within *their* value system.

HELP THEM FIND ANOTHER WAY TO GET THEIR NEEDS MET

Even if things were seemingly going a bit off course with one of my children, and I wanted to intervene by introducing some concepts or ideas that might be helpful, I still found it was wiser and worked better to honor their values than to impose mine. Linking what I thought might be useful to my daughter over to what she was interested in was much more effective than just telling her, "This is what you need to learn," or even, "This is what you should do," which would have been an exercise in futility in the long run.

For instance, one of my daughters wanted to leave home to live with her boyfriend because she was infatuated with him. A common parental response might be to forbid it, which would have only created a battle of wills. Instead, I recognized that one of her values was earning money. I routinely collect biographies of people who've done extraordinary things and then pay my children to read them and give me one-page summaries. So I found a biography relevant to my daughter's situation, someone who'd had similar options and made empowering choices. I then gave it to her and asked, "I'd like you to read this and give me a one-page summary, and I'll pay you by the hour. Do you want the work?" She said, "Okay," and was eager to do it.

She made a wise, informed decision. I never had to tell her what to do.

After she delivered the report I asked her, "What did you learn?" She said, "That woman went through the same thing I'm going through, and look what she did with her life!" So I said, "Well, then you could do great things with your life too! This is just a stepping-stone." She now had an inspiring role model and other options, and it expanded her world. As a result, she made a wiser, more informed decision, and *I never had to tell her what to do.*

Most parents get frightened when they see their child going down what might be termed a "bad road" or off track. I don't necessarily see it as a bad road because I lived it myself, so I have a different perspective. During my teens in the late sixties I was in a rock band. I lived on the streets in the drug scene, and I almost died of strychnine poisoning. But an elderly man named Paul Bragg intervened and transformed my life. One of the pivotal things he did was to see my genius potential while everyone else saw a messed-up child with a learning disability. And because he saw something different, he was able to catalyze my profound transformation. He awakened me to my inspired vision of becoming a philosopher, healer and a teacher, which I didn't think I could do. I had accepted my grade school label of "learning deficient" and allowed it to become a self-fulfilling prophecy. But Paul told me I was perfectly able to learn and do amazing things. "In fact," he said, "you're a genius." He made me promise to say one affirmative statement to myself every day: *I'm a genius and I apply my wisdom.* That's when I turned my life around.

They have a need and they're trying to find a way to meet it.

If not for those wayward years I wouldn't be where I am today, so I don't condemn it in others. I sure don't pass judgment or think, "Oh my goodness, they're screwing up!" What I see is that they have a need and they're trying to find a way to meet it.

It's far more effective to discover what that unmet need is and then provide alternative ways of getting it met—like my daughter wanting to move out. Show them they have options so they aren't limited to one thing, one path—the way Paul Bragg did with me. I simply ask, "Okay, whatever you're going through, how is it serving you and how can you use it to your advantage?"

Every child follows a unique path. I don't find that over protecting children from difficult things serves them in the long run. To do great things requires a challenging path. Many people who've done extraordinary things came from very difficult situations. When I did a search on celebrity orphans, I found hundreds of celebrities who had been orphaned—their father or mother died or they were abandoned. For instance, Sir Isaac Newton didn't have a father; his mother gave him up temporarily, and he went on to do the most extraordinary things. Truthfully, it's not about what you've been through or what you're going through. It's about how you interpret it and how you use it to fulfill what's inspiring to you. I try to teach my children that.

LIVING A VALUE-DRIVEN, INTEREST-DRIVEN LIFE EMPOWERS YOU

I explained to my children that any area of your life that you don't empower is set up for someone to overpower you. But it's important to realize you're not a victim of their overpowering; you're just not empowered. I tell them, "If you've got a bully in your life and he's pushing you around, it's partly because you're not guiding or governing your own life. You're not empowered in that area. Once you empower that area, the bully disappears. If you don't empower yourself, the bully just keeps coming in to toughen you up, to make you stronger so you empower that area. That bully is your hero because he is actually helping you empower yourself."

> Once you empower that area, the bully disappears.

This didn't happen often with my children because I urged them to live within their own values and become masters of their interests. In doing that they became more empowered and self-confident, and there was no need for a bully in their life.

A lot of children today are labeled ADHD. However, when they're doing what they love doing, often these same children can easily sit for six hours straight in front of a video game, learning things invisible to their parents and educators. Often these children are geniuses, but they're just not inspired when they feel that they have to do other seemingly meaningless activities other people are projecting onto them. As parents we are wise to learn how to communicate within their highest values. By doing this we wake them up. They're then ready to go out and do extraordinary things that inspire them, even though they live in a society with many boxes of mediocrity, and they're basically told to fit in them and be obedient. But if you look carefully, the people who have left their marks in history are the people who didn't fit into those boxes and were not mediocre. My own life is a testament to this.

The people who have left their marks in history are the people who didn't fit into those boxes and were not mediocre.

When I was in first grade, my teacher asked my parents to come to the school. As we sat in a little semicircle she said to them in front of me, "I'm afraid your son has learning difficulties. He has dyslexia and will never read, write, or communicate. He will never go very far in life; indeed, he will never amount to anything. I suggest you put him into sports because he likes to run." (I was born with a foot turned in and had to wear braces, so when I got out of them, I just ran everywhere.) That's why I dropped out of school and lived on the streets until Paul Bragg came along and showed me how to access and wake up my own genius.

So here's the irony. When my daughter was exactly the same age, her first grade teacher asked me to come to the school to discuss her concerns about my daughter. When she said almost the *identical* things, I simply burst out laughing. Quite irate, she asked, "You don't care about your child?" Still laughing I said, "No, I'm just so inspired, because from what you're saying, I know my daughter is going to do great things!" And today she is!

My children are young adults now, but I still communicate with them through their interests. And I watch them sometimes communicating the same way with those around them. I'm confident that when they become parents (if that is part of their mission), they will pass this same approach along to their children as well. My vision and hope for my children is for them to continually discover what's inspiring to them and be living from that state of being. My children are not here to live my mission; they're here to live their own mission, and wherever and whenever they are living congruently with their highest values, their genius appears. This encouragement is the greatest gift I can give them. If I can help them live like this, then I will consider myself a successful father.

"Everybody is a genius. But, if you judge a fish by its ability to climb a tree, it will spend its whole life believing that it is stupid."

Albert Einstein, a theoretical physicist and philosopher, who is widely regarded as the father of modern physics. He was awarded the 1921 Nobel Prize in Physics.

WHO IS JOHN DEMARTINI, D.C.?

John with (children) Alana, Breccia, and Dan

Dr. John Demartini is a model of determination, overcoming childhood obstacles to become a wealthy and renowned leader in human behavior. He is founder of the Demartini Institute, a research and education organization, and author of more than forty books. His Demartini Method is used worldwide by psychologists, psychiatrists, and other health professionals to evaluate and reduce stress and resolve conflict.

Labeled "learning disabled" by a first-grade teacher who announced—in front of him—that he wouldn't go far in life, Demartini dropped out of school at fourteen, illiterate. Through determination and the inspiration of a mentor, he earned a bachelor of science degree at the University of Houston, and a doctorate at Texas Chiropractic College. Demartini went on to build a thriving chiropractic practice before retiring to pursue a deep interest in human behavior.

Featured in the best-selling film and book *The Secret,* Demartini has also shared his expertise through such outlets as CNBC, *Oprah* magazine, and *Larry King Live.* He teaches that everyone has potential, stressing to parents that their role should be to understand their children's behavior and facilitate their reaching their goals.

Demartini is a citizen of the world, maintaining his residence on the cruise ship The World, a community of 165 private residences that continually travels the globe. He is the proud father of three adult children: two daughters, Alana Joy and Breccia Aurora, and one son, Dan David.

www.drdemartini.com

BEING THERE AND
HELPING YOU DECIDE

If I Were Your Daddy ... I'd do everything possible to be there for you. I'd teach you that the quality of your life depends on making good decisions. And I'd help you make good ones by weighing opportunities, risks, and outcomes.

GREG LINK
Corporate President & Marketing Expert

Life doesn't always give you a second chance, but I was blessed. I *got* a second chance, as a father, to be there for my kids. And I learned that one of the most important reasons to "be there" is to help your kids make good decisions.

When my first wife and I divorced, our daughters, Jennifer and Stephanie, were only three and six. Their mom got full custody, and although I got visitation rights, the circumstances she presented made it very difficult for me to spend time with my girls. I paid child support all the way, but that's only a small part of parenting. I just wasn't there for them. Looking back, I wish I had done whatever it took to see them—and demanded my visitation rights. But I was young, and I didn't.

Children don't know anything about messy circumstances, nor does it really matter. The only thing they know is whether you were there or not. If you weren't there, kids feel abandoned. They hear stories from the custodial parent that may or may not be accurate. My girls needed to know that I loved them unconditionally—which I did. But nothing speaks louder than being there, and that's why *not* being there is so damaging. I share this because it's the raw truth, and maybe someone reading this can learn from my experience. If I'd known then what I know now, I'd have done things differently. No matter how hard divorce and ex-spouses are, you've just got to do whatever it takes to be there for your kids.

No matter how hard divorce and ex-spouses are, you've just got to do whatever it takes to be there for your kids.

(Now this story does have a happy ending. When my girls turned eighteen, I finally had complete access to them, and at that point we were able to start rebuilding our relationship.)

A SECOND CHANCE

A few years after the divorce, I met and married Annie, the love of my life. It was difficult for Annie to get pregnant, so when Natalie was born, she was our miracle baby. We then adopted our son, Gavin, at birth.

I was very grateful to have a second chance at being a dad, and this time I was determined to do it right. The most important thing for me was to be physically present as much as I could—in a way I'd been unable to with Jennifer and Stephanie—and to let my kids know, every day, that I loved them unconditionally. Being physically present would allow me the luxury of imparting, day to day, the many things I did well: the life skills I knew I could pass on to help them become healthy adults. I've always done extremely well in business, excelling at problem solving and decision making, and I wanted to make sure my kids had these abilities too. I felt a foundation like this could make a huge difference in their teen and adult years. And now I was able to give it.

"NO" IS NOT SUSTAINABLE

For both Annie and me, it was important to start teaching our kids early how to think through a situation for themselves, and make a good decision. It's a big mistake to assume that our kids are helpless until they're twenty-one. Our natural tendency as parents is to protect them, and as a result we often hold back and *over*protect. We do things *for* them instead of teaching them how to do things for themselves ... and that includes decision making. When they want to do something, we see what could go wrong and often routinely just say, "No, I don't think that's a good idea." But if all we ever do is say "no," at a certain point we discover that "no" is not sustainable. It gives children no life skills to deal with the future. Kids need a process to think decisions through for themselves, or the parent becomes the "heavy." The sooner we can get kids to engage in adult dialogue and critical thinking, the faster we can get them to take responsibility for their own actions. Then, when "no" stops working, as it inevitably will, we have a system to replace it with, providing a smoother transition into adulthood.

THINKING FOR THEMSELVES

From the time my kids were eight, I saw that they started to have a sense of right and wrong and of the consequences of their actions. As much as possible, Annie and I treated our children like adults, capable of reasoning and making their own choices. Beginning when they were little, whenever they asked if they could go to this sleepover or that party or whatever, we sat down with them and asked a series of questions to analyze the request together. We used what we called the *four vital variables:* opportunity, risks, environment, and outcomes (O-R-E-O).

Teach kids early how to make a good decision by giving them a process to do it: O.R.E.O.

1. Opportunity: What's the opportunity?

2. Risks: What's the situation—what are the risks?

3. Environment: Where will you be? Who will be there? What's the maturity level of your friends? You'll be guilty by association so consider this carefully.

4. Outcomes: What are the likely or *possible* outcomes?

By going through these questions aloud and looking at the possible outcomes, our kids learned how to evaluate any situation. Then *they* made a decision whether to do it or not. By repeating this process throughout their childhood, they learned the skill of critical thinking, and making them part of the decision empowered them.

By repeating this a lot, they learned the skill of critical thinking.

As parents, of course we were part of the discussion, asking ourselves questions like "How important is it to them? Is it visibly important?" "If it doesn't work out, will it really ruin their lives?" and "How credible or mature is the child at this stage in life?"

We always tried to err on the side of giving our kids rope—though not so much that they could injure themselves or others. Wherever possible we said "yes." When the consequences were clearly dire, we said "no." We'd say, "I know you think you're ready for that but you're not. And you're not going to do it." And when we took this position, we stuck to it. There was no negotiating … but there was an explanation.

"WHAT HAVE YOU DONE WITH MY CHILD?"

What's wonderful about kids is that they never stay the same for long. And what's difficult about kids is that they never stay the same for long. They're always growing and changing, and as parents we have to be one step ahead, or we set ourselves up for trouble. We know that sooner or later our kids will become teenagers, but we're often caught off guard when those years actually arrive. We've been lulled into a kind of stupor with cute little ten- and eleven-year-olds who hang on our every word. We're comfortable relating to them as small, dependent children and forget they won't always be this way. Then, without warning, around age twelve or thirteen, they turn into monsters--full of so much attitude and rebellion that we're jolted into thinking, "Who are you and what have you done with my child?"

I've noticed that most parents struggle as their children move into this stage, and many are not very successful. Annie and I knew our kids would soon be faced with life-changing decisions about drugs, sex, and peer pressure—to name just a few—and they would face those decisions earlier than we had. We knew we could not expect them to make good decisions about these issues if we didn't teach them how.

Just like any other skill, good decision-making has to be taught and practiced. We knew if we waited until our kids were teenagers to start, it would be far too late. When parents are suddenly faced with a rebellious teenager with his or her own agenda, and try to invoke an adult reasoning conversation without a prior history of doing so, they usually end up desperately negotiating to maintain some kind of control. But negotiating with a teenager on these terms is like negotiating with terrorists; it does not work.

Using the O.R.E.O. process, we explored the risks and possible dangers together, but we let them make the final decision as much as possible.

It is my experience that young teens are perfectly capable of engaging in an intelligent decision-making dialogue, but only if they've been doing it all their lives. Because we implemented the four-point O.R.E.O. process early, our kids' decision-making skills were developed and cemented in place well before they were actually required, and long before they started resisting parental input.

When I later checked with my children, Natalie in particular pointed out that we always treated them like adults. "We weren't controlled and dictated to, we were talked with. And I always appreciated that."

When Gavin was around twelve, he wanted to go spring camping with some friends. Using the O.R.E.O. process, we explored the risks and possible dangers: there was winter runoff, and sometimes kids drowned in the streams in this area. We also went through how mature some of these friends were (they weren't very mature). We were concerned, but let him decide. After looking at all the facts, Gavin *himself* made the ultimate decision not to go.

When Natalie was not yet sixteen, she wanted to date an older boy. He was at least seventeen and could drive. We really didn't want her being alone with an older boy in a car, knowing some of the problems that might result, so we discussed it with her. We said, "Natalie, think about what's happened to some of your friends that you don't want to happen to you. Even though you know it won't, and this boy's different and all that stuff, give us some examples of what *might* happen (dating an older guy with a car)?" She offered some possibilities. We offered some more. We asked her, "Could you handle unwanted advances? Would you be prepared to handle this possibility?" After giving it some thought, Natalie decided of her own volition that she wasn't ready to go out with this older guy in his car.

Kids can reason and draw conclusions from their friends to help them make good decisions.

I've learned that kids are usually able to reason like this; they're able to draw conclusions from watching the friends around them, not for the purpose of judging but to learn from them. But there has to be a history of having that kind of conversation and developing those analytical skills. Then, once children become teenagers, the conversation doesn't show up on their radar as something intended to control them, but more as a resource to help them make good decisions.

We also discovered that even after all that hard work and preparation, at a certain point as they enter their teens, they tend to resist engaging. The minute we started the conversation, we'd get the rolling eyes, and "I know; here's the five reasons I shouldn't do this, blah, blah blah…" But even though kids may get a bit of an attitude about the whole process, the foundation of critical thinking is already in place. It still works amid the groans, and the kids are actually much more prepared for the bigger decisions of their teens. My kids acknowledged later that they would've been a lot worse off without those skills. We didn't insulate them from trouble (as if we could have), but we did give them tools they could use for the rest of their lives.

EXPERIENCING CONSEQUENCES

Beyond teaching our kids to make their own decisions, we also let them learn from those they had already made. Once the decision was made and the child went ahead, just allowing him or her to experience the natural consequences was very powerful. Perhaps it went well or perhaps it didn't. Too many parents short-circuit this process and help clean up messes, thus insulating kids from the natural consequences of their choices. In our family, treating our kids as adults meant holding them accountable.

Allowing kids to experience the natural consequences brings very powerful learning.

For example, when Natalie was thirteen, she wanted to go to a sleepover at a friend's house. We went through the whole four-point dialoging process. She decided to go, and at 3 a.m. the girls got picked up by the police for egging houses. So there were natural consequences, and Natalie got to experience them. She had to pay a fine, apologize to the homeowners, and experience the humiliation … and spend the next day helping clean up the house.

Another time, Gavin stole a camera from a party. The next day we made him return it to the family, apologize to the father, and own up to what he had done. He was incredibly embarrassed, but making kids clean up after themselves is a very powerful learning experience.

Remember, though, there's a massive difference between allowing kids to experience the *natural* consequences, and handing out a traditional punishment. In many ways, getting reprimanded or grounded lets them off the hook. Most kids would take a punishment any day rather than face the people they wronged and clean up their messes.

LESSONS LEARNED

Two final stories.

One day Natalie's young son, my grandson, threw a temper tantrum at Costco. He was on the floor screaming and kicking his feet. Usually parents in this situation are so embarrassed they'll give the child anything to get them to stop, thus reinforcing the negative behavior and preventing the child from learning an acceptable way to be heard.

Not Natalie. She calmly looked at her son and said, "Cardon, you know that's not going to work. I'm just going to stand right here, so you let me know when you're finished." And she did. She just let him throw his fit with everybody watching. She was allowing him to express his feelings but let him know that this behavior would not bring the results he wanted.

Natalie was passing down to her kids what she'd been given. She was talking and relating to him in an adult manner, and she was really being present to what served him most—not how she looked as a parent. When he got done with his fit, then they could talk, and

Teaching kids to communicate their needs in an appropriate manner is empowering them.

his wants would be heard and discussed. Natalie was teaching Cardon how to communicate his needs in an appropriate manner, and in this way, empowering him.

The other story is about my son, Gavin. He lived his life out of his heart, and I had lived mine out of my head. He had always been a free spirit, and for a few years he had some personal challenges to overcome. I let him go through those challenges (he was a young adult by then), make some unwise decisions, and live with the consequences. And I just kept loving him all the same. When we anchor children with a solid foundation, we've just got to trust that eventually they'll come around. Our role is to let them know they're unconditionally loved. And Gavin came through it all marvelously.

He'd been living in Hawaii with his sister, and going to BYU. Then, when he was twenty-one, he told us he wanted to go to Ireland. When we pooh-poohed it, he sold his truck and began taking steps to try and get himself there. About a week before he was scheduled to start working at a wilderness camp, he called me and said, "I *really* want to go to Ireland. Will you take me, Dad? I know it's impractical. Please!"

He knew how business-oriented I was, how I always planned things out, and that asking me to just drop everything and go to Ireland with him for five days was an absolutely unreasonable request. However, for whatever reason, *I listened to my heart and said yes.* I dropped everything and took him to Ireland.

We had a great time, we flew back, I drove him into the mountains to the camp, and then left. The next morning, Father's Day, we got a call telling us that Gavin had passed away quietly in his sleep. He was twenty-one. I tell you this: had I not trusted my instincts, followed my heart, and taken him to Ireland, I would have regretted it all my life. I had been given the miraculous opportunity to express a lot of things to him, literally the day before he died.

Make being present to them your highest priority.

At the funeral service in Hawaii, I got to re-know my son through the eyes of all his fellow college students. So many of them came up and told me touching stories about him. I had let him do what he needed to do, struggle through whatever personal lessons he needed to learn, and emerge from it all in his own timing—but I had never withdrawn my unconditional love. And I discovered he had become quite an extraordinary young man.

From Gavin, I learned the importance of following my heart—my instincts—and if I have one more thing to share with you, that would be it. Teach your children to make good decisions and become responsible, capable, loving adults. That teaching can serve as ballast through a storm. Make *being present* to them your highest priority. Then follow your heart and love them unconditionally, because you never know what the future will bring.

"*Those who know how to think need no teachers.*"

Mahatma Gandhi, world leader, whose leadership and nonviolent methods freed millions.

WHO IS GREG LINK?

Pictured: Greg with (wife) Annie, and (grandsons) Raleigh, Lincoln, and Cardon Norton

Greg would like to acknowledge his loved children and grandchildren not pictured: (Children) Jennifer Foulger, Stephanie Lavin, Natalie Norton, Gavin Link (in heaven). (Grandchildren) Cole Lavin, Ireland Lavin, and Gavin Norton (in heaven).

Behind every headliner—the bestselling author, the high-profile executive, the celebrated performer—there's typically a business mind like Greg Link's.

Stephen R. Covey, author of *The 7 Habits of Highly Effective People*, cites Link as instrumental to Covey's success and influence. Link masterminded the marketing and public relations campaign that led *CEO* magazine to name *7 Habits* as the number-one business book of the 20th century. It sold more than fifteen million copies in three-dozen-plus languages, including one million in Japan, making publishing history there. Link helped parlay this success into creation of the Covey Leadership Center, a $100-plus-million enterprise with offices in forty countries. He continues his decades-long relationship with what is now FranklinCovey.

Together with Covey's son, Stephen M. R. Covey, Link founded CoveyLink, a boutique consultancy committed to guiding business leaders in growing their careers and their organizations at the *SPEED of TRUST*. Based on the book of the same name authored by the younger Covey, Link serves as president and chief deal-making officer of the organization. Link is also the leader of the new FranklinCovey Global Speed of Trust Practice and is currently coauthoring a new book with Stephen M. R. Covey to be published in 2011. The working title is *Smart Trust: How People, Companies, and Countries Prosper from High Trust*.

Link's reputation opens doors globally. Covey and Link serve such A-list clients as Hewlett-Packard, IBM, Microsoft, Pepsico, DIRECTV, AT&T, Frito-Lay, and many others.

www.coveylink.com

INCLUDING YOUR CHILDREN

If I Were Your Daddy ... I'd keep you close by my side, and we'd learn about life together. We'd edify each other and those around us, acknowledging wonder and beauty wherever we see it. And we'd be each other's greatest hero.

DEAN KOSAGE

Amway Global Executive
Diamond Distributor

Have you ever heard someone say, "As soon as ..., then I'll ..."? Maybe it was "As soon as I make enough money, *then* I can spend more time with my family." Or the opposite, "As soon as my children are a bit older, *then* I'll get my life or career started," or "have time for myself." Something important is always being delayed by something else we think we need *first*.

When I found myself standing amid the ashes of a difficult divorce, it would have been easy to fall into this trap, and choose solving my financial crisis over being a present and involved Dad to my little girl. Although that choice would have been logical—certainly no one would have argued with it—it just didn't seem healthy. Even in the turmoil of the moment I recognized that choice as coming from a place of scarcity or lack, rather than from a place of fullness and abundance. I didn't want to sacrifice one for the other because the truth was ... I wanted to do *both*.

WHAT IF YOU ARE IN SURVIVAL MODE?

As many know, going through a divorce can cause both visible and invisible problems. In a very short time I had gone from a six-figure income to a six-figure debt. I spent a lot of days feeling completely helpless, my self-esteem torn apart as I battled in court for custody and visitation rights.

I did get custody of my daughter, Teagan, while her mother was rebuilding her life. My ex stayed in our house, so I moved into my mother's home and slept on her couch, with my two-year-old baby girl in my arms. Now I was a single dad, needing to manage both my and my child's life, grow my network marketing business, pay our bills, and feel good about my fathering. I wanted to do all this well, but the question was *how?*

After about three months, I was able to get a one-bedroom apartment and lease some furniture, and over the next year I found some very creative ways to rebuild my life, beginning first with my mindset. Change always starts on the inside. In the midst of this chaos I realized I could either mask all the pain I was going through, and plow on feeling the loss, or I could totally change the vision I held of what my family was going to be.

You can reinvent yourself at any time if needed, even if pain is your teacher.

I needed to reinvent myself and find something authentic I could support within the reality of my new situation. I learned a huge lesson from all this: you can reinvent yourself at any time if needed, even if pain is your teacher. That's a lesson I would want my daughter to learn too.

HOW DO YOU RAISE A CHILD AND TRAVEL FOR BUSINESS?

I don't want to minimize Teagan's mother's role in all this. In the midst of this chaos she was starting a new job, and did the best she could with her work schedule. I was expanding my business, and as my organizations grew across the country and around the globe, my need to travel increased, adding another level of complexity. So I did some research.

I asked myself, "What are other successful people doing who don't work nine to five? What does Lance Armstrong do, or other leaders who are not nine-to-five types? How do they see their kids?" Then I came across something I call a hybrid home school, and I discovered you don't have to be rich or famous to do it. When I figured that out, my first extra income did not go toward creating a better lifestyle. It went toward paying for a teacher.

HOME-SCHOOLING REINVENTED

I was home-schooled as a child, but I craved being with other kids, so I didn't really appreciate it. However, I've come to realize its advantages. Home-schooled kids are not put into a box called "go to school, then get a job." I hadn't ended up with that dependency on the system, but I had missed having friends, so that's what caught my attention about the hybrid school. Yes, it's home-schooling, but you find two or three other kids with like-minded parents, hire a private teacher, split the cost, and form your own little school. It often costs less than day care, and it's *way* less expensive than a private school. Tons of very qualified young teachers would love to teach four or five kids for about $2,000 a month, without the red tape of public school systems.

Finding a teacher who thought out of the box was easy. Many young teachers today have what I call the "Nike Generation" mentality. They want to be happy, healthy, and wealthy, and they believe they can really help children. But when they get into the system, they become disillusioned. I put an ad in the paper and started asking around for teachers who were also involved in personal growth. We were overwhelmed with applicants whose goal had always been to make learning as creative, fun, and cutting-edge as possible.

We hired a teacher and soon had four kids whose parents were also in my business. We called it the "CTU," short for the Counter-Training Unit! We gave the kids a logo and little uniforms, modeled after the Hogwarts uniforms from the Harry Potter movie that was big that year. The kids thought they were hot stuff. We wrapped the learning concept around what I called "the experience and the vision." For instance, if the kids were learning math, they needed to *experience* it and *apply* it to something in real life, like hitting a tennis ball over a fence or launching a little bottle rocket.

This experiential learning kept them totally engaged.

We decided we wanted travel and adventure to be part of the school, so if one parent was traveling for business or vacation, the entire school could decide to go along. It was always voluntary. This mobile school really allowed me to combine being a father, home-schooling my daughter, and running my business. Teagan got to travel with me and still be with her friends. When Teagan's mother's schedule allowed it, the teacher took the whole school to her place, about two hours away.

HELPING YOUR CHILDREN THINK OUT OF THE BOX BY NEVER PUTTING THEM IN IT

Today, as we mature, many of us have started educating ourselves to think outside the box. We learn to eat organic food and be responsible for our health and our lives. We open our minds to setting goals, realizing dreams, and releasing ourselves from any limitations we were brought up with. But at the same time we're doing that, we're putting our kids right back into the same box that got us there, the traditional public school system.

> We open our minds, but at the same time, we're putting our kids into the same box.

Don't get me wrong—it's not about the teachers—they're often the ones screaming for help. They want to a do a great job, but they know the confines better than anyone else: the curriculum and administrative rigidity, overcrowding, and scores of other problems. The system these teachers have to work within was designed to effectively "de-genius" children, and stifle creative thinking by perpetuating stultifying attitudes towards work, wealth, personal potential, and problem solving.

If you study some of the best teachers, or books like Richard Adams's *Watership Down,* you come to understand that the public school system was originally designed to turn out obedient hourly-wage workers, not to create beautiful, creative children. The system breaks a child's spirit to dream, much like a rancher breaks a horse. The horse is not physically harmed, but its spirit is broken, and after that it allows someone to ride it forever. To make matters worse, schools are increasingly becoming physically dangerous places.

The children of the wealthy have always received a different kind of education—education that encourages a child's creativity and independent thinking while enriching her mind and soul. I discovered that it's really not that expensive to do the same thing.

So by creating a different paradigm for education and for life, I've kept Teagan's creativity and uniqueness from getting stifled, and she's never had to fit into a box. And I kept her close to me during those years.

THE MAGIC OF THE RED CARD

Here's an example of how Teagan and her classmates learned. At the beginning of some school days, regardless of the lesson, every child got his or her own little red card. Inside was a simple age-appropriate question like, "Here is a picture of a bird. Today's lesson doesn't end until you can identify what kind of bird this is." At first the task would be simple, but it taught them to think through and find things. As the children got older, the question would require two or three levels of investigation. This process was designed to teach the kids they could find out about anything, any time. We made it a game, and it became very popular.

My daughter is twelve now, and watching her grow up with this outside-the-box education has been amazing. She's learning to be an independent thinker, and she's around people who are solution oriented. She's acquiring skills she might not even be aware of, but they'll become ingrained habits that will serve her well for life in the twenty-first century. If she has a problem, she has extreme confidence in her ability to find a solution. I saw this in action one day when she was only eight, and we were in Maui.

"Hey, Dad, can we can go see the dolphins at that other hotel?" she asked. "I really want to swim with the dolphins." A little fatigued, I simply responded, "Uh, I don't know. It's really late, and I'm not sure if they would help us." I was basically making an excuse because I was tired. But she said,

"Don't worry, Dad. I'll call the hotel front desk and concierge service. Someone will know."

At eight she already understood the concepts of outsourcing and leverage.

She gathered the information and booked the appointment, and my lame excuse was exposed. The unknown simply didn't scare her. She knew all she had to do was ask someone to ask someone to ask someone. At eight she already understood the concepts of outsourcing and leverage. She knew the unknown was no reason to stop, and she was perfectly capable of finding the answers she needed.

MAKE YOUR CHILD PART OF THE SOLUTION

With our weekday life handled, I had another concern. As a frequent speaker at major weekend events, I often had to leave Teagan alone with a sitter. I didn't like doing that—so again I got creative. My solution was to have other kids over to the house whose parents were also going to the event. Instead of having separate babysitters, five kids could easily be cared for by three people, reducing the cost. But I didn't want just babysitting; I wanted the kids to have an "activity day" or weekend, where they had an adventure or a team-building experience. One fun activity is to get a bunch of *huge* cardboard boxes, and literally fill up the back yard. Then give the kids the goal of creating a maze of cardboard houses. They can finger-paint the outsides, and create a city they can show off to the parents when they come home. This simple adventure becomes a game and helps the child avoid the "I'm just sad" feelings.

Other times, they all finger-painted a massive canvas or learned a skit from *American Idol.* Perhaps one of the babysitters was a dancer, so her job was to teach the kids a dance routine. More than once, as the weekend was drawing to a close, I received a message from Teagan saying, "Don't come home yet; we're not ready!" The kids were trying to finish up and perfect their project or routine so they could present it to us when we came to pick them up!

This approach turns what could feel like abandonment into a family adventure! While the parent is bringing home the money, the child is creating a show, and I found that to be a very bonding experience. But don't even think about coming home sooner than expected—unless you call!

This approach turns what could have felt like abandonment into a family adventure!

It was such a simple solution, but when I knew my daughter was excited and having fun, much of my anxiety was gone. All the parents involved felt the same. And Teagan really loved those weekends. Soon she was asking, "When is the next event you're going to, Dad? When can we do an activity weekend again?" At first she was the four-year-old, then suddenly she was the eight-year-old who'd been through it before. So she herself became part of the solution, planning and directing the weekends so they were really fun and special.

MAKE YOUR CHILD PART OF YOUR ACCOUNTABILITY

Accountability is a big part of success, especially if you're an entrepreneur building your own business. I discovered a way to involve my daughter in this accountability. Whenever I had a personal goal, I'd write it down and post it on the refrigerator. My goals were things like calling three people a day to keep my business moving forward, or meeting five new people a week, or eliminating sweets. So I got some of those green poison-control "Mr. Yuk" stickers, and every day the goal didn't get done I'd post one of the green stickers beside it. I then added another element by telling Teagan, "When I miss my goal ten times, you get to plan a day just for yourself." It was really motivating when Teagan said, "Dad, all you have to do is fail one more time and I get to go to the movies." Occasionally we ended up going to a movie, and that was OK. But more often, her playful taunting motivated me to get the job done.

Sometimes she'd see three, seven, eight, eleven, or even fourteen failures in a row. But when I finally succeeded, she got to see me put up a happy-face sticker, and we celebrated that together. So Teagan won either way. But the best part wasn't the accountability and motivating support she gave me; it was knowing I was teaching her that failure is part of life, and success often comes only after repeated failures.

Failure is part of life, and success often comes only after repeated failures.

If we parents share *only* our successes with our kids, when they get to college and fail three times at something, they're almost trained to quit, *because they've never seen us fail.* But when they've seen the process and the persistence it can take, the first time they fail they just say, "Oh, this is nothing." When they see their friends fail and quit, they say, "How can you possibly quit, Caitlin? I've watched my mom and dad fail fourteen times in a row! That's what it takes to succeed." I knew I was teaching my daughter a huge lesson in success— all by involving her in my journey.

LEARN TO EDIFY YOUR SPOUSE, AND YOUR CHILDREN

In my field of direct sales, a powerful thing we teach is to edify others, particularly your business team or upline. This means that you never speak badly about people in your organization. Instead, you look to see their greatness and praise them.

If this policy is good for business, I figured it's a good policy all the way around. Adopting the philosophy, I began to teach my organization to edify their spouses to their children. I began with me. Teagan's mother had become a police officer, so I said to Teagan, "I know right now you can't really see what your mom does, because it is too dangerous for you to go ride along with her. But I need you to understand that your mother really puts herself at risk to help people. Often she might be scared walking into a situation, but she's there to help or save somebody, and you should be very proud of her."

It's not about being a superstar, or wealthy, or wildly successful. It *is* about pointing out all the great things the child does not see in the other parent. For instance, you might say, "Your father is a carpenter, and he brings joy to people. People rely on him, and you'll notice he's the person who relieves everybody's stress at the barbecue. I want you to watch tonight how a lot of people count on your dad to be the breath of fresh air at the end of the day."

When you do this, you are giving your child a perspective— *an appreciation for beauty.* It's about taking a moment to slow the world down and point out something beautiful about that butterfly, or the sun sparkling on the water. Whenever you take a moment to

*A*cknowledge the beautiful, wonderful things around you for your child.

help someone else see something beautiful that's going on, your own ability to notice beauty in everything around you goes up. So the wisdom I've learned is to edify and acknowledge the beautiful, wonderful things around you for your child, and for others.

I've found that children need to see you edify and point out beauty about three times before they suddenly realize they've got that same skill: they can notice the beautiful, amazing things around them. When she was still very young, Teagan began to replicate this behavior. She started pointing out to other kids beautiful things going on around them that they had just taken for granted.

A few years ago, when Teagan was about eight, we were at a resort where there were lots of kids in the pool. Suddenly a couple of older boys swam over and took her swimming toys, really upsetting her. Well, another little boy went and rescued her toys and brought them back. The next day, Teagan went up to the boy's parents and said, "You know, what your son did was so nice because those kids took my toys. But it was especially nice since they were big, and he is a very small boy, and it didn't seem to matter to him." Her observation went beyond a thank-you. She recognized the beauty in the boy's courage, so she went to his parents and edified him.

BE A HERO TO YOUR CHILD

I discovered that edifying others includes edifying yourself. Children don't usually get to see what their parents do at work every day, so it's really hard for them to admire and respect their parents for how brilliant they are and how they help people. All the child sees when they come home is tired parents. But when a child gets to see his or her mother or father do something unbelievable in their special arena, it can cause the child to be really inspired and proud to say, "Hey, that's my mom!"

My own work often entails counseling families as they are building their businesses. Sometimes people come to the house, and sometimes we go to a beach or a park, but the kids are always playing nearby. Teagan would hear people say things like "Thank you, Dean; this has helped me tremendously. You've removed the guilt and shown me a way to run a business and be a mother, and not be in conflict."

I often forgot that my daughter was listening, but one day I found out she knew exactly what I was doing. She, some other kids, and I were watching the movie *The Incredibles,* about a family of superheroes. At one point, my daughter leaned over to the other kids, whose parents were in the same business I am, and said to them, "That's what our parents do!" She explained, "People come to our house all the time, and I don't always understand it, but I do know this: my dad helps them. He seems to make bad things go away." Later I taught her to take it further by saying to other kids, "When your mom and dad are working and doing something worthy, you can be proud of them too."

Provide occasions for your children to see your greatness, not just your parenting.

It's well documented that young people today want to be heroes. They want to make a difference by promoting social justice and helping others. Filmmakers and marketers appeal constantly to this desire. So if you provide occasions for your children to see your greatness, not just your parenting, you strengthen their bond with you.

A few months ago I met with an organization that honored world athletes. This organization had gathered together people who had ever won a world championship in anything—Olympics or otherwise—just to recognize them and say thanks. All their friends and families were invited. Now, some of these athletes had won their medals up to forty years ago—so their children had never seen them in that light. After the event, the children were walking up to their parents and saying, "Dad or Mom, I had no idea how unreal it is, what you did. I'm so proud of you." These former athletes were just overwhelmed with emotion, because they had never before had an opportunity for their kids to see them in that way. Eighty-year-old guys were in tears, because their children finally saw them in some of their moments of glory.

Common wisdom teaches how important it is for parents to let their kids know they're proud of them. But parents also need to be seen and known by their kids, so the kids can be proud of their parents. Including your children—bringing your work home or your children to work, whenever and wherever possible—accomplishes just that. We all need to be heroes, and to know we make a difference, and when kids get to see us in our work environment, seeing the way we're serving our community, we create occasions when our kids can see us shine. We make the most out of being their first and best teacher just by keeping them near.

This was my gift to my daughter—and her gift to me. And somehow along the way, in certain moments, we became each other's heroes.

"Kids spell love T-I-M-E."

John Crudele, author, speaker, and expert in the field of education. He is a frequent TV and radio guest, and former host of a national talk radio show.

WHO IS DEAN KOSAGE?

Dean and (daughter) Teagan

Dean Kosage is a survivor and thriver. When he became a young single parent, living in chaos and debt, he decided to follow the advice of the many authors and speakers he had studied, and to turn his pain into victory. He has risen to the highest level, Executive Diamond, at Amway Global, supporting thriving teams in more than thirty countries, and being recognized as a superstar in the direct sales industry.

Kosage is owner and operator of Kosage Motivation, Inc., and is recognized for his dedication, leadership, and excellence in all aspects of motivational consulting. His goal is to motivate individuals to exit "survival mode" and enter "success mode," by taking positive charge of their lives. Thousands of people, in multiple countries, have gained inspiration and made their own comebacks as a result of counseling with Kosage personally or through his CDs and seminars.

In addition to his motivation company, Kosage works on entertainment projects—funding movies and helping musicians remix albums.

Kosage's interests include surfing, hiking, playing music, brainstorming with other thinkers and people of passion, traveling, and meeting new friends who add stories and value to his life. Kosage writes, "We all have the seeds of greatness inside us. It's time to water them. All great stories have a beginning, and today is chapter one of your epic journey."

www.deankosage.com

YOUR INNER RESOURCES

If I Were Your Daddy ... I'd teach you that patience, perseverance, and love are needed to do anything well. I'd give you simple strategies for accessing and employing your deepest reserves of each.

BRIAN ALMAN, Ph.D.

Clinical Practitioner & Wellness Expert

I was in the middle of a family meltdown. There were three screaming babies and me, just me. My wife had just left me permanently. I was alone and, at that moment, not handling things all too well. That which fills diapers was, as the saying goes, hitting the fan.

My first three children—then ages one, three, and five—and I were in the kitchen when, at the exact same moment, a cacophony of life-or-death cries erupted at full throttle. Each child had a different primal need: number one was hungry, number two had a dirty diaper, and number three had a bleeding finger. As I turned to tend one child, the other two hollered even more loudly, commanding my attention. The air was pungent with the aroma of dirty diaper. It was a three-ring circus. I spun into overwhelm, thinking, "Oh, my God, I'm only one person! What am I going to do?"

Voices and judgments throbbed inside my head. I simultaneously felt desperation, impatience, pity, and guilt. I had three living, breathing, screaming full-time jobs in front of me, never mind problems of my own.

My script, as I recall, spewed out something like this: "This isn't fair; I'm just one person. I work all the time, and she [my wife] just checks out and leaves. I'm pissed that I have to handle this all by myself and pissed that I'm apparently unprepared to handle it all myself. I *should* be able to. What's wrong with me? What's wrong with this picture? C'mon, pull yourself together. Your parenting has to be twice as good as before, not half."

Suddenly, a strong inner voice cut in: "Brian, get ahold of yourself. When you need a helping hand, look at the end of your wrist." My mom had said this to me many times. So I stopped, just stopped. Letting the cries mount, I stood there, stalled in what seemed like so much ineffectiveness. But in that moment stopping was the most *effective* thing I could do. My pain, feelings, and judgments were doors to pass through.

We often find our greatest strengths in the crucible of intense moments.

I've heard it said that we often find our greatest strengths in the crucible of intense moments. I suddenly remembered a breathing technique I'd repeatedly prescribed to my clients, but never road-tested myself under duress. I'd developed it based on my training with world-renowned medical doctor Milton Erickson. When I combined what I learned from him, with what I'd learned traveling India and my work with thousands of clients, I came up with this 1-2-3 approach. As the three girls wailed on, I grabbed the exercise like a life preserver and started reciting the instructions as I would to a patient, except that this time the patient was me.

CALMING DOWN AND COPING AS EASY AS 1-2-3

The first step is to pay attention to your breathing. Don't try to make it better, different, or more relaxed. Don't count or judge it as good or bad. Just notice its pattern and depth, and accept it for what it is. Accepting our breathing as it is gives us a glimpse into what it feels like to accept ourselves as we are; it's is a wide bridge that carries us to our inner resources.

"Is it shallow and rough?" I asked myself. "It is," I answered, noticing.

I immediately felt a slight release just from accepting my breath, relaxing just a bit, and from knowing I'd actually seen this method bring miraculous calm and healing to others.

Next, be mindful of your *exhalations,* saying your name to yourself each time you breathe out. Inhale, slight pause, and exale "Brian," I responded to my own prompting. Again, inhale, pause, "B-R-I-A-N." saying it and exhaling more slowly this time. Inhale, pause, exhale "B—R—I—A—N" stretching it out longer and longer as I squeezed out more breath, and let go of more stress. I did this five to ten times, at which point I felt myself relaxing some more. The key is to let go of your stress on the exhales. *Letting go* is the master key that opens all the doors to be the best parent possible. When you let go, you can more easily connect to your inner resources.

The third and last step involves saying to yourself every time you inhale, the word "patience." Keep saying your name on the exhale. So—breathe in: "P-a-t-i-e-n-c-e." Breathe out: "B—r—i—a—n. Breathe in: "P-a-t-i-e-n-c-e." Breathe out: "B—r—i—a—n." I kept doing this, slowing down the words and repeating the sequence a handful of times. This 1-2-3 method opened up the acceptance within me, released my stress, and connected me to my deepest intentions. It freed me to be a hundred percent present, caring, and compassionate with the kids and with myself. Using this breath work, in a matter of moments I was able to transform my nervous break*down* into a break*through.* Now calm and connected to me, I was able to re-engage and lovingly attend to my three unhappy children.

> *I* transformed my nervous breakdown into a breakthrough within moments.

I turned to the child whose problem was most urgent. "We have to stop the bleeding," I said to her. "And," I looked at her sisters "I need your help." Their howling eased a bit. I asked the youngest to help me hold a cloth on her big sister's cut and the other to unwrap the bandage. We took care of the cut as a team. Next we changed the diaper together, one fetching a clean diaper while the other administered baby powder. Finally we fed the starving child together. Tears dried on their cheeks, and sniffles became fewer. I made up a silly little song whose singular lyric was "Cooperation. Cooperation. Cooperation. Cooperation." It became an instant hit complete with shaking our booties and other body parts in rhythm. As the girls giggled, we sang and helped each other and turned the scene around.

To handle the day-to-day challenges, you need practical tools.

In the aftermath of our collective meltdown I realized that to handle the day-to-day challenges of living, particularly as a parent, you need practical tools and you need to practice them. You need in your pocket an automatic 1-2-3 response that summons the patience, perseverance, and love you possess within, however buried they may be at the moment. From that day forward I used the above breathing strategy in my parenting every single day.

Fortunately, after seven years of being a single dad I met my soul mate, and as a single mother she was doing the same kinds of things with her daughter. As time passed and our family grew, we taught this approach to all six of our children. Today I have every confidence that I can breathe my way through any situation, and my children can do the same. We do it every day and on an as-needed basis.

In our big blended family, this breathing strategy went on to serve as a springboard for not only calming and collecting ourselves, but for reprogramming negative thoughts into positive beliefs. While the original version that day in the kitchen used the word "patience," any positive quality can be substituted as an affirmation, or goal stated to yourself. For instance, my children loved using "relaxed and confident," "brave" or "love" whenever they were feeling a bit needy in those areas. Any positive affirmation on the inhale and any version of your name on the exhale will do. I point out that affirmations must never involve another person, or the behavior we wish from them. A teenage girl breathing out "Tyler likes me" is imposing her will onto Tyler. "I am liked" is more in keeping with the spirit of the exercise.

Lots of people do affirmations, but inhaling them in this way sends them deep into your being, while exhaling provides immediate calm and comfort. You're breathing anyway and it's all automatic, so why not make it really useful! Over time, positive affirmations can shift your outlook, because usually things must first happen on the inside

We used positive affirmations to change our focus.

before they manifest on the outside. Spoken affirmations use the power of our voice to change our focus. That said, certain situations require an immediate infusion of a different perspective. For those, my children and I "went to the movies," so to speak.

SIT BACK, WATCH, AND WRITE YOUR OWN ENDING

One morning at four a.m. I had an epiphany inspired by my work with hundreds of different people facing different situations. If it could help them, it could help us. My family and I dubbed it, affectionately, "going to the movies," a three-step process I taught my kids to use whenever they were feeling fear or anxiety.

My one daughter studied tae kwon do for years. Although not a very aggressive child, when she was twelve she wanted to earn her black belt. To do this required that she go to a competition and spar with kids who generally had more experience. This felt like "fighting" to her, and she did not want to do it. But she did want to earn that belt, so with trepidation on her part we went, filing into the event with probably a couple of thousand other people. As the competition progressed, she was miserable and performing with more fear than confidence. She didn't want to hurt anyone. She didn't want to be there, didn't want to spar. She had trouble putting her learned skills into action against girls who were bent on winning. I knew that resisting competition wasn't serving her, and would keep her from her goal of earning her belt and doing what she loved.

So, right in the middle of the event, I knelt down beside her and said, "Honey, let's 'go to the movies.'" I asked her, "How are you feeling right now? What's happening on your movie screen?" This is step one.

She replied, *"I want to go home. I hate this."* I prompted, "OK, what else?" *"Why do I have to do this exercise? Can't I just skip this part?"* I responded, "No honey, you need to recognize and express your feelings in order to get past them. Just go ahead and say what you're feeling."

She spilled it all out. *"This competition is dumb. I hate it. I'm doing horrible, and I'm so embarrassed."* As I listened, I really understood. The event was intense. Almost any kid who wasn't cutthroat-aggressive could have related to what she was experiencing. I was grateful that I was there to serve as her sounding bound.

Whenever I use the "going to the movies" technique myself, I do my feelings-check-in silently, write them in a journal, or go for a solo walk or drive and talk to myself. The key is to be totally honest, accepting and expressing—without holding back, holding in, or editing—whatever feelings spill out that have been bubbling below the surface. When we repress our feelings, our bodies respond with either pain or stress. We can either repress (which is called stress) or express (that's called freedom). Expression can be verbal or nonverbal, released through breathing, walking, doing jumping jacks, and even dancing around.

I whispered to my daughter that she might want to go to the fifteenth row of the theater and see what her fifteenth-row judge was saying about her and the competition. So step two involves stepping back from the "movie" of your life at the moment, and retreating to the fifteenth row. That's the perspective from which your inner critic sits and overanalyzes, carrying on about how you'll never be good enough and expressing all manner of dissatisfaction. Instead of trying to repress your fifteenth-row critic, accept it and let it rip. This is the number-one place where athletes, both amateur and professional, get stuck. Everybody doubts themselves from that fifteenth-row perspective, and *nobody* gets rid of their inner critic. It's a lifetime membership! Learning at twelve or forty-two or any age to accept and express your inner judge moves you from simply coping, to creatively transcending something that hobbles millions.

> We can either repress (which is called stress) or express (that's called freedom).

My daughter then relayed to me the browbeating she was receiving from her fifteenth-row inner critic: *"You should be able to do this. Your tae kwon do teacher is here with his wife; they thought you'd be good at this. What are the other kids thinking? They think you're being a baby. Their parents probably think so, too."* Saying this aloud allowed her to really release a load of stress. See, you either allow that fifteenth-row critic speak and be heard, or it will, from the shadows, drive your action

Instead of repressing your inner critic, accept it and let it rip!

or inaction. The tough part is that nobody wants to know what his or her fifteenth-row critic is thinking, yet if it's repressed, its power and insistence only grow stronger. The critic *must* be heard if it is to be overcome.

Next I asked my open-minded/open-hearted twelve-year-old to now imagine herself moving to the last row at the back of the theater. This is step three, the big master move. The movie is playing on the screen. The critic is in the fifteenth row. From the perspective of the last row you can simply relax, and see all the feelings on the screen and all the judgment from the critic. From this calm, distant place you can ask, "What is the best way to deal with what's going on?" Your intuition will either give you momentary calm or deliver something prophetic. Just stay relaxed, be patient, and enjoy the connection to your whole self. From the last row, you're always going to get the answer, and it's always going to be one that's friendly and compassionate toward yourself and others. That's what love is.

"Do the breathing," I coaxed my daughter. Her eyes closed as commotion from the matches roared around us in the exhibition hall. We slipped into our own little world. "Accept your breath *as it is*," I said. "Inhale 'acceptance.'" Her lungs expanded. Exhaling, she mouthed her name. Her body began to relax. After a few breaths, she started substituting her affirmation on the inhales: "I enjoy sparring." Her once-tight face eased as her fears resided. From the last row, she could see that she needed to focus on technique and engage fully in each sparring match. This was the gift her intuition, the last-row perspective, revealed.

Think about how different it would have been had I barked, "Go on!

Stop resisting and just go for it!" Without the opportunity to vent her feelings and admit her self-judgments, she would have become an even greater muddle, and would have written me off as another stress agent pressing her to perform. Instead, these 1-2-3 breathing and "go to the movies" exercises worked because she performed them herself: she accessed her own inner resources, which are always available to her, and moved forward, thereby markedly increasing her self-confidence.

> *The perspective is always theirs, but I gave them the gift of access.*

Doing what she did, at age twelve, in just three steps is far better, and ultimately much easier than getting stuck in that self critical fifteenth row for days, months, or decades, which is what happens to most people. Our best decisions and resolutions are found within, but tapping into them, particularly during times of duress, requires that we be in a state of relaxed acceptance—that we be in the last row. My two daughters and son who came later in life, plus their three sisters, are living proof that with time and practice, with love and perseverance, anyone can learn to go there automatically. The perspective is always theirs, but I gave them the gift of access.

So how did my daughter do in the sparring competition? Newly relaxed and present, she went from having virtually no points to placing first—and winning her coveted black belt.

We celebrated together, each a different but precious victory.

"You have to leave the city of your comfort and go into the wilderness of your intuition. What you'll discover will be wonderful. What you'll discover is yourself."

Alan Alda, actor, director, and screenwriter with five Emmys and six Golden Globe Awards.

WHO IS BRIAN ALMAN, Ph.D.?

Brian finds it hard to get all the kids together at once.
Brian with (wife) Tracie, (children) Rebecca, Shishana, Michael, Brittany, Deanna, and Alaina

Dr. Brian Alman is one of the world's leading authorities on mental fitness and mind-body wellness. During his thirty years of private practice, he has coached and trained more than ten thousand people, including health care professionals, on such quality-of-life issues as weight loss, stress reduction, pain control, problem solving, relief from addictions, and disease management.

Alman reaches many hundred thousand more through his company, TruSage International, a mind-body wellness company that helps clinics, hospitals and specialists deliver high-quality, personalized follow-up through wireless technology.

Alman has worked with dozens of world-class organizations—including Apple, Harvard Medical School, Kaiser Permanente, Kraft, Procter & Gamble, Sony Pictures, the University of California, and the University of Paris. He is the author of five books: *Self-Hypnosis: The Complete Manual for Health and Self-Change* (1983), *Thin Meditations* (1994), *Six Steps to Freedom* (1999), *Keep it Off: Your Keys to Weight Loss for Life* (2004) and *The Voice* (scheduled for release in December 2010).

Though successful in so many ways, Alman considers fathering his most impressive accomplishment. As a single parent with sole custody of three girls for seven years, Alman eventually married "the love of my life," Tracie, and became father to three more children, raising a total of six.

www.TruSageInternational.com

HOW TO NEVER FAIL

If I Were Your Daddy ... I'd pass on the best advice my father ever gave me: you never fail until you stop trying. I'd give you a spiritual perspective and faith in life, and help you see every loss as a lesson, a step closer to success.

DINO ROSSI

Retired Washington State Senator
& Real Estate Investor

My father taught me a formula for success that I believe was responsible for some of my greatest triumphs. Over and over, my dad would say, "You never fail until you stop trying." Today I repeat those same words to my own children, and my father's wisdom is passed on.

I first discovered the power of this formula as a teenager when I tried out for the community basketball team. When I didn't make it, I was heartbroken. My father's only comment was the gentle reminder, "Dino, you never fail until you stop trying." With those words he shifted my disappointment into the context of a bigger picture—where achievement is a process, not a one-shot deal. It was up to me.

In the midst of my angst I understood. I realized that I would never fail if I continued improving my skills and kept after my goal. Only if I quit now would I actually fail.

So I reframed my loss into something positive. Maybe I just wasn't ready that year. Maybe not making the team was actually a good thing. With this new perspective, I set out to make next year's team as a much better player. I began to consistently practice on my own, and a year later I not only made that team, but

Reframe your losses into something positive.

was one of its star players as we went on to become regional champions. I never knew failure because I never quit.

In 1992 I ran for state senate in Washington, and lost by a slim margin of 1,051 votes. Remembering my father's words, instead of quitting, I reshaped my efforts. In the next election I knocked on some fifteen thousand doors and got bitten by four dogs! I won that year, the only Republican in the state to defeat an incumbent.

Feeling discouraged may be the normal acceptable response after losing the first close race, but it was not the response I chose. I'm not saying I was happy about the outcome, but by that point in my life I was well conditioned to view defeat as temporary. With that in mind, I focused all my resources on moving forward. It would simply take more time and persistence.

HANDING IT TO THE NEXT GENERATION

As I've passed this wisdom on to my own four kids, I've seen clearly how my dad's approach to life has helped shape them into resilient, determined individuals. They've become people who decide their own destinies. I haven't encouraged my children toward success; *they've found it themselves.* This approach to life creates successful people.

My first daughter learned the power of this approach at only eight. Like me, Juliauna loved basketball, so she signed up for the school team. I took her to the first practice. Holding hands as we often did, we walked onto the court and silently surveyed the scene. There were two basketball courts, side by side, both of them packed with boys. Juliauna whispered in a strained voice, "Dad, *there are no girls here.*" Sure enough, she was the only female in sight. The rest were all boys.

"Yeah, honey, it certainly looks that way. Do you want to stay?" Summoning all her courage she said, "Yeah, I'd like to try."

When Juliauna was introduced, the boys all rolled their eyes the way boys that age do. Ignoring their silent commentary, she went out on the court and they began playing. Suddenly, she had the ball. She looked at the basket, put the ball over her head, and without hesitation she shot, the ball spinning with beautiful rotation, and *swish!* Two points!

Her face beamed with joy until she became painfully aware of what everyone else already knew: she'd put the ball in the wrong basket. She was mortified.

Well, that was all those boys needed to totally exclude her. They didn't pass the ball to her again and immediately demoted her to the lowest possible "girl" ranking. And no one does scornful dismissal better than boys of that age.

During our long and quiet drive home I asked, "Do you want to continue playing?"

"I don't know," Juliauna replied.

"Well, if you want to, I'll help you," I said. "We have a basketball hoop in the driveway, and I can show you some moves." I continued, "You know, my dad always told me that you never fail until you stop trying. I've lived my life by this and it really works. So as far as you're concerned, and as far as I'm concerned, you have not failed. It's quite clear you're capable of making a basket, and you've got the rest of the season to do all sorts of things."

> Celebrating a child's progress—every single little victory—is key to building self-confidence.

"All right," she said quietly, "I'll try again."

We worked out on the driveway for a couple of hours that day. I taught her how to box people out, and to stand between her opponent and the basket.

Just defense. I figured learning defense was going to be a big part of her recipe to success.

Juliauna continued to improve her skills and became a good little basketball player. I acknowledged her every improvement. I knew that celebrating a child's progress—every single little victory—is key to building self-confidence.

Despite all her hard work, Juliauna didn't get to practice her new skills with the team. The boys simply would not pass to her, so she never got to touch the ball. This went on for many games. While her teammates remained oblivious or uninterested in her improvements, I noticed the boys on the opposing teams were frustrated because they were having such a hard time getting past her. She was quick and always in their way. With each game, it was becoming increasingly difficult to score against her. Juliauna was becoming a valuable member of the team and therefore not failing. Still, she had no opportunity to go for the hoop.

Finally, it was the last game of the season. In the final moments of play, a rebound ended up in her hands. I gasped. No one had passed it to her: she was still in exile. Juliauna moved up and took her shot. The ball hit the backboard, swirled around the rim, and dropped in. And believe me, it was the right basket!

There was a moment of stunned silence, of real awe. Then the bleachers erupted in screams and cheers. Those two game-winning points were the ultimate payoff to Juliauna's persistence and patience. She had become the team hero!

OBSTACLES AS TEMPORARY SPEED BUMPS

After that experience, Juliauna beamed with confidence and determination, following through on goals with tenacity beyond her years. Obstacles became temporary speed bumps. She fully embraced the wisdom, "You never fail until you stop trying." Not giving up left only one option: to tap into her internal resources. Offering excuses, blaming others, feeling that life has handed you a raw deal when you don't get what you want—all are eliminated with the simple choice to look within and keep moving forward. As a result, her successes meant more whenever the journey leading up to them required extra effort. From this early age, Juliauna knew she was in the driver's seat, totally responsible for her life's "failures" and successes.

Not giving up leaves only one option: you have to tap your internal resources.

When she was sixteen, Juliauna came to me and said, "Dad, I want to apply to do a church mission somewhere in the world. It's eight weeks, and I have no idea where they will send me." Now despite her many successes, and the fact that she was now sixteen, she was still Daddy's little girl, the one who used to fall asleep on my chest when she was a baby. Being Italian, all of my protective instincts took over.

I said, "Honey, I don't know where they're going to send you, but you're not going anywhere." My daughter knows I'm usually a sucker for a sales pitch from her, so she had a good one ready. "Dad," she said, "I think it's going to help with my faith formation." Then she followed up with a laundry list of reasons why it would be a good thing.

But I was stuck in protective mode and said, "I still don't know where they're going to send you, and I'm not going to let you go." She continued her campaign to convince me, asking in different ways, coming at me from different angles, never giving up. I too remained steadfast, unrelenting. Then, about a week later, I overheard her girlfriends talking about what they had done the previous summer. Things like hanging out at the mall and so on. And I thought, "Dino, you're being an idiot! Just let her apply."

She had already been pretty involved in the church, and managed to put together an impressive resume all on her own. She applied and ended up being one of sixteen girls from six countries who were chosen for an eight-week Catholic mission in Rome. She had six audiences with the pope; she shook his hand. She did missions with the elderly and disabled during the day, and at times she slept on parish floors at night. This was life-altering stuff. But it was a long eight weeks for Dad, I can tell you. Every Sunday I waited for that phone call, just to know she was okay.

This was the same girl, my little basketball star, working with that same wisdom: she wasn't going to quit. This is now the way she operates, and I'm sure part of it is a result of what I instilled in her. But I can't take all the credit; her mother played an invaluable role as well. My wife is the greatest blessing of my life, and while we're not perfect (no parents are), together we've done the best we can. You can give your children daily guidance, you can give them morals, you can give them an education, and you can give them straight teeth. But they need more. They need a foundation that will set them on the right course that will allow them to succeed beyond that—to make sound decisions later in life.

> *You* can give your children guidance, morals, education, and straight teeth ... but they need more.

That's what Juliauna did. She didn't listen to the naysayer—her loving but overprotective dad—for her dream. She kept pushing it and never gave up. And she was successful, just as she was in basketball.

GIVE THEM A SPIRITUAL PERSPECTIVE, A FOUNDATION OF FAITH

Our faith is very important to me and my wife, and we believe it is part of our duty as parents to provide our kids with that spiritual perspective. We believe that with that foundation, no matter what they might decide to do in their teens or twenties, some day children will want to look for something bigger than themselves. We wanted to make sure they had somewhere to look.

On September 11, 2001, our son Joseph was five and in preschool. Joseph is our stubborn child who liked to do things his own way, period. My wife says he'll be a great CEO one day—if he survives the exasperated people around him. He is a loving child, but ever since he could walk and talk, he resisted doing the basic things we asked—like cleaning up his room. Although he smoothed out later, at this time in his life he was defiant about everything. About a week before September 11, my wife and I were discussing how we needed to keep this kid on track: stay tough, and keep on him so he continued to head in the right direction.

Then 9/11 hit. We didn't talk too much about the tragedy at home, but we said a prayer that night at dinner for the people who had lost their lives.

The next day, Joseph went back to preschool. When I arrived to pick him up his teacher asked, "Can I talk to you for a second, Mr. Rossi?" I said, "Oh God, what did Joseph do? Did he cut off some girl's pigtail or something?" But she said, "Oh no, it's nothing bad. I just want to tell you what he did today."

"All the children were sitting down," she began, "and they all started talking in their own little five-year-old ways about what happened yesterday. You know—'Some bad guys flew some planes into the buildings, and a lot of innocent people died.' They were just kind of piecing it all together. And then Joseph raised his hand and stood up and said, 'I know what we need to do.' 'What's that, Joseph?' I asked, and he said, 'We need to pray for those people.' And then your five-year-old son led all the other children in praying for those people."

When she finished telling me this story she was almost in tears, and so was I. I called my wife and said, "You know, I don't know what's going to happen with Joseph, but I think he'll be fine. Let's just keep doing what we're doing, because something is getting through." This experience reaffirmed for me that we were on the right path.

Keep trying; something will get through, and then they'll shine!

Day after day when you think you're not getting through to your kids and you wonder why you bother, you just have to keep trying *because something's getting through.* You don't know how, you don't know when, then out of the blue comes a moment when they just shine. It's that same wisdom again: you never fail until you stop trying.

Starting with my father and continuing in each of my children, in our family we know that no matter how poorly a pursuit might begin or how long it might take, you never fail unless you give up trying. If we want something, we reframe the loss into something positive, find a way to improve our skills or approach the goal differently, and remain expectant that we will eventually win. In short, we *keep after it.* And ultimately and gratefully, we succeed!

"Successful people know that failure is not falling down—it's not getting back up."

Keith Cunningham, multimillionaire business guru

EVERY FAILURE A SUCCESS: THOMAS EDISON'S ATTITUDE TO FAILURE[1]

Edison could not conceive of any experiment as a flop. As historian (Paul) Israel puts it, "He saw every failure as a success, because it channeled his thinking in a more fruitful direction." Israel thinks that Edison may have learned this attitude from his enterprising father, Sam Edison, who was not afraid to take risks and never became undone when a business venture crumbled. He would simply brush himself off and embark on a new moneymaking scheme, usually managing to shield the family from financial hardship. Israel says, "This sent a very positive message to his son—that it's okay to fail—and may explain why he rarely got discouraged if an experiment didn't work out." In addition to teaching him what wouldn't work, Israel says, failed experiments taught him the much more valuable lesson of what would work—albeit in a different context.[2]

[1] Excerpted from an article on the Edison Papers project by Kathleen McAuliffe: http://www.theatlantic.com/past/docs/issues/95dec/edison/edison.ht

[2] Paul Israel, a historian preparing a biography of Edison based on the Edison Archive

WHO IS DINO ROSSI?

Dino with (wife) Terry, (children) Julianna, Jake, Joseph, and Jillian

Dino Rossi is a third-generation Washingtonian whose devotion and service to his state have touched the hearts of many. In 2004, the *Wall Street Journal* called him one of two politicians to watch in America. The other was Barack Obama.

A state senator from 1997 through 2003, Rossi was a leader on state budget issues, working across party lines to address the largest dollar deficit in Washington history, and balancing the budget without raising taxes. For this, Rossi received the Defender of Liberty Award from the Evergreen Freedom Foundation, as well as six different awards from the developmentally disabled community for protecting funding for the most vulnerable.

In 2004, in the closest and most memorable governor's race in the history of Washington State, Rossi was twice certified as governor-elect. He is founder of the Forward Washington Foundation, a nonprofit, nonpartisan organization dedicated to improving the business climate for small- and medium-sized businesses. Rossi has a long-standing career in commercial real estate as well.

He and his wife, Terry, have been married since 1987, and have four children.

www.dinorossi.com

FUNDAMENTALS FOR WINNING IN LIFE!

If I Were Your Daddy ... I'd encourage you to dream big and live your dreams by understanding the fundamental "must do's" for success. You would welcome failure—and always have a backup plan. You'd learn to give back.

CHRIS DUDLEY

Foundation Executive, Businessman,
Retired NBA Player

One year when our three kids were still young, we went to the Mecca of childhood fantasy—Disneyland. For them everything there was magical. For a few days, I experienced that magic along with them. It was a real "Aha!" moment for me. As an adult I was tempted to analyze, "How'd they do that? How do they make that work?" But my kids didn't do that. To them, it simply is magical. As I stepped into my children's imaginations, seeing through their eyes and listening through their hearts, I saw the grandeur of that view.

Dreams are like that. They're magical and they're powerful. A dream can set you in motion to do things that may be totally impossible for others to do, but somehow it's not impossible for you. That's precisely why it's *your* dream and not someone else's. All great achievement starts like this, as a vision—a dream. The next step is to make a dream reality, which requires some fundamentals to be in place. These fundamentals are the thoughts and actions that set you up to be successful. As a parent, I consider it a privilege to model these fundamental principals so my kids grow up using them daily, as a habit. This way their lives will not only include imagination and fantasy, but they'll move those dreams into successes as well.

As a child, I was fortunate to have two amazing grandfathers as role models. These two exemplified success but in distinctive ways, and together I formed a balanced way to live life—something I want to leave with my kids as well. One grandfather was a pastor who came from communist Hungary. He was so appreciative of life in America and for his newfound freedom that he made his life all about giving back. My other grandfather was a gifted businessman who rebuilt his father's insurance company to new heights after the Great Depression. He voluntarily stepped away from his business success to serve as a pilot during World War II, and returned home covered in medals. He went on to become the United States of America's Ambassador to Denmark. In my eyes he became greater than life.

There is more than one path to success. But there are fundamentals that are key to achievement.

Because my grandfathers excelled in completely different ways, I learned very early that there is more than one path to success. But no matter the path you take, I believe there are certain fundamentals that are key to achievement during your life's journey.

FUNDAMENTAL #1: BELIEVE IN YOURSELF

Before you can accomplish anything, you have to first believe that you can. I have always encouraged my three children to try many different activities, so they have lots of successes. This helps form an internal belief system that *"I can accomplish anything I set my mind and heart to do."* This is key: kids must believe in themselves and be proud of *themselves,* first and foremost.

This means that one of my primary roles as a father is to be my kids' biggest fan. A perfect example happened one summer when our family was visiting an area in coastal Oregon known for its spectacular sand dunes. We decided we would climb up a particularly large sand dune, but it was really hard for my daughter, Emma, who was just four at the time. She really wanted to climb with the rest of us, but getting good traction was tricky and she found it really tough going. More than once, her mother or I were tempted to just pick her up and carry her. But instead, I started chanting *The Little Engine That Could* motto "I think I can, I think I can," And I kept that going with her all the way up. It was a funny scene—a six-foot-eleven dad towering over this little tiny girl—and cheering her forward. Her cheeks were red, her little legs were wobbling, and she was gasping for breath, but she just kept panting with me, "I think I can, I think I can." The next thing she knew she was at the top, and you could just see in her face the pride she felt in her accomplishment. If we had given in to the temptation to rescue and carry her, we would have denied her that wonderful success. Kids don't need to be carried; they need inspiration, encouragement, and support to do it themselves.

> *Kids don't need to be carried; they need inspiration, encouragement, and support to do it themselves.*

With my oldest son Charles, encouragement takes a slightly different tack. His nature is to hang back a bit, and he hesitates when it comes to stepping out of his comfort zone and trying new things. With him, my support is usually to just get him past his initial fear. When I urge him to stretch himself and just go for it, his first reaction is sometimes, "I don't want to practice, I can't do this or I can't do that." So I talk him through it and then he finally tries it, and he's so proud when he can do it. Time after time, he'll say something like, "Dad, I'm so glad I did that! That was awesome. That was great!" It's just so important to really encourage your children to believe that if they give it their best, they can accomplish great things.

The belief that "I can do anything I set my mind and heart to" cures a lot; it means success is attainable and achievable, and it provides internal strength. When this message has been reinforced enough times, kids expect to win or to keep trying until they do. Bullies aren't attracted to them because they've built a mental fortress—they believe in themselves, which is the first fundamental to success.

FUNDAMENTAL #2:
DREAM BIG AND EMBRACE FAILURE

The power of a dream can help you persevere through struggle that might give you the inclination or the excuse to quit. For a long time, I didn't tell anyone about my dream of playing in the NBA because I feared people would laugh at me. And I wouldn't have blamed kids for that. After all, I almost didn't make my eighth-grade team, and I did not make the varsity team until my senior year of high school. Then, at age sixteen—before I even finished high school—I was diagnosed with Type I diabetes. Even though no one with the disease had ever played in the NBA, I held on to my dream. This dream was *essential* to my success; it helped me believe in myself enough to make it happen, and I expect it will be the same for each of my kids' dreams.

While some kids know at an early age what they want to be when they grow up, my daughter, Emma, is set on being a veterinarian. More often than not, kids don't know what they want, or they need to explore many areas. The best support parents can give is just to encourage them to figure out what they *love*. As a parent, it's a great thing to help them identify what their passion is, and once it becomes clear, to just give them as much help as possible to follow it.

Instead of being afraid to fail, consider failures as signposts to make adjustments.

I think people sometimes set the bar too low and then don't realize they could have gone a lot further. I believe this has more to do with being afraid of getting something wrong than anything else. Being afraid to fail will make you tentative. It'll take you out of the game even before you begin. A tentative athlete, for example, is not a very effective athlete. I encourage my kids to consider failures as signposts directing them to make adjustments along the way, much like the many improvements I had to make to scale up my basketball skills before I could go pro.

If there is someone out there who has never failed, what it really means is that he or she never tried. I remind my kids about the many famous individuals who failed a lot while pursuing their dream. Thomas Edison failed more than ten thousand times before he figured out the perfect set-up for the light bulb. Walt Disney couldn't get a loan because nobody believed in his dream of an amusement park. Michael Jordan got cut from his high school basketball team. J.K. Rowling, author of the best selling *Harry Potter* book series, was turned down by more than ten publishers before one took a chance on her. Jack Canfield and Mark Victor Hansen kept going even after the first *Chicken Soup for the Soul* book was rejected by 144 publishers. They have since gone on to sell over a hundred million copies! Simply put, life would be a lot smaller if everyone stopped pursuing big dreams.

FUNDAMENTAL #3: APPROACH LIFE WITH BALANCE: ALWAYS HAVE A BACKUP PLAN TO SCORE

In the game of basketball, you can often feel a successful shot the moment it leaves your fingertips. But, you still prepare for the unexpected—the tip or the block that might prevent the ball from going in. You get yourself in position to get that rebound. The same is true for life because you may need to pivot and change direction.

One thing you have to be careful of when you're talking to kids—they'll say that they want to be a professional athlete, or maybe a rock musician or a movie star. While it's absolutely important to

Don't limit your life by putting all your eggs in one basket.

support them in that dream, you also want to encourage them to stay balanced in their life and take care of schoolwork. "I want you to dream big and follow your dreams, but don't limit your life by putting all your eggs in one basket," I tell them. This balanced approach to life is really important, and it may mean having a back-up plan. This is especially true in sports where if you get injured, your dream could quickly be derailed. Things can happen—you just don't know. It's all about balance. The key is to throw your heart and soul into working on your dream, but also make sure you are working in other areas of your life as well, so if you have to change direction, you're prepared.

Having balance means if you have to change directions, you're prepared.

Even when I was dreaming of becoming a professional athlete, I made sure I took care of my schoolwork and set myself up to have options. I was aware that most people would have said I wasn't going to be in the NBA. From the outside looking in, it was a long shot. But this was MY dream, and I wanted to see it through and try to make it happen. I knew I might not make the NBA, so when I had the opportunity to go to Yale, even though it wasn't exactly a basketball powerhouse, I took it. I believed that if you were good enough, the NBA would find you. And if they didn't find me, I knew I'd have a good education from a good school, and I'd have options.

This is critical wisdom I emphasize with many athletes and older kids I talk to, including my own kids. It's important to not limit yourself. I had a successful sixteen years playing pro basketball. Now, I run a charitable foundation, work at a financial investment firm, and I just entered politics. Each path has taught me a great deal and helped me to live a full life.

FUNDAMENTAL #4:
THE IMPORTANCE OF GIVING BACK

Perhaps the most important fundamental in living a successful life is to live your life not just for yourself, but for others as well. Inspired by my Hungarian grandfather, I opened the Chris Dudley Foundation in 1994 with the mission of helping young people with Type I diabetes reach their full potential. Every summer, the foundation sponsors a basketball camp for kids with diabetes. My entire family is involved with the camp, and we all agree it is one of our favorite weeks of the year. I take great pride in the fact that all three of my kids—Emma, especially—are always thinking of different causes that need assistance, and are out there raising money for them. The example my grandfather set for me is now being passed on to a third generation.

For each of my three kids, it's such a privilege to be their dad. I get to fan their flames of desire and hope, and encourage their dreams. Step by step they build mighty internal "I can" beliefs that get them over the hills and into position to win no matter what life brings. And all along, I tell them I love them no matter what! Just these principles alone are the makings for great professional successes, but when you add the last fundamental—giving back—it's like winning the playoffs. It's true success; it's a rich balanced version.

With these principles there are great successes, but add giving back and it's like winning the playoffs.

These are the secrets to happiness and success, and the best part about it is everyone can have them. They are completely free! You'll find you don't need Disneyland to make your dreams come true!

"*Success is neither magical nor mysterious. Success is the natural consequence of consistently applying the basic fundamentals.*"

Jim Rohn, American entrepreneur, author and motivational speaker. A self-made multi-millionaire, Rohn is commonly regarded a legendary icon in the personal development industry.

WHO IS CHRIS DUDLEY?

Chris with (wife) Chris Love, and (children) Charles, Emma and Sam

Chris Dudley is the epitome of someone who followed his dream—and attained it. Diagnosed at age sixteen with Type 1 diabetes, Chris set out to prove that obstacles are not necessarily roadblocks.

Several years after the diagnosis, he went on to play basketball and earn a degree in economics and political science at Yale. When he began his pro basketball career, no one with diabetes had ever played in the NBA. Today, after living with the disease for twenty-nine years, he is a leader in the effort to find a cure. With his wife, Chris Love, he founded the Chris Dudley Foundation, dedicated to kids with diabetes. Through the foundation, Dudley was able to establish the only basketball camp in the country for children with the disease.

In 2005 and 2006 Dudley addressed United States Senate committees on the topics of diabetes funding and research. His awards include the J. Walter Kennedy Citizenship Award, *USA Today's* Most Caring Athlete Award, and the Freedom Corps Award.

After leaving basketball in 2003, Dudley served as senior vice president at M Financial, and is now a partner in a small financial company in Oregon. Dudley and his family serve on countless charitable boards and participate in a wide range of activities, from coaching youth sports to raising funds for the Oregon Health Science University Circle of Giving. Dudley and his wife are also the authors of *Chris Dreams Big,* a children's book about overcoming adversity.

www.chrisdudley.org

UTILIZING SUPPORT

A WORLD OF MENTORS

If I Were Your Daddy ... I'd take you with me, and together we'd learn from a world community of extraordinary mentors.

THOMAS MOORE, Ph.D.
Theologian & Best-Selling Author

My two children, now young adults, learned the most valuable things in life through osmosis. Character, values, and attitudes seeped in like spring rain into thirsty soil. I sought out rich, colorful environments filled with positive and expansive influences, and I placed my kids in the paths of people who were living the values I most admired. This was a conscious decision. Rather than teach by direct moral lessons (you *should* do this), I allowed my children, through association, to naturally adopt strong qualities and character traits from the mentors around them who embodied those qualities and traits.

I learned this approach in part from my uncle, whose influence was profound. I grew up in Detroit, but spent my summers on his farm in upstate New York. My uncle didn't teach me anything *explicitly*, but I learned a tremendous amount from his example. I saw the simplicity, honesty, and strong work ethic that lived in this magnificent man who lived a life close to the earth, with a strong sense of the environment and the animals in his care. He modeled and I absorbed. Although he was a man of few words, he spoke volumes.

My father was another strong influence. He's ninety-seven as of this writing. He taught plumbing all his life and was a great teacher. When I teach, I always feel my father as part of my work; I feel that he's part of my blood and that I teach the way he does. His way of teaching was to put us kids in an environment and stand by as we learned, offering help as it was needed. He never told us how to do something. Instead, he encouraged us to have our own experiences, and we learned through our solo explorations and repeat efforts.

One time I saw my father teach a young boy, a stranger, how to bowl. To fully appreciate this story, you have to realize that bowling is taken seriously in Detroit: it's been known as "the city of the big Bowling Ball."

My father was playing with several of his teammates while I sat nearby doing my homework. Off to the side was another young boy of about fifteen who was watching them. When my father noticed him, he went up to the counter and rented an extra pair of shoes. Then he went over to the boy, offered him the shoes, and invited him to bowl with him and his team. The other men didn't like this much, saying, "He's a kid. We wanna play our own game." But Dad replied, "Take it easy. He'll learn quickly and it'll be great."

Well, then he had to teach the kid how to bowl! He showed him how to hold the ball, then stood back and said, "Now you try it." The boy threw the ball down the alley, and it was OK. So my dad said, "That was pretty good. Now, here's where you can put your finger," and so on. Within about fifteen minutes he had that kid bowling pretty well. He wasn't being pushy. He was just letting the boy have the experience, gaining self-confidence by his own improvement.

I've never forgotten that moment of noticing how masterfully my dad taught a skill. More important, he showed me that fathering doesn't have to come from "Dad." At that moment, he saw a child in need

Fathering doesn't have to come from "Dad."

173

of attention and some parenting, and he gave it to him, subtly, almost invisibly. Little did I know that this observation—at a bowling alley, of all places!—would set a precedent for how I would approach teaching my own children.

When parenting is limited to *you*, it's limited to you! Since we tend to carry the same problems and behavioral issues our parents had, and their parents had before them, we tend to repeat the same parenting patterns—the good, the bad, and the ugly. It's hard not to. I didn't come from a violent family, but some people do and it passes down, kind of like a family inheritance. Whatever it is, we need to become conscious of these bad inheritances and make a deliberate decision to heal the generations by parenting differently, by choosing not to carry bad patterns forward with our own parenting.

> We tend to repeat the same parenting patterns—the good, the bad, and the ugly.

As the saying goes, "We don't know what we don't know," and you can't teach your children what you don't know yourself. Our parents were limited by this, as are we; by extension, so are our children. Even when we recognize something we want to do differently, seldom is there a blueprint for change.

EXPANDING PARENTING BEYOND YOU

While I joyfully accepted the responsibility of parenthood, I kept this principle in mind. I looked for ways to expand my parenting beyond the influences and predispositions of our immediate family. My solution was to invite the world to raise my children with me. I deliberately sought out positive influences beyond our home, and as a result, I watched my two children develop in ways that eclipsed their mother's and my comfort levels, talents, and abilities.

The people I sought to surround my children modeled the kind of values I admired: intelligent men and women doing something extraordinary, not just fitting into the cookie-cutter mold of finding their job and their place. Hard-working, honest people, people *off the grid,* individuals who were not just concerned with their own affairs, but who considered and embraced a global community. Extraordinary people who would provide models of adults who would help our children make choices in their own lives as they grew up.

As I encountered them, I began to invite these people to our home. We had lively discussions, with the children always within listening distance, if not in the same room. I remember my diapered daughter toppling over in a circle discussion, unable to sit up unassisted for very long. They were *that* young when I first began creating environments of people, discussions, and ideas that included them, and I continued this throughout their childhood.

The most valuable learning was taking place outside of school.

As I lectured at conferences and spoke to small groups and with individuals, I took my kids with me. It soon became clear that the most valuable learning was taking place outside of school. Perhaps one of the most positive experiences was bringing my children with my wife and me on a teaching engagement I was offered at Schumacher College in England during the summers while they were growing up. A wonderful place in a beautiful part of England, it's what they call an "Adult Education Center." People go there to immerse themselves in community living, which includes the study of ecology and the maintenance and care of the facilities. You can get a master's degree in ecology there just by being a part of the group.

Schumacher isn't an elite, aristocratic place. Far from it. Based on a Gandhi approach to education and community, it's the perfect environment for engaging with people contemplating global issues, whatever your age. I didn't take the position for the minimal income it offered, but for the nonmonetary wealth I thought it would bring to my family. My estimations proved correct.

Although the environment was perfect for expanding one's awareness of world challenges and possible solutions, it was unprecedented to bring young children into the setting. So I made my agreement to lecture conditional upon my whole family's being there. The school had never had children on the grounds before, and the administration wasn't sure it would be a good idea to have them running around during the "serious business" of teaching. They finally relented, and so it was that two little heads came to bob amid a sea of grownups for many a summer. Once the youngsters were there, the faculty and students loved them.

Being around others who are concerned with making a contribution to the world tends to rub off.

For the next six summers the children sat in on a few classes and participated in events that interested them. They got to know the people who were teaching and taking courses. We didn't push them toward a curriculum or agenda. We simply plunked them down in an environment rich with people concerned with solving global, social, and ecological issues. Over the years I saw the tangible impact these people had on our children, starting with the director of the school, Satish Kumar, who has a great sense of belonging to the world and making a contribution. A warm person, he's become like a member of the family and has helped the kids a great deal. Being around others who are concerned with making a contribution to the world tends to rub off.

THOUGHTFULLY MAKE IT HAPPEN

There are many ways parents can accomplish a like-spirited approach. Our path was unique to our family and to the nature of my work as an author, lecturer, and teacher. We are all, however, exposed to people we admire. Creating opportunities for children to be with those extraordinary individuals makes a critical difference in their development.

Parenting doesn't have to be limited to you if you don't limit parenting. As I had seen for myself, introducing my children to the many faces of parenting beyond Mom and Dad gave them many creative role models for doing positive things for the world. These influences eventually bore fruit inside my children, who accomplish things far beyond my comfort level and ability, and with mastery and ease. I am awestruck by their depth of character, even as young adults. Had my wife and I raised them alone, just the two of us, they no doubt would have been good people. But how much more capable are they now because we opened the world for them to receive? These rich environments and positive role models took

We are all exposed to people we admire. We created the opportunities for our children to be around these people.

each of us beyond the limits of our family heritage. This in itself is a step toward healing the generations, and one of the greatest gifts I have given my children.

"Alone we can do so little; together we can do so much."

Helen Keller, American author, political activist, and lecturer; the first deaf-blind person to earn a Bachelor of Arts degree.

WHO IS DR. THOMAS MOORE?

Thomas with (wife) Hari Kirin, (children) Abraham and Siobhán

Dr. Thomas Moore is a former monk, a father, and an extraordinary writer. After the success of his *New York Times* bestseller, *Care of the Soul,* and its companion, *SoulMates,* he became a full-time writer. He has now published more than twenty books in the areas of archetypal psychology, mythology, and the imagination.

Born in Detroit, Michigan, to an Irish Catholic family, Moore joined the Servites, a Catholic religious order, where he served for twelve years. He earned degrees in theology, music, and philosophy, including an M.A. in Theology from the University of Windsor and a doctorate in religion from Syracuse, and he taught at Glassboro State College and briefly at Southern Methodist University. Moore practiced as a psychotherapist for sixteen years, first in Dallas, then in New England.

One of his most recent books, *Care of the Soul in Medicine,* represents Moore's vision for improving health care. It spells out how health care workers can care for their patients as whole persons—body, soul, and spirit. While sharing stories from his personal and professional life, Moore gives advice to both health care providers and patients for maintaining dignity and humanity, providing spiritual guidance for dealing with feelings of mortality and threat, encouraging patients to not only take an active part in healing but also to view illness as a positive passage to new awareness.

Moore is married to Hari Kirin and has a son and daughter. He lives in New Hampshire with his family.

www.careofthesoul.net

LIVING WITH TRADITION AND COMMUNITY

If I Were Your Daddy ... I'd model, by example, the importance of good health and healing at all levels. I'd teach you to honor a foundation for life based on traditional values, supported by family and community.

ROBERT MIRABAL

Grammy Award-Winning,
Native American World Musician

I'm a traditional native musician and artist on the world stage, but I'm also a farmer, a son, a grandchild, and a father. I was born and raised in the Taos Pueblo in northern New Mexico, and I have three girls. We live at the foot of sacred Taos Mountain, and my girls are being raised traditionally as full residents of the Taos Pueblo. As a family we take part in all our community's traditional ceremonies.

One time we were right in the middle of the harvest ceremonies. I was in the center of this group of men singing, and over there I saw my three beautiful daughters dancing around to these songs that were composed thousands of years ago. I also saw my mother, my wife, my niece, and my grandmother. It was such a profound moment, because I saw myself as being in the middle of something so deep and ancient and timeless, I knew something was working. In my commitment to my role as a father in this traditional society, I knew life was flowing and moving forward in a continuum as it should, and something was working.

Taos Pueblo is a living Native American community. It's been designated as a World Heritage Site and is also a National Historic Landmark. My family lives in one of two multi-storied adobe buildings that have been continuously inhabited for over a thousand years. Today about 1,900 people live on Taos Pueblo lands near their fields, and they maintain homes in the pueblo, which they use during our traditional ceremonies. Only about 150 of us live in the pueblo full-time.

I live a pretty committed lifestyle based on the traditional values I inherited from my grandparents, and they from theirs, and this is the most important thing I'm passing along to my daughters. Our Tiwa language is not written, so that in itself requires a community because to survive it must continue to be spoken. Most of the traditional cultural practices happen in that language, and to fully understand the value of our community, you really have to speak and understand it.

I've always been interested in the world at large, and I began playing music at a time when world music was becoming popular. I've been fortunate enough to travel to many places to study arts and cultures. As a father I'm doing the best I can in this day and age, because as our traditional society is impacted by the greater culture around us, it is rapidly changing. Change began in the simple form of a book, then radio, then television, and now computers. English is the first language of the kids nowadays, and we have to work with that reality. Living in two extremely different worlds like this presents many complex issues. There are only about two thousand of us left. We're dwindling, and we could easily fade away in one generation. Each generation faces a powerful lurking force; are we the ones who will lose it? Just two thousand people—is it enough? For now it is, and we enjoy the fact that there's something still alive, still magical; we can make rain and the gods and goddesses still listen to us. The elders have said this; you won't find it anywhere else, and nobody can come into this world and teach us how to do it, so we have inherited this responsibility.

FATHERING

I don't think we can *effectively* father our children individually; it really does take a community. First, the traditional lifestyle encompasses the whole being. There's no such thing as a generation gap. The grandparents are there, and those values are passed down. My grandmother is there, my mother is there; next come my mother's brothers and sisters, my aunties and uncles, and then the external family. Those are the teachers; they have lived through a lot of the cultural and traditional practices, and

We can't *effectively* father our children individually; it really does take a community.

it is their job to pass them down to the children of the Pueblo. From that point it goes to the son and the sisters—or to my sister. Son and daughter, we become the aunties and uncles that guide the child, and then it goes into the community.

This place doesn't have electricity or running water. Our fresh water is supplied by the river that runs through the village. While these traditions encompass the historical value of the community, they also have direct implication to ceremony and to all the elements we're living with. From there, it goes into food because we are an agrarian society. Every springtime families till the earth and plant their seed, and this encompasses the traditional dances—the buffalo dances, the corn dances, the male and female aspects of the dance, all of which my daughters will learn as full members of this community. From there, it encompasses more of a spiritual connection to the larger self—the community and then to the world. All prayers and dances are for the world and not just for us, making it a full circle.

The role of a father, for instance, is somewhat different here than it is in the greater culture around us. In my community, it's the father who opens the door for you as a son, but I grew up without a father. As a result, I was shy and withdrawn in my early years. When I was older, I connected to my grandfather, and he became a surrogate father for me—a pillar in my life. It could have been an uncle or someone else who played this role, but for me, my grandfather became my role model.

Because I didn't have a father—and because the role of father in my community is so different from that in the larger world—every experience, every week, every month, every year has become an extremely difficult task for me to understand as a father in a world that's changing so drastically. So what I'm doing is giving my daughters what was missing in my life. I'm just totally showing up for them in all issues.

On many levels, I can't say I can teach my children much. So much of the day-to-day learning about culture, tradition, language, and values is taught by the grandparents and the extended family. I think mostly I learn from them; I think my children are my best teachers.

Just because you're a father doesn't mean you're healthy or wise. Just because I'm a parent doesn't mean I see the truth in everything. I am as feeble-minded and as ignorant as they come. I am made up of mistakes and faults, but I'm also made up of honor and love, and the best thing for that is to revitalize myself through the negativity from a place of committed effort. This culture encompasses a very strong individual—both man and woman. To be that it is imperative to be healthy, and I think the best I can give my girls is to be committed to my own health and wellness, a life of curiosity, a life of pursuing love and understanding. I must honor my people, my heritage and my family, and then because I am part of that I must honor myself by living a life that is worthy. For the sake of my children I must become a pillar and a warrior. If I can become a strong example of that for them, then they will search for those examples for themselves. And what does wellness and vitality mean? It's everything—the language, the culture, the dance, the food, but the only way I can become all those things is by committing myself to my own healing—and that means physically, emotionally, mentally and spiritually. Despite all the other teachers in their lives, my children will learn nothing if, as their father, I'm not healthy or strong or a good example of what we are trying to teach. It seems simple and naïve, but staying strong and committed to healing is a very powerful entity.

> *Despite all the other teachers in their lives, my children will learn nothing if I'm not healthy or strong or a good example.*

Today we must go beyond our parents and our grandparents, because this generation faces the real possibility of the culture being lost. But how do you keep it alive? You heal. How do you heal? You learn the language; you commit yourself to proper foods and a solid program of wellness and traditional values. I must do this, and this is the example I must give to my children. When I do this, it means me showing up to their life, and to the values handed down to me from my great-grandparents.

This way of life and thinking is different from that of white America. As a father and man, I need my children as much as they need me, because as my oldest daughter reaches puberty, she has ceremonies. She will become the young woman who's part of a culture that is dying out, but for her it is brand new. Her mother and her grandmother and her aunties must bring in the power, because they went through the same changes. But as her father I must bring in the light for her, the light of knowledge, the light of direction, as well as the water—which is sustenance, healing, and strength. It encompasses a spiritual path of light as well as a literal path—whether it means the special wood they need, or the special water they need, or the special food they need. It means to bring light to their whole existence, and bringing in this light is the responsibility of the man—to himself, his family, and his society. This is what I must do. As the father, I must become the true male that takes care of the mothers, the grandmothers, and the aunties, and then finally the daughter. As my daughter becomes a young woman, she can dance with me the different dances, and she becomes a teacher to the next generation.

As her father, if I don't create and pursue my own healing, she will be schooled by an artificial form of expression and learning and that will contribute to a deteriorating society. The only way for me to do that is to be strong physically, emotionally, mentally and spiritually, and this provides a foundation for her to lean on. And I hope she will do the same for her children.

> As a father I must bring in the light—the light of knowledge, the light of direction.

This same foundation is what I've used in my music and travels and studies. Hopefully, instead of creating chaos and mental confusion, it will bring solace and peace. It all depends on how well I can convey through my art those places of conflict as well as those places of peace, how well my own foundation supports my efforts in my music, as well as being a father.

Parenting is a full-time job, and I believe it takes a whole community. We can't be putting our children into public schools and think that's going to father them. We can't create initiation rituals by putting them into a university or a war overseas, because children need the admirable qualities that only we teach, so they can become who they are. As a parent, I fear I will fail. I think most parents have this fear, and in that place of fear we may lose faith in ourselves, and in our children. But if we can just step back a little and actually see our children grow and evolve, we will see some of the most amazing developments we would never expect, and I think that is the beauty of parenting. I love that.

> Children aren't here for us; they're here for everybody in the world.

My first child was not born until I was thirty, and I can honestly say it's the best thing that's ever happened to me. I can also say it's the most difficult. I can't see my life without my children. I want to do the best I can as a father, and I've come to realize that to just stay on a healing path is the most important thing I can ever do for them. And even though I approach this from the context of my own culture, I think it is wisdom that has a broader base— for all fathers, for all parents. We have to heal our own issues, our own pain, and commit to being a role model of a healthy lifestyle for our kids to give them a foundation they can hopefully apply to their own lives. Their journey is their own. Children aren't here for us; they're here for everybody in the world. Hopefully we will be there for them, and hopefully the path my children will take is the strong, committed spiritual path I taught them. When they come to a crossroads, this healing path will say, "If you need help, your father stuck to the healing path." Hopefully because they have that example, instead of struggling they will follow that road.

I have conversations about these things with my daughters every day. I tell them to challenge their teachers, challenge their friends, and challenge us. Our children chose us. They have their own spirit, and we're obligated to challenge them on many levels—physically, spiritually, and emotionally. I tell them, "If you think something is wrong, question it. Be the beacon. Find the source of this strangeness, this feeling of not clear, not right. Question the heart. Question the mind: find the answers through others or through yourself. It'll set you free." It's like planting a seed of curiosity; something will grow.

While it is true that our life in the Taos Pueblo is unique, I think there are some basic truths about parents and children and community that are universal. First, I think every child needs to find something that is a constant, something that will sustain them. I was educated outside the community so I have a broader world view than some of the others. I wanted my daughter to have that broader education as well, so I put her into a Steiner-Waldorf school. I really liked the Rudolf Steiner philosophy. It seemed to be less of a restrictive public-school environment and more of a tribal community atmosphere. But out of the whole school, probably half of them moved away. And then the school administration people moved away. My daughter couldn't understand why people were leaving and moving away, and there was no consistency, no continuity, nothing to sustain her.

> *Every child needs to find something that is a constant, something that will sustain them.*

So I brought her back to the pueblo school where teachers have been there for thirty-five years. I think this concept has to be seen and felt, and I think in America we're in dire straits with this type of thinking. How many people actually want to live where their grandparents and parents live, or in the community they grew up in? But if we are committed to that lifestyle, there are places where we can find it in small bits and pieces of our world.

Community brings you back to your strength and foundation. My girls have seen death and understand what death is all about, and they understand what birth is all about. They've seen it on many levels. I don't shy away from the difficulties they're going to face in life. I speak to them as adults and spiritual beings. What else could I do? I have no book to tell me. I read somewhere that children don't come with instructions, and if that is so, then I guess they must be our teachers, so I consider them the best teachers I have. As much as I feel like I sometimes have the answers, every day as they grow, I grow too. As they learn new things, they challenge me to push myself. The best thing I can do as a father is to stay vital and well. And I pursue that constantly.

I know I'm on the right path because I had an experience once doing a concert, and all three of my children were there. When I looked out into the audience I could see them as young women and I could see them as old women. It was a profound generational experience. It was magic, and that moment was created for me, so as a father I could see the beauty in all of them.

They taught me that what I'm doing is very important because I saw it in their eyes.

I guess my message for other parents is if you give up on yourself, then you give up on your children and everybody else. Stay on your healing journey, and don't give up. Don't give up on your pursuit of becoming a pillar, a warrior. They are your teacher, and you are their light and their hope.

"Example is not the main thing in influencing others. It is the only thing."

Albert Schweitzer, prominent theologian, organist, philosopher, and physician.

WHO IS ROBERT MIRABAL?

Robert with his three daughters.
Photograph by Lewis Kostiner, from *FATHERHOOD: American Stories*

Robert Mirabal is a two-time Grammy winner who chooses to live a traditional Native American life with his family at the foot of sacred Taos Mountain in northern New Mexico. "If you live a traditional life," he says, "you see things differently—spiritually and musically."

Mirabal has been described as a Native American "Renaissance man," with major successes as a traditional flute player, flute maker, composer, painter, poet, actor, screenwriter, horseman and farmer. His flutes have been displayed at the Smithsonian's Museum of the American Indian.

Mirabal's awards for his music include two awards as Native American Artist of the Year, three as Songwriter of the Year, a 2006 Grammy Award for his album *Sacred Ground: A Tribute to Mother Earth,* and a 2008 Grammy for *Johnny Whitehorse: Totemic Flute Chants.* He has been featured in two Public Broadcasting Corporation productions, 1998's "Spirit: A Journey in Dance, Drum, and Song," and 2002's "Music from a Painted Cave." He also partnered with John Tesh for the PBS Millennium program "One World."

In 1994, Mirabal published *Skeletons of a Bridge,* a book of poetry. He is currently writing his first novel, *Running Alone in Photographs.* He says, "What I create comes out of my body and soul in a desire to take care of the spirits of the earth."

Mirabal and his wife, Dawn, have three daughters whom he calls his teachers.

www.mirabal.com

CONNECTING AND PLUGGING IN

If I Were Your Daddy ... I'd help you create daily habits to connect you with your inner self, with others, and with nature. You'd learn that there's a peaceful, resting place inside of you.

FREDDIE RAVEL
Grammy-Nominated International
Recording Artist & Speaker

It's seven o'clock on a lovely morning in southern California. Still covered in dew, the grass is sparkling in the early morning sunshine, and it's a bit chilly. Our eight-year-old daughter, Jasmine, slips on her jacket and sandals and makes her way over to our raised vegetable garden built of old railway ties. After I built it we planted all kinds of different herbs and vegetables like mint, cilantro, basil, rosemary, tomatoes, carrots, and scallions. Now in the morning when she's getting ready to go to school, I often say, "Jas, here are some scissors. Go out and grab a few herbs."

As recently as twenty years ago this was a normal activity for a child. But today, I'm astonished at how many kids don't know where food comes from. They think you go to the market and it's just there. They've lost entirely the connection between people and the natural process of growing our food. Watching my child connect with life through this very fundamental activity is extremely satisfying for me. I'm excited to see her close to the soil, and understanding about little bugs and worms and all the things that live in our garden, and how we are part of the great dance of life that nourishes us.

As a professional musician, my life is all about making connections; planting a vegetable garden in our yard is just one way I'm teaching my children about the basic human need to connect. Not the superficial, illusionary connections of text messaging or amassing "friends" on social networking web sites, but deep, lifelong connections with themselves, with others, and with nature. I want my kids to be connected to the greater life force that flows through all of us, along with the trees, the wind and the waves, and the animals on our beautiful planet.

CONNECTING TO SELF

Some years ago I had the pleasure of working with, and becoming friends with, Deepak Chopra. From him I learned a daily routine which has become a practice I truly love. When my children were still babies I introduced them to a routine to help them create the unique experience of being able to connect within.

This routine begins in the morning when Jasmine, Max, and I gather on our big Oriental rug. I'm in my bathrobe, Jasmine is still in her PJs, and Max is in his diaper. Mom is still upstairs catching a bit more sleep. We start the day quietly—even if only for a few minutes—to connect with ourselves and have a moment of stillness. Little kids have their own interpretation of "still," and that's just fine.

I introduced my children to a daily routine to help them connect within.

We begin by facing north, ready to greet the new day. We "salute the sun," a series of yoga poses or "asanas" that include stretches and breath work, and follow that by performing twelve simple yoga asanas, which we do about five times. We follow that with a few minutes of "reverse nostril breathing," a breathing exercise designed for physical and emotional balancing.

We've been doing these same three things every morning since the kids were barely two years old. I cherish the two photos I have of Jasmine and me doing "downward dog" and "cobra" positions, with me in my bathrobe and her in her diaper! By the time Jasmine was six she knew these exercises well, and her baby brother would imitate her as best he could.

Finally we meditate, legs crossed, hands on the knees, with our thumb and middle fingers touching. We close our eyes and quiet the mind. Now eight, Jasmine is getting very good at meditation and manages a couple of minutes of silence. When Max was three, he could last about ten seconds before breaking into laughter, really extraordinary for a baby. Now five, he's up to about twenty seconds.

> *There's more than the noise of the world: there's a resting place inside.*

Silencing the mind in meditation, experiencing nothingness, no activities or thoughts—even for a few seconds—can be absolutely transformational. For children, it helps them understand that there's more to life than just the noise of the world; there's a resting place inside of them.

Taking small steps, we just have fun with our morning routine. Acquiring any skill, accomplishing any goal, requires daily self-discipline. Just like becoming an accomplished musician, you don't practice just when you feel like it. The daily habit of practice is learned and established, and that's the kind of discipline I want my kids to have.

With our morning routine, I know it's my daughter and son's entry to acquiring self-discipline and healthy habits, while their brains are still getting wired up. Practicing this daily routine with kids definitely takes patience, but by rooting this habit deeply within them now, I'm giving them an invaluable counterbalance to the speed of the world.

CONNECTING TO OTHERS

I'm beginning to see results. In Jasmine I see an extraordinary self-composure, a broad, calm, nonjudgmental and open way of being with other people. Whether she's welcoming a rock star, like the group Earth, Wind and Fire's Verdine White, or a teacher and author like Marianne

Williamson, Jasmine is open to anyone who comes into our home. I credit at least some of her developing maturity to the stability our morning routine offers, and to an inner calm we are cultivating daily. Jasmine doesn't have to be always entertained. There's a still place inside her that has been found and nurtured, and that others can sense about her.

Rather than shut myself off, I chose to include them.

Stilling myself to be present in this way has helped me find balance personally. In fact, it's one of the most valuable things I've ever learned to do. When I became a dad I knew I wanted to pass this gift along to my kids, so rather than shut myself off in silence in a room away from them, I chose to include them. I simplified my routine to only the steps mentioned here, and I've been doing it with them almost every day.

CONNECTING TO NATURE

Connecting to the inner world is closely tied to connecting with nature: we need both. The year Jasmine was six, on Earth Day, she and I were excited to embark on our daily bike ride to school because it was our first trip on our new tandem bike for two. We arrived to find the playground filled with over six hundred kids. Like us, many of them lived nearby, but we were the only ones arriving by bike. One bike out of six hundred kids!

Since they were two years old, I've been taking Jasmine and Max everywhere by bicycle—helmets on, strapped into their own seats—usually for about a fifteen-minute ride. I love cycling because when you're on the bike you're not trying to talk over the hum of an engine or radio. And forget about cell phones! It's just the wind, your voice and your child's voice in your ear, and you have really delightful conversations. Moving relatively slowly, you're able to point things out, and your children can really digest your words.

"Oh, honey, look! There's a jasmine flower, the one you're named after." Or "Take a look at that cactus. Do you know that if you burn the spines off that prickly pear, you can actually eat it?"

"You've got to be kidding, Daddy! You can eat cactus?!"

"Oh yeah, if you burn off the spines you can!"

These conversations couldn't happen in a car, because you're moving too fast. On the bike your children can hear the birds, feel the temperature outside, and enjoy the sun and the breeze. It's a visceral, dynamic sensation to be embedding in your children's memory when they're this age! We've consciously chosen to live near our kids' schools so the places we go daily are accessible by bike. It's one way we stay connected to nature.

> These conversations couldn't happen in a car, because you're moving too fast.

I grew up on the central coast of California, and from my father I developed a deep love and appreciation for nature. I went through Cub Scouts, then Boy Scouts, and I was camping by the time I was seven. I just loved that connection to nature; it's really a big part of who I am.

So once a year I make sure to take my family camping. We pitch tents, sleep in sleeping bags on air mattresses, and hike during the day. Last year's family trip was to Big Sur, California, with my mom, sister, and dad along, as well as the kids' eight-year-old cousin. I try to teach my kids something new each year, like how to build a good cooking fire, and cook on it, or look after the environment by handling our garbage properly. After dinner we'll take flashlights and go exploring, roast marshmallows, and tell stories—all the regular camping and nature experiences that many kids are sadly growing up without.

Camping takes us out of the man-made world and into the God-made world, where you are a small part of something greater. The learning is purely experiential so it provides a profound sense of connection. One afternoon I saw some clouds forming, and knew we were in for some rain. While six-year-old Jasmine and her cousin watched, I filled a kettle from a nearby tap and poured water on the ground so the girls could see how the water was going to flow around our tent once it started to rain. Based on where the water went, the girls then used a little fold-up shovel to dig a trench around the tent to prepare for the rainstorm. They laughed themselves silly the whole time moving the dirt around. Then when it rained, they actually saw the water going around the tent in their trench, and they learned something about the world. Another time my father saw a moth on a tree which nature had camouflaged to resemble a dead oak leaf. "Jasmine, let's clean the tent," he said and continued, "Would you pick up that 'oak leaf' for me?" When she went to pick it up she discovered it was actually a moth! And this led to a discussion about camouflage and how nature survives in different environments. It was a fabulous lesson that she talks about to this day.

I'm planting a homing signal in my children.

With these experiences around connecting with nature, I'm planting a homing signal in my children, the same one that my folks planted in me when I was a boy. When the kids are older, they will come back to this experience in any way they can, and hopefully hand it down to their children.

Ten years ago, who would have thought we'd even need to talk about the benefits of getting our kids (and us) out on bicycles, or going camping? But one by-product of this electronic age is that almost everything, including sports, can be done from our couch. Activities we once did readily and spontaneously must now be consciously planned and scheduled. And sadly, if they don't get planned and scheduled, they don't happen.

For this reason, I'm very passionate about keeping my kids organic and not dependent on creature comforts, which means taking them camping, hiking, and on longer family bicycle outings. It's part of this connection to nature that today, in our society, we have to consciously preserve. If we, as parents, don't teach and emphasize spending time in nature, our kids may likely never find it, nor will they be as motivated to preserve it for future generations to come.

CREATING BOUNDARIES = STRONGER CONNECTIONS
"Give me boundaries so I can truly be free." —Igor Stravinsky

When my wife and I started our family, we realized the world our children were growing up in was different from the world of our childhood. On the surface, people seem more connected than ever before. The average person has access to masses of information on any subject, at any moment, for any reason—but it's mostly on a sound-bite level.

As a boy I had a lot of close friend connections. But the word "friend" meant somebody you liked, trusted, and did things with. It involved integrity and loyalty and being a good listener, and it had a lot to do with being in the moment, present and available. The word friend wasn't used for casual relationships, as it is in today's social networking web sites.

So I've asked myself, how will my children form real friends and build solid connections in today's age? The answer I believe is that they need to have boundaries and a container. Within those boundaries, great things can happen—especially for a developing mind.

Boundaries are actually very empowering for children.

In an experiment, children were allowed to play on a couple of acres of land with no boundaries. The result: they were all scattered and not engaged. In the second experiment, they took the same area but this time created a small fenced area in the center. Suddenly the kids began to focus, connect, and do things together. The lesson from that experiment? Boundaries are actually very empowering for children. I've adopted this lesson with my own kids, and together we set specific and strict electronic boundaries. My goal is not to deprive them, but empower them, and help their minds develop in a healthy way.

At my daughter's school I already see four- or five-year-olds with their noses in their PDAs and smart phones. Now I'm not advocating we eliminate the flood of electronic devices we have today; I use hundreds of thousand of dollars in computer gear in my studio on a daily basis. But like many adults, I stand at a threshold between the analog world and the digital world, concerned about my kids' healthy, whole development.

CREATING BOUNDARIES WITH ELECTRONIC DEVICES

Kids today are immersed early in a digital world, but as their brains are getting wired up, they need to *first* learn about the world in an "analog" way.

They need to make real friends, play real baseball, fish in a real river, climb a real tree, swim in a real lake, and see real animals. If they are exposed only to a virtual electronic world, truly an illusionary world, they don't learn to be present to the reality around them.

Kids need to learn about the world in an "analog" way first.

I'm not yet ready to allow my eight-year-old daughter to have a cell phone, because today it's really a pocket computer. A "smart phone" sounds enticing, but that term means easy access to the Internet, exposing our kids to places we don't allow them to go on computers.

When Jasmine asks, "Daddy, can I get a smart phone? Can I get a iPad? Can I get anything?" what she really means is "Can I get something so I can look cool and hip with my friends?" So she says, "Dad, the phone's really cool and after school it gives me a way to reach you."

And to that I say, "Honey, before cell phones, parents somehow managed to pick their kids up from school. So I'll pick you up by the flagpole at three fifteen." That's what we've been doing all year, and it works just fine. I know the time is coming when we're going to have to let Jasmine have a phone, but not yet.

In this virtual age, I also think there's something special and important in our children's learning for them to actually process information with a pen or pencil, on paper. On a recent trip to New York City, I took my kids to the American Museum of Natural History, a fantastic place. My phone was stashed in my pocket, and we brought no other electronic devices. Instead we brought some note-pads from the hotel, and I said, "Let's write things down." When we got to the dinosaur exhibit, Jasmine began drawing pictures of the dinosaurs and writing down different words to describe the era of each one. By the end of the day, she had filled about ten pieces of paper, and had learned something important about processing information in an analog way.

CREATING BOUNDARIES AROUND DINNER

With the emergence of all this new technology, my wife and I are on the same page, and very careful. We don't really watch TV, but we do have a collection of DVDs, including some good educational ones for the kids. There are many good things you can use media for, but there are few things that replace the wooden train set, the building blocks—the tactile world of old-fashioned toys that require imaginative building.

Sitting in front of the television or computer is a huge part of the emergence of childhood obesity, one of the greatest problems in our society, because kids are not as active as they need to be. Eating in front of a television is a double whammy, first because kids connect emotionally to whatever is on the screen, and second because they connect eating with something completely detached from it.

In our home the dinner table is sacred. The cell phones are turned off and there's no television, but because music is a big thing in our family, we do play classical music very softly in the background. We reserve this time for old-school family discussion, like "What can you share about your day today?" There is always prayer, where we give thanks for the blessings of the day, for the people we had connected with, for whatever good is happening in our lives right now.

CONNECTING TO OTHERS

I wanted to make my family a part of my work and expose them to what I do, so I decided to build my music studio into our home, and make it a rich hub of activities, people, and influences. I could have easily kept my studio outside my home, and perhaps by doing so I would have composed and recorded more, but it would have separated me and my work from my kids and family. Rather, integrating my kids into my work life teaches them through experiences that life is about relationships, about one voice being answered by another. Success is never about what we do individually, what Daddy writes or sings, but what we are able to accomplish together.

In my work I consciously seek out diversity, which not only enriches my music, but blesses our whole family by planting seeds of cultural openness and tolerance. I include my kids as much as possible, and they've learned to be respectful and just watch while Daddy works with clients in his studio. Although the people who come through our door look quite different, and have different faiths and beliefs, they do share a common core value: a desire to embrace the beauty in humanity, namely *Namaste*. Loosely translated, *Namaste* means, *"that which is of God in me greets that which is of God in you."* Although language may differ, they are all positive, world-embracing individuals, and this core value of real connection is what unifies the influences they bring to my work and to my family.

Success is never about what we do individually, but what we are able to accomplish together.

I've drawn my own professional boundary: I simply won't work with people who don't share this mind-set because my influences also influence my children. My offering to them is to be mindful to form expansive, world-embracing, and positive connections, and nothing teaches it more powerfully than seeing it lived, day after day, by many different people.

When we're young, it's easy to form habits, good or bad. By giving Jasmine and Max healthy habits of mind, body, and spirit, early on I'm preparing them to be present, self-congruent, and truly connect—to others, even in the midst of an increasingly electronic age. For me, there is no greater gift I can give my children than bringing them real connection, not superficial "virtual" association. By opening the doors for them to know themselves, experience nature, and embrace others, I'm helping my children grow into healthy, whole, loving adults, who one day will hopefully pass these same habits and values on to their own children.

A complete description of Freddie's family yoga routine can be found at
www.ifiwereyourdaddy/freddieravel.com

"OUTDOOR FUN IS GOOD FOR KIDS
AND THE PLANET"

Excerpts from the article by environmentalists David Suzuki and Faisal Moola

"Now, according to author Richard Louv, only six per cent of nine to 13-year-old children in the U.S. play outside in a typical week. This is reflected by a dramatic decline in fishing, swimming, and even biking. Mr. Louv, cofounder of the Children and Nature Network, noted that in San Diego, '90 percent of inner-city kids do not know how to swim' and '34 percent have never been to the beach.'

Our children have exchanged the experience of outdoors and nature with the enclosed world of electronics, resulting in 'nature deficit disorder.' For those of us who are concerned about the state of the biosphere, this is disturbing because a person for whom nature is a stranger will not notice, let alone care about, environmental degradation.

That's why many environmentalists are concerned with the way young people are growing up. Computers, television, video games, and the Internet offer information and entertainment in a virtual world without the hazards or discomfort of mosquitoes, rain and cold, steep climbs, or 'dangerous' animals of the real world — and without all the joys that the real world has to offer. Unless we are willing to encourage our children to reconnect with and appreciate the natural world, we can't expect them to help protect and care for it."

David Suzuki, cofounder of the David Suzuki Foundation,
is an award-winning scientist, environmentalist, and broadcaster.
Dr. Suzuki lives in Vancouver, British Columbia, Canada.
Visit him at
http://www.davidsuzuki.org

Read the whole article at
www.ifiwereyourdaddy/freddieravel.com

WHO IS FREDDIE RAVEL?

Freddie with (wife) Marie France, (children) Jasmine and Max

"The purest moments," says Freddie Ravel, "come when I'm just sitting at the piano letting all of this flow through me to make music that speaks from the heart."

For music aficionados around the globe, Ravel's music has indeed spoken from his heart to theirs. As a keyboardist, composer, and producer, he has performed and recorded with many iconic artists, including Carlos Santana, Earth Wind and Fire, Phil Collins, Quincy Jones, Madonna, Al Jarreau, the Boston Pops, and Prince.

Born in Los Angeles with South American and European roots, the bilingual Ravel became fascinated with music at the age of five. By age twenty-three, he was performing worldwide with Brazilian master Sergio Mendes. Universal Music discovered him and then released three solo albums that topped record charts: *Midnight Passion, Sol to Soul* and *Freddie Ravel* featuring the #1 USA hit, *Sunny Side Up.* The critics call it "Sensual and fiery," and Ravel's solo albums continue to have extensive international airplay.

Ravel's lifelong commitment to raising human potential through music gave birth to a powerful interactive performance program in 2002, which he named *Tune Up to Success®.* In this "Keynote Concert" he reveals to audiences ranging from teenagers to *Fortune* 500 companies, how music can connect and empower their personal and professional lives.

With rave reviews from clients that range from NASA to the *Fortune* 100, and renowned visionaries such as Dr. Deepak Chopra and Jack Canfield, Ravel's musical inspirations enrich audiences worldwide. This philosophy also drives Ravel's philanthropic work. For the past decade he has been spokesperson for Angelcare, a charity dedicated to saving lives and giving hope to underprivileged children.

Ravel is married to Marie-France and lives with his two children in California.

www.freddieravel.com

ENVIRONMENTS THAT MAKE OR BREAK YOU

If I Were Your Daddy ... I'd be mindful of the environments that make up your world, and I'd help design them so you grow. I'd encourage you to adopt supportive beliefs to create a happy, healthy, and wealthy life.

JIM BUNCH
Entrepreneur & Ultimate Life Coach

I got to see something I hope every man will get to see. I watched my wife, Michele, fall completely in love with the baby inside her. For nine months, every day was magical for her.

My experience as the soon-to-be dad, however, was somewhat different. The reality is that not every man bonds with his child at the same time and in the same way as a woman does. For me I just felt one step removed from the whole pregnancy experience. The child was growing inside of her, not me. I worried, "Shouldn't I be more in love with this being? What if this is an inconvenience? What if she and I don't have sex anymore? *What if he and I don't get along?* I knew things were going to change, but how much? Beneath all these questions was a deep-seated fear. I was afraid I would screw up being a dad, and do something, be something, or say something that would let my son down, as my father had repeatedly done with me.

Now, four years later, I adore my son, Teagan. My fears faded pretty quickly, and I can't imagine life without him. But back then, I was a pile of raw, mixed emotions—excited and concerned over the coming responsibility.

Luckily one of my good friends, Don, helped keep me from doing something stupid. He told me that before the birth of his first child, he was used to having 100 percent of his wife's attention and energy. Then suddenly the child came along and became number one, and he became number *zero*. He wasn't getting any of his needs met: no attention, no caressing, no whatever. His wife, on the other hand, was now getting all her needs met through the baby. He started resenting both the baby and the mom, and pulled away. As a result, they eventually divorced.

When he remarried and had another child, it all started again. But this time, he realized what was going on, and went to his wife and said, "I realize I'm starting to withdraw from you because I'm not getting my needs met, and what I should be doing instead is looking for ways to connect with you." They worked the problem out, and he remained happily married—and became a very present dad too.

Shortly after Teagan was born, I began having the same experience. During those first few weeks, my wife and I were both incredibly tired, but she was still getting her needs met. Only now it was through the baby. I was starting to resent my new son and my wife, and having thoughts like, "Maybe this marriage isn't going to work; maybe I'm not going to get my needs met; maybe I need to go somewhere else." I started wanting to withdraw, but then I remembered Don's story and realized why I was having these irrational thoughts. So from a place of brutal honesty, I explained my feelings to Michele.

*B*rutally honest, I explained my feelings.

"I just need us to hold hands again," I said. "I just need to spoon with you, and at some point, when your body has recovered, maybe we could have that thing called sex." So rather than staying in resentment and then withdrawing, I was able to ask my wife for connection and attention. Things changed immediately. If Don hadn't felt open to share this very personal stuff with me, I might have done something really dumb in order to get a basic need met. Instead Michele and I, and baby Teagan, got closer.

Once Teagan was old enough for us to leave for a few hours, Michele and

I scheduled a regular weekly date night to maintain good communication. Being somewhere different once a week—just the two of us, talking things out—helps us remain open with each other. We say all the things we didn't air or resolve during the week. Having a fresh environment frees us up to communicate what's working and what's not, and a little sake and sushi help too!

THE SUPPORT ENVIRONMENT: THE POWER OF NETWORKS

I didn't have the best role model for how to be a father. My biological dad did the best he could, but he was a Vietnam vet with a lot of issues to deal with. My mom divorced him when I was a year old, and married my stepfather when I was five. When I was little, my dad would call up and say he'd be right over to pick me up, except on the way he'd make a "quick" stop that often grew into a "long stop." I'd sit there on the porch waiting, sometimes through the night, and often through the weekend. One day I finally stopped waiting or hoping for *anything* from him. When I became a dad, I realized there was a lot about fathering I just didn't know; I'd never experienced it, so I never learned it. Therefore, I began talking to my friends about their kids, and watching how they interacted with them. I wanted to know what worked for them, and why they did those things.

There was a lot about fathering I didn't know. So I began talking to my dad friends: "What works and why?"

For whatever reason, guys don't naturally share stuff like this; you have to ask. But I had a burning desire to be a great father, so I started asking. I asked men I respected on many levels, so they were credible sources for me. Because I used my network to support me in becoming a better dad and husband, I didn't limit my knowledge of parenting to my own experiences growing up. As I've expanded my network and used it to have real conversations with fellow dads, my son's life has expanded as well.

We all have networks of colleagues and friends—these environments can either hold us back, keep us rigid, or propel us forward and help us grow. Because I learned long ago to surround myself with people I respect and who inspire me on some level, my associations propel me forward and continue to help me be the kind of father I want to be.

THE HOME ENVIRONMENT: SUPPORTIVE OR NOT?

When Teagan was still a baby, we rented a beautiful three-story six-thousand-square-foot Tuscan-style villa, with an option to buy. High on a hill, it overlooked the ocean and was very private. The first time we walked in, we knew this was Michele's dream home!

The whole top floor was the master bedroom suite. The next floor down—the main floor—had a huge TV and entertainment area, dining area, grand foyer, guest room, and Teagan's room. The house was so big that Teagan, then three, would ride his tricycle from his bedroom to the TV room. We didn't realize the impact this huge house was having on us—and our son—until much later.

Although beautiful, the house had a few drawbacks. In a large home, communication can be a challenge. There was no intercom system, so Michele and I were constantly yelling across the house, simply to be heard. Watching us communicate this way, Teagan naturally started yelling too, in and out of the house. Then, at his Montessori preschool, he started having little bursts of anger and hitting other kids and his teachers. Teagan had always been such a curious, happy, and sociable kid, and this behavior was so unlike him. One day the school called, and asked us to take him home.

At first, we had no idea what was going on, but then we started to notice a few other things. We felt greater stress and tension in this house than in our previous home, and as a result, Michele and I weren't getting along as well. When we considered this fact, our son's new behavior, and the financial demands of the house, we realized that something needed to change. We decided to move, and within a week, Michele found a much smaller, less formal beach house to rent. As soon as we walked in, we took a breath of fresh air. The house came fully furnished, so we put our own furniture in storage. Very quickly, everything in our life was different.

Renting a fully furnished house had some advantages. Most people drag their stuff from one place to the next when they move. We love our own furniture, but I know that possessions create mental and emotional anchors. When people stay in the same environment for ten, twenty, or thirty years without changing anything, this doesn't stimulate them to grow. The purpose of our environments is much like the purpose of our goals—to help us evolve. Moving to this new place, with new furnishings, gave us a fresh start.

> The purpose of our environments is much like the purpose of our goals—to help us evolve.

Sure enough, we saw a change in our marriage relationship, and more importantly, in Teagan. The new house is smaller, so we don't yell anymore. It has a lot of glass so it's very bright and airy. The upper level is one big open space, so we can see each other and feel more connected. Teagan's bedroom is only steps away from ours. We all fall asleep to the calming sound of distant ocean waves.

In the first few months at the beach house, we spent more time outdoors, in nature, than we had the whole time we lived at the huge house. And there were more kids for Teagan to play with. So Teagan's connection to nature and to others improved overnight.

From my friend Jack Canfield I learned that the two most important things to put in your child's bedroom are pictures of you and your kids laughing and having fun together, and a picture of your child succeeding at something. That way, your child sees positive, happy images every day. So we followed that advice. In Teagan's new bedroom we hung lots of new happy, smiling pictures of us all together. Updating children's rooms periodically supports their evolution and growth.

Any one of these factors can change a child's view of the world, and sometimes changing one thing is enough. But because our son's environment changed totally—new home, new neighborhood, new furnishings and pictures—the results were immediate! Looking back, it's so obvious that much of Teagan's destructive behavior at school resulted from a lack of connection and security. His physical environment had been the biggest *barrier* to getting his needs met. With this insight, I imagined what it must have felt like for a three-year-old to wake up in the middle of the night, and have to scream at the top of his lungs just to be heard. Looking at the results, I worked backwards to figure it out.

Not getting your needs met is like a gaping hole. You'll do whatever to satisfy it.

Back at the huge house, we'd tried to address our son's behavior problems directly, but it was really an uphill battle. Environments are like that; they either help us grow or keep us stuck. The moment a person doesn't get a primal need met, it's like there's a gaping hole. I had felt it with Michele in my new dad experience, then Teagan had that feeling too. When I work with coaching clients, I tell them that when people—even little ones—aren't getting a need met, they will do whatever they can to get it satisfied. A child will start fights to get resolution hugs, or bite to get attention. When we fixed the environment, for Teagan the problem was solved.

THE SCHOOL ENVIRONMENT: WHAT IS HE DOING RIGHT?

When Michele and I were called to the school, the experience was very intimidating. As we sat down with the principal and two of Teagan's teachers, we felt like we were in front of a parole board. Michele, especially, was really nervous, thinking, "Oh my God, am I a bad parent? Our son is hitting other kids!"

Then I remembered an approach I'd learned from my friend Alex Mandossian. Faced with a similar situation, he had redirected the conversation by asking the principal, "OK, great, that's what my daughter is *not* doing well, but tell me what she is doing well. Where is she excelling? Is she incredible at math? Is she good at putting things together? Does she show generosity? Does she apologize when she's done something wrong? Tell me about the things she does *right,* and the progress she is making."

So when the principal and teachers began discussing Teagan's situation, I stopped them and said, "Before you dive any deeper into what our son is doing wrong, I want all three of you to tell me something positive you see in Teagan that makes him different from any of the other kids."

They weren't expecting this; we could see the shift as they repositioned themselves. After a moment one teacher said, "Well he's one of the most loving kids. He's very thoughtful and kind, but he just has these outbursts." I said, "Good. What else?" Another teacher said, "He has a memory that's just great. And his language is so far ahead of the other kids; you must talk to him like an adult, not like a child."

I said, "Yeah, we do. I really appreciate you saying these things, because *that's how I want you to see my son.* If we're having behavior issues, as his parents we'll deal with those at home. But as his teachers, I want to make sure you're focusing on his strengths, gifts, and talents because when he's older, that's what I want him to express."

All three of them agreed to take that approach. The good news is we didn't have to return to the principal's office, and soon we had reports that Teagan was back to the fun, happy, loving, playful child he had been before.

If the focus is always on what needs to be "fixed," the child eventually hears "I'm not good enough."

In the outdated approach that most schools still use, a child is evaluated against an expected standard of accomplishment and behavior. Meeting that standard is taken for granted, and the focus is then on what needs to be "fixed," on the ways the child is not good enough. *Yet* "I'm not good enough" is the single most destructive message a child can receive, and parents and teachers alike must focus on delivering the opposite message, by continuously acknowledging a child's strengths, abilities, gifts, and talents.

THE "SELF" ENVIRONMENT: HERE'S WHERE YOU'RE GREAT!

The best way I've found to recognize and emphasize all the things Teagan does well is to acknowledge him for it in the moment, so it's more likely to stick. For example, when Teagan was playing with a friend I whispered to him, "You notice how Bella gets excited and happy when you're around? That's because you make people feel good." Part of what I'm doing is helping my son become aware of himself. This is what I call the "self" environment, which is made up of our personality, gifts, talents, and strengths. If my son recognizes his strengths and great qualities, he'll be able to use them and have a healthy self-image. If not, he'll grow up and be a mystery to himself and likely feel lost. So I'm helping him take stock of what's great about him as he grows.

We all have beliefs about ourselves and the world which become the filter through which we see and experience everything. Most people are limited by their own beliefs about themselves, and what they're capable of, so we've started doing affirmations. One of our favorites is "Teagan, you can do anything…," and he completes the sentence, "…I set my heart and mind to. Yeah!" or I'd go into his room when he was sleeping and say things like, "You're here to make a difference. You're a global leader. Mom and Dad love you no matter who you are or what path you choose." My whispers—whether he's awake or asleep—are building his belief that "anything is possible" and "the world is constantly supporting me."

THE PARENTAL ENVIRONMENT: HOMECOMINGS

As a kid, when I came home from school, my mother would often be asleep on the couch with a migraine. I'd have to go past her to get to my room, and if I was hungry I'd have to tiptoe into the kitchen. Because she had a migraine, she'd be upset if I woke her up, so I'd walk on eggshells every time I came in the door. I concluded—as kids do—that "Mom doesn't love me and I was a bother." This wasn't the case at all, but as I child that was my immediate conclusion from my homecoming reception.

I didn't want that for my son—in fact I wanted the opposite. I've added a glass window to my home office to make the room visibly open to my family, yet still give me some privacy. When my son gets home from school, I'm often on the phone or engaged with something. Because of my experience with my own mother, I realized that when Teagan gets home, he's going to be either excited to see Dad or fearful to see Dad, and it will all be based on how I respond to him. The message a child receives in that moment goes a long way towards letting him know whether he is important or not.

Always pause and celebrate their homecoming.

One day I caught myself closing the door when Teagan came into the house, and suddenly realized I'd done it before. I remembered Alex Mandossian telling me that when his kids show up and he's working, he'll pause the phone call and celebrate their homecoming. So now I do that. If I'm doing a radio interview or something, we'll at least put our faces and hands up to the glass, as if to say, "Hey, I'm excited to see you." If I'm teaching a telecourse, I'll bring him in and say, "Hey, everybody, Teagan's here, and I'm going to celebrate that!" and give him a hug and a kiss. From this experience, reinforced daily, my son *knows* he is more important than any phone call. I make sure that "coming home" is a supportive environment; I show him I'm excited to see him, and guess how he now responds? When he comes home he's excited to see Dad, too!

THE "DADDY" ENVIRONMENT: IMMERSION

If I could relive my first ninety days with Teagan, there is one thing I'd do differently. During that time Teagan did not have the same strong connection with me that he had with Michele. In particular, he didn't really respond to my voice. Then when he was just a few months old, I gave a keynote address for a local company. The setup had me on stage with big video screens on both sides. Michele took Teagan, and for the next two hours, Teagan sat hearing my voice and seeing me on the big screen. After that experience, he began responding to my voice in a different way.

I realized that for the nine months Michele was carrying him, her voice and vibration became a primary part of his environment. But until that day at the keynote, he'd never been immersed in me for very long at one time. If I were starting over as a dad, I'd make sure that, early on, my child had more immersion in me, and I would do this with a recording. I'm a big believer in putting things on CDs and playing them in the background. So I'd record the top ten beliefs I'd like my child to have in my own voice. Then I'd play the recording back while he or she sleeps, and see what happened. I think this would create a baby more connected to Dad—and Dad to baby.

THE POWER OF ENVIRONMENTS: CREATING WORLDS

We each create and design our own world, and as parents it goes without saying, we create our children's world and emotional experiences. Their whole reference for life is rooted in the worlds we expose them to or build for them. Most of their core beliefs/programming comes from their environments from birth to seven years old. We can create those worlds and environments either by design or by default. Most people, even very loving parents, do it by default which means they just pass on the same beliefs they were given about their health, wealth, and happiness.

If a person or a child's environment is not growing and evolving as he grows and evolves, he will be living in a state of drag—low energy, resistance, slow movement—rather than in a state of inspiration. One way or the other it will show up. When you overlook something, the way I did by missing the impact of the large house on Teagan, you can use the effect as *clues* to determine what part of the environment is interfering with your success. You talk things through directly, but then you must also change the environment.

Most of our core beliefs come from our environments from birth to seven.

As human begins, we are all directly affected by our environments, including our physical space, the people we spend time with, the books we read, and the thoughts we think. To most powerfully support my son,

I can help him craft everything in all his environments—both inner and outer—to support his development. As he gets older, I will teach him how to do this for himself. Intentionally crafting your environment is easier than trying to use willpower to gets things done, which can only take you so far. So my wish for my son is that he live in a world he creates by intentional design, not by default.

> *Intentionally crafting your environment is easier than using willpower.*

By teaching Teagan the power of environments, I'm passing forward a little-known secret to purposefully create happiness, health, and wealth. I'm setting him up to more easily achieve his life mission—and be the amazing human being he is, and was born to be.

To learn more about the nine environments to reach and sustain success, and other cool stuff Jim has to say, go to
www.ifiwereyourdaddy.com/jimbunch

"You are a product of your environment. So choose the environment that will best develop you toward your objective. Analyze your life in terms of its environment. Are the things around you helping you toward success—or are they holding you back?"

W. Clement Stone, a "rags to riches" businessman, philanthropist, and self-help author, who reportedly gave over $275 million to charity.

WHO IS JIM BUNCH?

Jim with (wife) Michele, and (child) Teagan

Jim Bunch is known as "The Ultimate Life Entrepreneur," with a mission to inspire happiness, health, and wealth worldwide.

Whether it's launching a new business venture or helping someone upgrade his or her life, there's a common thread in whatever Bunch does—and that's bringing out the best in the companies and people he works with, while personally maintaining an "Ultimate Life."

Bunch solid track record of success means he speaks from experience. In 1999, he was part of the team that built Bamboo.com, a virtual tour company that brought in more than $30 million in its first ten months and attracted more than a hundred thousand clients in its first year. Other clients include Century 21, Coldwell Banker, Frito-Lay, Pitney Bowes, Prudential, and Xerox.

Bunch is a member of the Transformational Leadership Council, with such leaders as Jack Canfield, John Gray, John Assaraf, and many others from the movie *The Secret*. He has more than eighteen years of professional speaking experience and has given more than a thousand presentations on personal and professional development.

Bunch founded The Ultimate Game, Inc., and created *The Ultimate Game of Life*, which combines seminars, coaching, and technology. He and his coaches have helped more than seven thousand people make major life and business changes. Bunch has been featured in numerous articles and radio and television programs.

When Bunch isn't out creating and inspiring change, you won't find him far from his wife and young son near their Del Mar, California, home.

www.jimbunch.com, www.theultimategameoflife.com

AN EARLY ADVANTAGE

If I Were Your Daddy ... I'd expose you to learning from the moment you were born, and make sure none of your natural abilities are hindered so you can develop to your greatest potential.

VISHEN LAKHIANI

Entrepreneur & Internet
Marketing Expert

By nature, I tend to question everything, including what I learned in school, my religion, my culture—everything. I've always loved digging up new information, doing research online, and looking for innovative new thinkers in different fields.

When I first learned I was going to be a dad, this same need, to discover the newest innovative strategies, kicked in. Education and learning are really important to me, and I wanted to know why some kids are super-smart in intellect, self-esteem, and confidence, while others are not. I also wanted to know what parents could do in the early stages that would give children the best advantage possible, to help them fulfill their own maximum potential later on.

CULTIVATING A LOVE OF LEARNING

I grew up in Malaysia. My mom was a teacher, and my dad was a successful entrepreneur and prolific reader, so I learned to love and value education from an early age. My dad was a self-taught man, and every corner of our house was full of books. When I was seven, my mom bought me the *Encyclopedia Britannica for Children*. This was around 1984— well before the age of the Internet. The encyclopedia was just gorgeous, and I read its thousands of pages the way other people read regular books. I even memorized it. I was just crazy about learning.

When I turned seven, I was very excited to finally go to school. In my class, there were about forty other boys just like me. At some point on the first day, the teacher needed a break between two lessons, so she told us to just sit at our desks and be quiet for ten minutes. This made no sense to me. Why would I have to do this? I was not learning anything by sitting quietly at a desk. So after a few minutes of trying my best to sit still, I got up and went to her and said, very politely, "Excuse me, Ma'am, what time is it?"

This woman yelled at me, "I SAID GET BACK TO YOUR DESK!"

I was not used to being spoken to this way, so this first-day event instantly made me dislike school. In life, if you walk up to anyone and politely ask, "Do you have the time?" he or she is not going to yell at you. So what right did this teacher have to yell at a seven-year-old? I realize now that she was trying to teach me discipline. But her Victorian era style of dealing with kids instead made me adamant to spend as little time in school as I could.

For the next six years I hated school, and I would actually manifest illness—fall sick with a fever that would last six days, so I would not have to go. The Malaysian school system is similar to the U.S. system. It's not that it's bad, but so often you get teachers who do not love children or teaching; to them it is just a job that provides a paycheck. While most teachers were using archaic and punitive modalities, there were a few amazing teachers who got us to think on our own, and drew us into discussions. Sadly, they were in the minority so I developed, and was left with, an enormous dislike for school.

Although I managed only a C average, I was still three or four grade levels ahead of my peers, because my parents had over a thousand books in our home, and reading is what I did for fun.

DISCOVERING A BETTER WAY

It goes without saying that when my son, Hayden, is old enough to be in school, we will place him in a more nurturing and stimulating environment than the ones I was sent to. But through all my years of schooling, I maintained a deep hunger and love for learning that got me through the tough schooling years. This love, which I learned at home, prepared me to be successful now. So when Hayden was born, I went online and began searching for everything I could find from researchers and experts on early infant education. I researched the best methods available to begin educating Hayden early, hoping to instill in him the same love for learning that I had. I believe that if you teach a child to truly love learning, no amount of bad teachers, or a broken education system, will ever hold that child back from truly being smart. This is what I set out to do—to teach Hayden to truly embrace the idea of learning.

I began searching for everything I could find on early infant education.

I read about researchers who were doing fascinating things with early infant education, even prior to birth, like putting headphones on the mother's abdomen and playing classical music. I found a book called *Kindergarten Is Too Late,* written by Masaru Ibuka, a Japanese researcher and co-founder of the Sony Company. Ibuka discussed the enormous amount of evidence indicating that infants are way smarter than we think they are. Most people believe babies should be strapped into a baby carrier or car seat, or just bundled up and held in someone's arms. Normally we do not start seriously teaching our kids until the age of three or four, when we ship them off to prekindergarten.

Today we know that this approach is exactly the *opposite* of what a child needs in order to learn. Babies are actually super-sponges when it comes to learning. Learning is biological, evolutionary, and connected to communication, which babies need and crave for survival. So you should expose a new baby to as much learning as possible, as early as possible.

Because babies don't learn to speak until a little later, people just assume the infant is not intelligent or ready to learn. The truth is that babies actually learn to understand and think long before they learn to vocalize. Human beings are born with genius abilities; the only reason we do not keep those abilities throughout our lives is because they are not cultivated at a young age. So as soon as Hayden was born, my wife and I immediately began implementing some of these ideas with him. We communicated with him, and treated him like a person who understood everything we said and did. I assumed he was super-intelligent and just temporarily lacked the ability to speak. So I spoke to him very respectfully, almost as if I were talking to an adult.

We lose our genius abilities when they're not cultivated.

DISCOVERING THE DOMAN ADVANTAGE

When Hayden was about a year old, I discovered the Doman Advantage books and took their related parenting course in Philadelphia, at the Institutes for the Achievement of Human Potential, run by Janet Doman, daughter of the founder. We loved the concepts, and quickly discovered that like all kids exposed to this program, our son just naturally loved learning. A lot of the institutes' strategies are based on using different sets of brightly colored reading cards, which babies just love.

An interesting fact we learned was that when a baby is first born, everything in the body is interconnected and develops simultaneously. For instance, a baby's ability to inhale oxygen is directly related to his or her ability to process information, to learn, and to develop neuron pathways in the brain. This creates a direct link between physical exercise and learning. So rather than leaving our son confined to a stroller all day, we did specific exercises with him to help develop his chest and lungs. This work at the very beginning of his life is going to accelerate everything he will be able to do. We also worked with his cognitive development by allowing him to keep moving all the time. Movement and exercise help develop a baby's neuron pathways, so as soon as Hayden was mobile, I gave him all the opportunity to run, jump, and climb. We would wrestle. We would do mock fighting—anything to get him moving and exercising. He is extremely fit for a child his age. When we go to the playground, he always comes back with bruises, but that's OK, because I do not believe in sheltering him.

All this physical exercise gives Hayden more confident use of his body. At the pool, we would teach him to dive underwater; at the playground, to pull himself up with his hands on a bar. He really loves the monkey bars, and whenever he sees a bar anywhere—in an elevator, for example—he will jump up and start swinging himself on it. While it is really cute to watch, I also know that what's going on is that Hayden is also developing confidence in reading, math, and physical exercise—all at the same time.

It is so important to do all this learning before age six.

The pathways in a baby's brain are pliable, fluid, and constantly developing. It is not until children reach six that these pathways start to lock in and become hard, almost like concrete. That is why it is so important to do all this learning *before* age six. After that it gets harder for the brain to learn and absorb information, although it will still retain everything it learned earlier.

TEACHING NUMBERS WITH DOT CARDS

We immediately began teaching Hayden to count using the dot cards, a method pioneered by Glenn Doman, who founded the Institutes for the Achievement of the Human Potential. For instance, for the number one, we hold up a dot card with one dot on it and say, "OK, this is one." Then we show him a card with two dots and say, "This is two," and three dots and say, "This is three." These cards show only the true quantities of the number, not the numeric symbols. The child is not shown the numerals "1," "2," or "3."

We go like this all the way up to one hundred. When adults look at a card with seventy-seven dots, there is no way they can perceive seventy-seven; they have to count them. But young babies can perceive the number instantaneously: they can look at a flash card with seventy-two dots and without having to count them one by one, instantly perceive the idea of seventy-two. It's amazing to see children who learn numbers this way do this! By being exposed to this method early, Hayden's brain will retain the ability to process numbers this way. Math will always be easy and fun for him. If we had waited, he would have lost this ability. Most kids run into issues with math at school because parents do not use this window of opportunity to expose their kids to such things. This is why Doman teaches using only the true quantities of numbers.

TEACHING READING WITH WORD CARDS

Normally, reading is taught with phonics and individual letters, but Doman teaches babies using the whole word. Over time their brains will deduce that *dog* is *d-o-g*. When they see *frog* their brain remembers that *o-g* is the *og* sound. Even though you have never taught them, they just get it. The human brain can learn all these things even before the vocal cords are fully developed or functioning. It is only later when we try to teach children phonics that it's hard for their brains to learn that way.

We worked with common, everyday words, and also with Hayden's favorite words. At one point his favorite word was *shoes,* so I would show him shoes, and then different shoes: "These are sandals" or "These are sneakers." He learned words like *hippopotamus* and *refrigerator* well before age three. We began by teaching him one word like *dog,* then added a word and showed him "little dog." Then we made it a sentence like "Little dog runs." After that, we made a simple little book using all these words and sentences that

By reading a book at age three, it increased his self-confidence and his interest in learning more words.

Hayden liked and had already learned, including *shoes,* and by age two he was able to read it all by himself. That was the only book he could read, but he got into the habit of understanding what it means to read a book, which only increased his self-confidence in reading, as well as his interest in learning more words.

I've met six-year old Doman-educated children who read Shakespeare, and a four-year-old who can do advanced mental math without a calculator. By the time they are seven, kids raised with this perspective are memorizing encyclopedias, not because they have been forced to, but because *they crave learning.* In fact a key idea behind this methodology of learning is the fact that learning *must* be joyful. The child must choose to learn; it is never forced on the child.

LEARNING MULTIPLE LANGUAGES

During this journey I have also learned the importance of teaching a young child multiple languages. When children are young it is very easy for them to learn many different languages, and they actually learn them with a different part of their brain than you or I would as an adult.

My son is not quite three, and he already speaks five different languages, which he is learning simultaneously. My wife and our nanny are both Estonian, so that is the language he hears the most. My mom speaks Hindi, so he is learning that. I speak to him in English, my mother-in-law speaks to him in Russian, and he is learning the local Malaysian language—that is five languages for a kid under three. Right now Hayden communicates primarily in Estonian, but recently, I told him a story in English, his second language. His English is a little limited: he knows maybe a thousand words, but he understood the entire story and at the end he was actually able to tell me the point of the story. I was completely surprised because it was fairly complicated, and I was using big words and complex sentence structures, yet he understood. It was very clear that Hayden's ability to absorb and process information is far superior to his ability to vocalize. I believe this is why parents and teachers have traditionally underestimated children and their ability to learn.

My son now has multiple vocabularies in five languages and he speaks to everyone around him— in all of them! I would never have guessed that a two-and-a-half-year-old child could simultaneously engage in conversations in five languages, as well as read and translate.

NURTURING NATURAL ABILITIES

If none of Hayden's natural abilities have been hindered by the time he is twelve, only then will I know that I have been a successful father. Sadly, most of the ways we currently "parent" hinder a child's natural abilities. Exposing children to a lot of television before the age of two can get in the way of a child's time to explore, play, and interact with parents and others. The first two years are considered a critical time for brain development, and with daily interaction and active play, a child is learning and developing healthy physical and social development. By waiting until children get to kindergarten before exposing them to learning, we hinder their abilities from developing as powerfully as they can. By not allowing toddlers to run around freely because we fear they will fall and injure themselves, we hinder them from developing their physical intelligence.

By waiting till kindergarten ... we hinder their abilities from developing as powerfully as they can.

The most important thing for me is to give Hayden the complete freedom to be Hayden. Part of being Hayden is being a crazy, wild kid who wants to learn everything. So I give him all the learning opportunities that are available. He has all his natural abilities fully nourished to become whatever he wants to become.

The one thing I noticed far more than Hayden's quickness in learning is the bond that has developed between the two of us. The way I nurture and support his learning capabilities is based on fun interaction, not on force or fear. Hayden loves learning, and the best thing is that he loves to learn with me. When I fully immerse myself into my child's learning path, when I fully dedicate my time to helping him develop his abilities and to nurture his mind, I feel that Hayden senses that and reciprocates by wanting to learn more, and to spend more time with me. Just as in my childhood, he's developing a love of learning that will be seeded among his earliest memories, a love that will not just see him through school, but through life. With a love of learning, it's likely even challenges will be seen as learning opportunities; life opens wide to all sorts of possibilities.

All of this is because a love of learning was nurtured and developed, and he was given an early advantage. And when he has grown, I will know I did my job as a parent. I will have shown him, even as a baby, how amazing the world of books and ideas are, how amazing it is to explore new things and have new adventures, and what an amazing—genius—creature he is. As a father, what greater gift could I give him than that?

To find out more about the Doman Advantage and Vishen's passion to teach his little boy and help parents worldwide nurture their child's genius, go to
www.ifiwereyourdaddy.com/vishenlakhiani

"As the proverb says, 'What one likes one will do well,' and there is no education method more effective than engaging a child's real interest and enthusiasm. For this, the parent's main role is in arousing that interest: instead of teaching the child how to count, the parent should interest him in numbers, and instead of teaching the writing of letters, interest him in writing itself. In other words, the parent's role is to prepare the child for education.

… As long as a good bud has been implanted in the child in the most critical early years, he will grow up to be a strong child capable of surmounting any trying circumstances."

Excerpts from *Kindergarten is Too Late,* by Mararu Ibuka, a book that claims that the most significant human learning occurs from ages nine months to three years. Mr. Ibuka was a Japanese electronics industrialist, who co-founded what is now Sony.

WHO IS VISHEN LAKHIANI?

Vishen with (wife) Carrie and (son) Hayden

As his web site says, Vishen Lakhiani is "intense, a little bit crazy, and really good at what he does." At the age of thirty three, he has built a multimillion-dollar company, created a remarkable place to work, and become a major speaker.

Lakhiani's company, MindValley, is a new kind of publishing company, one that merges software, mixed media, video, and social networks to put authors in the personal development movement directly in front of the Internet generation, bypassing traditional print media.

When Lakhiani began to interact with major personal development authors, their ideas began to shape his company. Over the last few years, MindValley became a testing ground for new, experimental ways of doing business. MindValley has won two consecutive World's Most Democratic Workplace Awards and has attracted employees from some twenty-one countries—employees whose growth and learning is a top priority. In the last year, MindValley saw a 500-percent revenue growth.

Lakhiani's quest is to redesign the global education system and heighten human consciousness by combining marketing and technology to help spread enlightened ideas. It's no wonder that he's a marketing and technology consultant to some of the world's top authors and thinkers in personal and business transformation.

As a highly successful online entrepreneur, Lakhiani has become one of the most sought-after speakers in the world of online business building. He has shared platforms with such speakers as Sir Richard Branson, the Dalai Lama, Jack Canfield, and South African president F. W. DeKlerk.

www.mindvalley.com

MONEY & RESPONSIBILITY

PREPARING A KID TO STAND ON HER OWN

If I Were Your Daddy ... the best thing I'd do for you is not to do it for you. You'd learn through watching and doing, not through lectures from me. I'd be your greatest cheerleader, help you to be a great loser, and show you life's secret to being happy.

*B*OB ROTELLA, Ph.D.

Olympic and Professional Sports Psychologist

It was the day that fathers of daughters both dream of and dread. My only child, Casey, had just gotten married. I'd walked her down the aisle and given her away to start a new life with her young husband. Now the reception was in full swing. As I began tapping my champagne glass, the music died down and the room grew silent. My plan was to give a memorable father-of-the-bride toast, congratulating the new couple and sending them off with heartfelt best wishes. I stood up, but when I opened my mouth to speak ... nothing came out. It was pretty amazing really. There I was, a noted professional speaker, and I just broke down. In front of all my friends and family, including all the guys who would roast me about it later, I couldn't utter one intelligible sentence. I looked hopelessly and apologetically toward my daughter and wife, and then just sat down.

After twenty-four years of being my little girl, Casey was leaving. Part of my choked-up speechlessness was joy and thrill, and part of it was missing her already. She was a college graduate and now a wife, with dreams of becoming a mother and teacher. Our daughter was leaving home, just as nature had perfectly designed.

When Casey was born I called my mother for some advice. She and my father had raised five kids, and three of us have a Ph.D., so with that success I figured she'd have some tips to share about how, exactly, they had done that.

"All of us turned out happy," I said. "I'd like your thoughts on parenting." To my amazement, my mother said, "I had absolutely no idea what I was doing. I wake up every day and just can't believe you all turned out OK."

"Mom," I said, "I'd like something a little more detailed."

"I'm telling you. I had no idea what I was doing," she replied.

Mom may not have known how she did it, but she and Dad still did it. And I don't believe we all turned out well just by chance. As in sports, luck favors the prepared, and for this I give my mom and dad a lot of credit. They gave us rock-solid fundamentals.

In much the same way, my wife, Darlene, and I figured we had eighteen years to prepare our daughter and get across the fundamentals—what we valued, what we believed in, what was important. The rest was up to her.

TEACH VALUES SO KIDS HEAR AND ADOPT THEM

Like my dad, we put education at the top of our list of values. So we *filled Casey's environment* with reading and exploration. Many days while still in her crib, she had so many books she'd fall asleep on a pile of them. We made learning fun. We read together daily, she saw us reading—we made it important. Darlene was a second grade teacher with a master's in reading, so she spent a lot of time with Casey on reading and schoolwork. It paid off because our daughter excelled in school, and it all began when she was a baby.

Darlene and I also wanted to prepare Casey early on to deal with the peer pressure that happens in school. Year after year it seems to get worse in the schools; the drugs and sex are just out of control. Today there are so many more temptations, and so there is much more pressure to conform, that if children can't stand on their own and decide what they value, if they allow other people to control them, they are at risk. A lot of kids just aren't armed to do that because their parents don't know how to equip them. Our solution was to help Casey think for herself rather than tell her what to think.

Help kids think for themselves rather than telling them what to think.

In addition to books, we filled our daughter's environment with supportive influences. We surrounded her with people who were independent thinkers and exposed her to rich experiences so that when she was faced with peer pressure at school she'd be strong enough to make her own decisions. One such place was the infamous "Rotella basement." Throughout Casey's childhood we always had professional athletes, musicians, singers, and business people at the house. From an early age she would bring her toys down and play in the corner, seemingly not listening yet clearly listening, because later she would say or do something that confirmed that she'd absorbed it all. Most people concern themselves with who their kids are hanging out with, and rightfully so. But we also considered the quality of *our* friends, acquaintances, and houseguests. Just as practicing with better players raises your sports game, we surrounded our daughter with people who were striving to be better, who were passionate and excellent at their craft and actively giving to others.

Exposing Casey to people like this instilled in her the values we wanted for her far more effectively than our lecturing her. As I told Casey many times, "Friends will have a big impact on what you're like, how you live, how you behave, and how you treat people, so pay attention to who you hang around with and listen to." Darlene and I also paid attention and chose accordingly.

When kids are told what to do, what to believe, and how to live, at some point they strike out for independence. But when kids *observe* certain principles or wisdom in action, they get to choose for themselves and

*W*hen kids are told, they resist. When kids observe, they get to choose and there's no friction.

there's almost no resistance. I never sat Casey down and said, "Now I'm going to talk to you about attitude." And I don't think she's ever read one of my books on sports psychology. But as she got older and started playing sports, when we played golf with two of her friends, they would ask me questions nonstop, and she would always be listening. Also, I purposely took her along when I worked with an athlete so she could learn by listening and watching. As a dad I found it worked much better to teach Casey indirectly, letting her observe me and others, listening and drawing conclusions for herself.

BE YOUR CHILD'S BIGGEST CHEERLEADER

After coaching a lot of high-level athletes, my biggest "aha" with my daughter was learning how to relate to her as her father, and not as a coach. With my athletes, part of my job is critiquing, lecturing, and directing them. But this approach didn't work with Casey, so instead I became her biggest cheerleader. I always get asked by parents of athletes, fathers in particular, "What can I do to support my kids so they win?" My advice is always the same: "Be their greatest cheerleader." We tend to think of cheerleaders as being upbeat and positive. Well, that's exactly what's required. I would go even further and advise parent cheerleaders to never say anything critical. Although this might be an overgeneralization, my experience is that children, including my daughter, never hear constructive criticism as constructive. Casey generally took it way too personally, and your kids will likely do the same.

I discovered this one day on the practice green when I made some comment about her swing and immediately regretted it. I could tell by her wounded expression that she interpreted it as me saying something about her as a human being, and she was crushed. She likely heard, "I'm disappointed in you; you're not good enough," though of course I didn't mean that at all. As a coach, when I critique players, they know I'm critiquing their *skills*. But if Dad or Mom critiques a child, there's much more emotion there, and the child takes it as if you're saying something about him or her personally, like a knife to the heart.

It worked much better when I noticed Casey doing the right stuff and acknowledged, rewarded, and encouraged that. That afternoon on the practice green I decided that, going forward, it would be best to let the school golf coach critique her game and I'd stick to being her cheerleader. Keeping my close relationship with her intact was more important than building a sports star. Though she did become one of those too.

Every champion and every kid needs someone who can see his or her potential, *especially* when it's most hidden. Mine came from my Aunt Josephine. When I was young, every time I went to her house she'd always say, "Oh, Bobby, you walk just like an athlete." Nothing she might have said could have meant more to me than that. She saw something in me that was just beginning to grow—something I wanted and she encouraged. She was my cheerleader.

Every kid needs someone who can see his or her potential, especially when it's most hidden.

FIND SOMETHING IN COMMON AND SPEND LOTS OF TIME TOGETHER

When Casey was still a little girl people often said to me, "Well, I suppose you want your daughter to be a professional golfer," and I'd say, "Not really. It's not about what I want; it's about what she wants. My dreams are for her to be happy and have a good life." I never played a role in getting her to start anything, including golf, and I'm glad no one did that with me. I don't think you can make somebody want something, and if you try it will probably backfire at some point.

The only thing I required is that once Casey joined a team she had to finish the season, and this speaks to keeping your commitments, another value we uphold. In high school she was undefeated in tennis, and then at the end of the year she came home and announced, "I'm going to quit tennis and take up golf." If I had told her to choose golf as her sport, she probably wouldn't have done it.

Having said that, if your kid happens to love something you love, it gives you a huge opportunity to be together. And if they don't, I recommend finding something you both like doing, and then do it together . . . a lot! I've heard that the Reverend Jesse Jackson once said, "Your children need your presence more than your presents," and I wholeheartedly agree. From the day she took up golf, any day that I was home when she got out of school and during the summer we'd go to the practice area or the short-game area and play until dark. We spent *millions* of hours there. Everyone thought I was working on her swing. But here's the truth: early on I learned to let someone else teach her golf swings, so half the time I was teeing up balls for her and the other half I was just being with my kid.

Finding something you both like doing, and then do it together ... a lot!

Spending time with her gave her the chance to tell me about some situation that happened in school that day, or how somebody treated her in a way that broke her heart, or about someone cheating and getting away with it and affecting curfew. More than anything else, I *listened.* (And if you knew the size of my mouth, you'd know this wasn't so easy!) Yes, I was happy she excelled at golf and I wanted her to do well, but I was happier that we could just hang out together. I learned who she was and what mattered to her, and that was what it was about for me. I didn't have a hidden agenda. I didn't need to improve or guide her. I was just being there with her.

Going into her teen years, my way of being around her kept her communicating. While other teens may clam up with their parents, or wrestle with issues alone, or figure it out (badly) with their peers, Casey felt comfortable talking to me. I tried not to offer feedback unless she specifically asked, asking questions instead, to help her sort things out on her own. I let her talk if she wanted to, and didn't press

I didn't need to improve or guide her. I was just being there with her.

her if she chose not to. If I'd lectured her rather than listened, I'd have lost her in about three minutes.

TEACH KIDS HOW TO BE GREAT LOSERS!

I definitely had mind-sets I wanted to pass along that are fundamental to success. One is a great attitude about losing. Although this sounds counterintuitive, learning how to lose is absolutely essential to winning. Casey often won championships in both tennis and golf, not to mention a golf scholarship to the University of Notre Dame. But she wasn't attached to outcomes; she didn't define herself by whether she won or lost. As a result, she wasn't afraid to mess up. When she played well in a tournament, whether she came in third or thirtieth, I always acknowledged her afterward for all the parts of her game and attitude where she did well, for being in a good mood and happy, for trying hard and giving it her best. I'd say, "Sometimes you give it your best and you come in thirtieth, and sometimes you give it your best and you win. You did your best, so you have nothing to regret."

Casey sat in on a lot of talks I gave over the years, and the line she always loved most was, "Don't take life too seriously. None of us are getting out of here alive anyway." That's pretty much how she's approached sports and life. If she had a poor performance, it took her five minutes at most to let it all go. She adopted what I call a "winning losing strategy" and it served her well. Casey connected her self-worth to *the effort* rather than the results. Once athletes climb the ladder of success and the competition starts to get better, they need a philosophy that works across the board. If you have a philosophy that works only when you win, you're probably going to get destroyed. The same is true for life. I tell my athletes that

If you have a philosophy that works only when you win, you're probably going to get destroyed!

if they connect their self-esteem to results rather than effort, sooner or later they'll wind up hedging themselves, afraid to even try. The competition just gets better as they do. So one of my beliefs is don't get seduced by results, but lose yourself completely in the process *and just accept the results*. Once again, I didn't lecture Casey on this directly; she was just surrounded by it. I believed it and lived it, I taught it to others, and I acknowledged her efforts. That's how I presented that mindset. And she definitely picked it up.

THE SECRET INGREDIENT TO HAPPINESS

Darlene and I deeply believe you need to treat others with respect regardless of how they treat you, and regardless of the consequences. We also know very well this can be a tough standard for kids to meet. In today's schools, if you're nice to everybody it often makes you decidedly *not* cool. Regardless, we let our daughter know we expected her to treat everyone equally well. I'd say, "I don't care if the kid's cool or smart, or not cool or not smart, we want you to treat people with respect, the way you'd like to be treated, because that's a value we hold about how we live our lives." And while saying this is important, experiencing it is another—and far more profound. So we looked for ways to have her experience it.

I spent about seven years working with handicapped kids; Darlene taught special education kids and I worked a lot with Special Olympics. I saw amazing acts of persistence, strength, and courage from the athletes that left me inspired on such a profound level. With this kind of reference, I easily delivered the message to Casey that others deserved our value and respect no matter what their talent or skill level. And she got it.

The longer I live and work, I'm absolutely convinced that a big part of happiness in life is helping others. In a world filled with self-absorbed people, being compassionate ensures your personal happiness. If I spent all my time thinking about me—my accomplishments, my achievements—I'd be mighty miserable. But when I spend at least part of my time doing for others and thinking of others, it's easy to be happy. It's fundamental to one's success, and we prepared Casey by showing her just how happy you can be when you give.

HELP THEM GROW AND LET THEM GO

I've spent the better part of my life preparing athletes for game day and teaching the fundamentals. As a coach, I've also learned that when you get out in the sports field on game day, you've got to just let go. If it's true for athletes, it's even more so for children. Kids don't become self-reliant if you're always doing things for them or bailing them out. Some of my friends complain about still financially supporting their adult children, saying, "I don't know when it will end!" But they continue to do it. My take is the opposite. I wouldn't step in and help her financially now that she's out of school, even though I could, and unless it was a dire emergency, my daughter wouldn't ask either. I'm sure glad no one helped me. Both she and her husband have great educations—Notre Dame educations! So if there's something they want, I trust they'll figure out how to get it.

I told my friends, "When they first got married they were living in a crummy basement apartment in a lousy neighborhood—kind of like

> *Kids* don't become self-reliant if you're always doing things for them or bailing them out.

the one her mother and I started out in, and like my mother and father started out in. It's up to them to figure out how to get a nicer place. It's up to them to make of their life what they want. The best thing I can do for them is *not* do it for them." We were following in my parents' footsteps. They didn't call and lecture me as a young adult nor did they bail me out of financial responsibilities. My foundation was already laid and they trusted it. And now it was my turn.

As Casey's wedding reception drew to a close, I reflected on the journey of raising my daughter behind us, and the new phase of life now unfolding before us. Darlene and I had accomplished what we set out to do—we raised a self-reliant and happy person.

Casey has definitely developed her own mind and values—heck, she's even stronger willed than me! She is off living her life, involved with her husband and making her own way in the world. My wife and I kid around from time to time, saying, "Maybe we should've brought her up to be totally *dependent* so she can just move in next door." We don't mean it, but still we laugh about it.

And then Casey found out she was pregnant. And the phone started ringing again.

"I don't believe in team motivation. I believe in getting a team prepared so it knows it will have the necessary confidence when it steps on a field and be prepared to play a good game."

Tom Landry, legendary American football player and coach, holder of the NFL record for longest winning streak, twenty consecutive winning seasons, including two Super Bowl titles.

WHO IS ROB ROTELLA, Ph.D.?

Bob with (wife) Darlene, (daughter) Casey

Dr. Bob Rotella knows sports—and he knows psychology. That combination has made him the world's best-known sports psychologist, and the author of the best-selling sports psychology book of all time, *Golf Is Not a Game of Perfect*—which also ranks as one of the three all-time best-selling books on golf.

Selected as one of the "Top 10 Golf Teachers of the 20th Century," Rotella has directed the prestigious University of Virginia program in sports psychology and has served as "mental coach" to the New York Yankees, San Francisco Forty-Niners, New Jersey Nets, Texas Rangers, and the U.S. Olympic ski and equestrian teams. His golfers on the PGA Tour have consistently been winners, including British Open Champion Padraig Harrington and Trevor Immelman, the 2008 Masters Champion.

Rotella is a columnist and editorial board member for *Golf Digest* magazine and contributing editor of the *Sports Psychology Journal*. His other books include *Golf Is a Game of Confidence, The Golf of Your Dreams, Life Is Not a Perfect Game, Putting out of Your Mind, The Golfer's Mind, Parenting Your Superstar,* and his latest, *Your 15th Club: The Inner Secret to Great Golf.* Rotella has served as president of the North American Association for Applied Sports Psychology.

The demand for Rotella's expertise has extended into the corporate world, where he has consulted with Merrill Lynch, General Electric, Ford, Time-Life, Coca-Cola, Chrysler, Newsweek, Pepsi-Cola, Taco Bell, and Pizza Hut.

Rotella and his wife, Darlene, have a daughter and two grandchildren.

www.practicelikeapro.com/Dr._Bob_Rotella.php

IT'S ALL ABOUT "EARNERSHIP"

If I Were Your Daddy ... anything in life that is of value, you'd have to earn. But you wouldn't be alone; I'd help you to uncover your gifts, your blind spots, and your divine agenda in life's great laboratory.

SHORE SLOCUM, Ph.D.

Professional Speaker & Educator

"I really want to go!" my nine-year-old son, Josua, pleaded. "Dillon said it was a great camp and really cool, and I would love it!" Dillon was a friend of ours in the industry, and he had told Jos about this acting camp in Los Angeles that the kids all go to during the season when networks like Nickelodeon and The Disney Channel are making pilots. My wife, Loren, and I knew Jos had a gift for acting, both drama and comedy, and he loved taking lessons, attending camps, and being in local productions.

Caught a bit off guard, I said, "That's really great, Jos, but we live in Henderson, Nevada, and that camp is in Los Angeles, California. Mommy or Daddy would have to go with you and figure out how to live there for a month, and it would cost a lot of money. Then there's your school to consider. It would be complicated, but let's look at it." I wasn't exactly dismissive, but I didn't jump all over his idea either. Maybe this was a passing interest that would fade with time.

A couple of months later Jos brought up the subject again. "I really want to go," he reminded us. Finally, Jos came into my home office one day and said, "Dad, that camp is starting in forty-five days." Digging into his pocket, he pulled out a wad of dollars and coins and put something like $217 on my desk. "This is all the money from my piggy bank, and I'll take all the money from my savings to pay for it because I know it's expensive. But I really want to do this."

As I studied Jos's earnest expression, my eyes filled with tears of pride and joy. If my baby boy wanted something badly enough that he was willing to do whatever it took to get there, how could I stand in his way?

"Okay, Jos," I said, "let's get your mom in here and we'll figure it out."

So we figured it out. I would stay home with our younger son, Quinn, while Loren went to L.A. with Jos.

The program was hard, but Jos loved it and thrived. Every afternoon the kids do acting or voice lessons, go on set, meet directors, and learn the industry. But just like working child actors, they have to do their regular schoolwork, studying on their own for four hours a day. Jos's days began at 7:00 a.m. and usually finished at 9:00 or 10:00 p.m. By the end of the month he was doing so well that he wanted to stay another month. Loren and I decided, "This is his deal. We've *got* to support him." After that we alternated weeks living in L.A. with him.

One night, about two weeks into the second month, Jos became overwhelmed. "I can't finish my homework," he said in despair. "I can't get ready for tomorrow. I need a night off." Loren was with him, and said, "Jos, you've given it your all. You've done everything you can. It's okay, sweetie. I love you." Then she gave him a hug, picked up the phone, and called the airline to book tickets home.

"Mom, what are you doing?" Jos cried. Excusing herself from the agent, Loren said, "We're done. You've done everything you could and we're going home now. I'm so proud of you," and returned to the agent. Not expecting this response, Jos quickly grabbed the phone, told the agent to cancel the booking, and hung up. "Mom," he explained, "I'm not done yet." Exhausted or not, he wasn't ready to let go of his dream.

Loren's response that late evening was nothing shy of inspired parenting.

It sent the message that being at the camp was a privilege based completely upon his efforts, even when it was challenging.

Jos persevered, did a stellar job completing the program, and even got straight A's in all his schoolwork. The final camp event was to create headshots and resumes, send them out, and find an agent. With a clear vision of what he wanted, Jos directed the photographer down to every detail of the photo shoot, and his mom and I kept our opinions to ourselves. Most campers are thrilled to get one or two invitations from agents; five would be a huge home run. Jos received twenty-three! It was at this time that I coined the word "earnership," because I saw, so clearly, how important it is.

EARNERSHIP: THE MAGIC THAT REVEALS PURPOSE

Earnership expresses the idea that anything of value we get in life we have to earn in some way. It's a universal principle that holds true in the spiritual as well as the physical dimension. You don't just get things; you have to earn them, and it's in the effort and the challenge where the most light and gifts are revealed. Loren and I maintain this approach in parenting. We're willing to be the support staff only as long as the child takes the lead and provides the manpower, and they know this. The price of privilege is responsibility.

We're the support staff only as long as they are the locomotive. The price of privilege is responsiblility.

While at acting camp, and later on TV show sets, Loren and I watched as many parents pushed their kids, and man, these kids were miserable. They didn't want to be there; they were there for their parents. In contrast, when the drive comes from the child himself—as it did with Jos—it works out. This is the value of earnership, and it's inexstricably linked to finding and honing your purpose. The children discover for themselves what they can do and how far they can go. Limits get pushed and confidence blossoms, and as with Josua, it's pure magic to see.

It's been said that the man who is handed the world on a silver platter is going to let it tarnish. It's a natural tendency to want to give your kids the world—every advantage, every boost—and Loren and I are blessed that we can. But we *don't*, because earnership is the value.

The man who is handed the world on a silver platter is going to let it tarnish.

One night we were getting ready for dinner, and my youngest son said, "You're the coolest dad ever!" Touched, I replied, "That's really great, Quinn. Thank you for that," and then gave him a big hug. "But your dad's not always going to do stuff that you like," I warned.

"I know," Quinn said. "Sometimes you have to be tough and stuff."

"That's true," I agreed, "because first of all my job is to be your daddy and then I can be your friend."

This is an important distinction. A lot of parents want to be their kids' best friend, and then they forget to parent. They get so caught up wanting to be liked by their kids, wanting their approval, that they don't set guidelines for them, they don't help them understand consequences, and they don't help them earn it on their own, even when it's hard.

Although it's a popular tradition, we don't give our kids an allowance either. They have to earn their money. Our children have chores because they are part of our family. They can then earn money by doing additional chores. For instance, weeding the garden is worth twenty dollars. I shuttle my sons across town to mow lawns. Sometimes it feels like it would be more efficient to just give the boy sixty dollars, but then he wouldn't learn earnership and the value of money. Part of the way Quinn makes extra money is by cleaning dog poop out of three neighbors' yards. Most kids probably wouldn't want to do that, but he wants the money, so he's earning it. It's a powerful lesson, and a lot of this kind of thing gets thrown away when you want to be your kids' friend and forget to be their parent first. I hope I'm my kids' friend, but it's my job to be their parent, to help them uncover their gifts and figure out why they're here.

HELPING KIDS UNCOVER THEIR GIFTS

Everyone has unique skills and talents to share, a *divine agenda*. The big question is what that agenda is. It can be a lifelong treasure hunt of sorts, and as parents, we get to facilitate it. While it can be exhausting, I know my first job is to pay attention to what draws my kids, what lights them up.

Each of our three kids is totally different. Our younger son, Quinn's, gifts are still being uncovered, so we're creating a wide berth for him to identify them by getting him involved with as many things as he shows an interest in. We noticed, for example, that when his math homework is done he wants to do extra stuff, so we buy math books and we put a math program on his computer that he enjoys working on. I don't know what this might lead to, but we're paying attention. When see your kid get lit up by something, that's a big thing. It's a sign.

Watching a child explore his interests can sometimes be tough; you're tempted to wave a "warning" and "danger ahead" flag. Although I've got thirty more years experience than my son, I'm continually asking myself, do I really know what best *for him?*

When Josua was exploring acting as a profession, I could have quoted statistics about the number of unemployed actors and said, "You can't make money in acting, so I'm protecting you. You need to pick something sensible." But this invalidates the child's inner direction and truth, and then what's he left with? Confusion, self-doubt, frustration, resentment, or even depression. Being pulled away from your calling, what you came to this world to do, can't be a good thing! Sadly, people do this to their kids all the time, but at what cost? Instead, Loren and I honored what was emerging in Jos, no matter how impractical it may have seemed at the time. We let go of our agenda in favor of his.

THE SOUL'S CORRECTION

I consider life a great laboratory. Not only are we discovering and ideally living our passions and purposes, but we're also here to learn, to make corrections. Each person comes with specific issues to address, a blind spot that Soul needs to work on, a task equally as important as living one's purpose. And it's interesting how, when you do start living your purpose, you're usually in the perfect situation to deal with the issue that needs attention.

For example, the part of my nature that I push up against is an inclination to retreat to a mountain cave and meditate in silence. But my gift of communication and working with people is my purpose, and it requires that I be fully involved in the world. So my Soul's correction is my daily walk, and I do it to stay proactive and take action.

Usually the hard thing to do is the right thing to do.

Facing corrections usually goes against your nature. There's a great line in the movie *The Weatherman* that captures this: *"Listen, son, you've got a decision to make and it's a hard one. Usually the hard thing to do is the right thing to do."* This idea truly expresses what I want to get across to my kids. When we face making our correction, usually the thing that seems the hardest will reveal the greatest reward. The hard thing to do is the right thing to do.

Overcoming my monk tendency is revealing the most good in my life, and that's the second part of parenting: to help our kids uncover their challenges without doing it for them. Each of my kids has a unique challenge that is different from mine or Loren's. If you're watching, you start to see the patterns, but it's still theirs to fix.

Quinn, for instance, will start doing his homework seven or eight days before it's due, and if he's not done a few days before that date he freaks out. So learning how to balance responsibility with carefree curiosity might be one of Quinn's corrections. We just tell him, "It's okay, Quinn. Go play on your skateboard or go ride your bike. You're doing great. Don't let the weight of the world be on you."

With Jos it's the opposite: the weight of the world *was* on him because he always put things off until the last minute. He lives in the moment a lot and is not a big planner. He'd pay no attention to his homework until the morning it was due. His biggest challenge was to learn how to discipline himself and plan ahead.

Helping your children identify their correction is a first step, but at some point they have to feel the discomfort and pain it causes so they have motivation to change. This is the meat of earnership: taking full responsibility for yourself, including both the triumphant and the less triumphant parts. It's not easy to stand back and watch a kid fall. Like most parents, I admit that my gut instinct is to protect and save my kids from pain. But at a certain age pain can be a great and necessary teacher, as long as children know they have a safe place to come back to.

EARNERSHIP IN THE CORRECTIONS DEPARTMENT

Because Jos needed to feel the consequences of leaving things until the last minute, it was definitely time to let him feel the pain of his less than ideal choices. It was difficult for us to let him trip and fall in school, and maybe get an F on a homework assignment. Like most parents we want our kids to get straight A's, so for many years *our* desire justified our incessantly reminding (nagging) him to do his homework. When the next school year came, we saw the same pattern starting to repeat with three book reports he had to write. So Loren and I decided to let him go through the process and figure it out for himself.

Predictably, he didn't do so well on that first report and it rocked his world. When he was in that moment, upset and uncomfortable with his results, he asked us for help. The key here is that Jos had to see the results of his choices, then seek a solution *himself,* or else it would never be his own. Imposing our sense of necessity and order would have defeated the whole purpose.

"If you want help Jos, just ask." Then I walked away. Soon after, he found me: "I want help, Dad." I said, "Can you imagine being organized so you don't miss due dates and you get your work done on time?" He liked the idea, so off we headed to the office supply store, where we bought calendars and planners and files. I let him design the solution, and I supported him by asking questions and offering suggestions.

Where his mother and I did help, however, was in helping him to stay on the new system. In the beginning it was a struggle, because it was against his nature to put things away, track assignments, and start things early. Every day we monitored it asking, "Did you put your homework in the files? Did you check your calendar? Did you... ?" Typically, it takes about forty-five to sixty days for a person to make a new behavior a habit, and indeed it took Jos two months for the system to become ingrained. But once it did, we didn't have to monitor it anymore.

> *It* takes about forty-five to sixty days for a person to make a new behavior a habit.

What a relief! By letting Jos feel the pain of the fall and take responsibility, we replaced years of ineffective nagging with something better—self-motivation. He became accountable to himself. He found his own solutions. And he got straight A's that last quarter. He was on fire!

When our kids overcome that tough thing, the thing that goes against their nature, we really celebrate it! Celebrating wins are huge for a child's esteem and self-evaluation.

One morning, Josua said, "Dad, I think I'm going to do my system for the summer. I've got a lot of activities planned, and I don't want to miss anything. Do you think we could pick up more supplies?" "You're a brilliant kid!" I said, and gave him a great big bear hug.

THE EARNERSHIP PART OF PARENTING

Parenting is the hardest job I've ever had—it's all the time, there's no break—but it's the job I love the most. We have married friends who decided to never have kids, and we think, "You don't know what you're missing." They see the late nights, the dirty diapers, the loss of freedom. What they don't see is all the great stuff that goes along with having children.

When my baby girl smiles—she's got those two bottom teeth coming in and one fang on the top—it's a big goofy grin that makes me melt. It's those moments, bringing all three of my kids into the world, that humble me. That's when I say, "Thank you, God. I know you're entrusting me to lead these Souls where they're supposed to go."

Parenting is about the magical moments and the challenging moments, holding kids close and letting them go. They are your children, but they're not "your" children. They've got a destiny and a Soul purpose of their own. They need your love and support, but not so much your direction. They're going to jump and fall. Very few people accomplish what they set out to achieve on the first try, and those who do rarely appreciate it.

Earnership and helping your kids live true to their calling = a happy life!

I say keep that box of Band-Aids near, but let your children go, let them earn it. It's the priceless prize of life and the noblest gift of parenting. Earnership and helping your kids live true to their calling leads them to fulfilling their Soul purpose and, best of all, having a happy and successful life.

"What can you give your children to enhance the probability that they will become economically productive adults? In addition to an education, create an environment that honors independent thoughts and deeds, cherishes individual achievements, and rewards responsibility and leadership. Yes, the best things in life are often free. Teach your own to live on their own. It's much less costly financially, and, in the long run, it is in the best interest of both the children and their parents."

From *The Millionaire Next Door: The Surprising Secrets of America's Wealthy,* by Thomas J. Stanley, Ph.D., and William D. Danko, Ph.D.

WHO IS SHORE SLOCUM, Ph.D.?

Shore with (wife) Loren, (children) Joshua, Quinn, and Asher

Dr. Shore Slocum is on fire. His early loss of both father and stepfather ignited a passion in him to learn more about the human body and the healing process. Since 1990, he has turned that knowledge into a highly successful speaking and consulting career, serving elite and *Fortune* 500 companies ranging from Quaker Oats to Southwest Airlines.

Drawing on his experience as a businessman, author, successful entrepreneur, and father, Shore combines compelling and humorous stories with engaging exercises and success principles—allowing him to connect with virtually any audience. Slocum's unique Speaker's Bootcamp trains corporate and community leaders to find their authentic voices and speak with greater impact and motivation.

Slocum earned his bachelor's and master's degrees in religious and spiritual studies, and in early 2007, he was awarded his doctorate in holistic theology.

Slocum has seen amazing things happen when people take responsibility and action toward their own well being. His strong belief and enthusiasm for what he calls "integrative synergy" are powerful and infectious. In 2010, Shore has been creating his most compelling venture to date: a worldwide movement to help "wake up the world" by taking the world's best wisdom, wrapping it in entertainment, and supporting it with a community that has a purpose. It is virtually based, and the site is called "Soul Needs."

Of all his roles, Slocum is proudest of his roles as husband and father. His wife of fourteen years, Loren, is a successful writer, speaker, and seminar leader in her own right. They have three children: Josua, Quinn, and Asher.

www.soulneeds.com, www.shorespeaks.com

DEVELOPING WINGS

If I Were Your Daddy ... I'd lead by example, nudge you out of your comfort zone, and refrain from jumping in to do what you can do for yourself.

NICK NERANGIS

Real Estate Developer & Franchise Owner

My parenting style first emerged one Friday evening when my four-year-old son, Steven, tears rolling down his cheeks, brought me his tricycle with a loose seat wobbling like a rag doll. "Daddy, fix it. It's broken," he sobbed.

A few years earlier I had left the Navy because I wanted to see my family grow up; I didn't want to be out at sea all the time. Now here I was, exhausted, having clocked seven eighteen-hour days in a row in my newly opened franchise restaurants. But at least I was home. In my fatigue, I was tempted to grab the trike and quickly dispatch the repair myself. I somehow found the good sense to come up with a different approach. Scanning the bike, I said, "That little bolt under the seat is loose and needs to be tightened. Wait here, I'll get you a wrench." Handing my son the tool, I sat back and relaxed. After staring at me for a moment, Steven turned his attention toward the trike. Concentrating with all his might, he wrestled with the seat with his little fingers and managed to tighten the nut a bit. That done, he triumphantly wheeled the trike back over to me. His wide grin and sparkling eyes told me he'd done it—he'd fixed his bike all by himself! Only after he went to bed did I quietly follow up on his repair for safety's sake. I felt he slept more peacefully that night, resting as an able and masterful captain of a great feat for a four-year-old.

I remember that rush of accomplishment well, though as a child I was prevented from knowing it very often. Growing up in Poughkeepsie, New York, I wasn't allowed to play football, baseball, or basketball because "someone might smash into you." No scouting or vacationing with friends was allowed either, because both involved overnight trips, similarly perceived as perilous. My father was a Greek immigrant, who over the course of four decades worked his way up from being a busboy to vice president of Metropolitan Life Insurance Company. He had gumption and a strong work ethic, both admirable qualities, but he was also the stereotypical European immigrant head of the household. Things ran his way, with no discussion or leeway. Dad's way was an overprotective one that confined much of my childhood. His response to almost everything I wanted to do was, "It's too risky. You might get hurt."

When I *was* allowed to pursue something, or I snuck away to assert some independence, I threw myself into the task and loved the exhilaration of successfully doing a task well. After living for so many years restricted and unchallenged because of my father, I made a conscious and deliberate choice to be a different kind of parent. When I became a dad, I pushed my three children ever so gently past their comfort zones, challenging them, one situation at a time, to think and do for themselves.

> *I* wanted more than anything for my children to astonish themselves.

As they got older, I sought and considered their opinions, contributed my thoughts, and then dropped the responsibility squarely in *their* laps. I sent them out of the home, out of our family business, and out of the local community to find their strengths and self-respect away from their father's spheres of influence. It's simply astonishing what young people can do when they must, and I wanted more than anything for my children to astonish themselves.

Now, this wasn't some abrupt push for which they were unprepared. Their mother and I had been nudging them toward age-appropriate autonomy all along and they always managed just fine. What started with a trike grew into intentional family practices that helped our children develop solid thinking and communicating skills. When it came time to stand on their own, they were ready.

DISCUSS AND CONQUER

As a family, we had weekly family meetings that created a base for great communication. My wife and I encouraged our children to weigh in on decisions. Most were simple day-to-day choices (what to have for dinner, where to go on vacation, and so on), but some were more complex. The children sat at the table, skinny legs dangling from chairs, feet not reaching the floor and considered the questions. They listened to their siblings' and parents' views, voiced their opinions, and felt heard and respected. They were learning self-confidence and how to solve problems.

Through weekly family meetings, they practiced listening, persuading, and negotiating, all key business skills.

They were practicing listening, persuading, and negotiating, all key business skills. They were participating in a democracy in which everyone had a vote and consensus ruled. Having been part of the decision-making process, they then voluntarily assumed responsibility for whatever followed rather than just being told what to do.

AND THEN CAME THE DOG

We were living in the country at the time. One day all of us were on the front lawn when a beater of a car rolled to a halt, its passenger door flew open, and a collie dog was flung into the ditch. As the car sped away we froze in horror. The poor dog chased the car down the road with all its might. Realizing it wasn't going to catch the car, the dog finally gave up and came back to exactly where it had been dropped and sat, panting and spent. There it sat for a full day, waiting for its owner's return. We put out food and water, of course, and the kids lavished it with love, petting it and pleading, "Please, Daddy, please, can we keep him?" "No! Don't even think about it!" I replied, thinking our life was complicated enough already.

When I came home from work the next day, I found my daughter in tears. "Daddy, a truck from the city took the dog away!" I realized, as my children had earlier, that the collie was going to be put to sleep. So we called a family meeting and the children petitioned their case. The older two championed the virtues and lessons, the exercise and companionship, that having a pet would afford them. The youngest simply wanted a "doggie." When we outlined the responsibilities of dog ownership, they assured us they were ready to assume them. "The dog cannot become Mom and Dad's responsibility. If you vote yes," I cautioned, "it will be all yours. You need to consider carefully." When the vote was taken, there were three yes votes. Imagine that.

When kids take part in decision making, they readily accept responsibility.

Off we went to the pound. The collie was indeed there and slated for euthanasia. With its rescue by us nearly certain, the kids were all abuzz trying on names for him: "Rex? Rover? Sam?" Overhearing this, the shelter attendant whispered to me, "You realize, of course, that he's a she and she's pregnant." *What?* We'd voted on one dog, not ten! Upon learning that they'd won the canine sweepstakes, the kids quickly vowed to handle everything. Amidst squeals of great joy, we loaded the mother-to-be into our car and took her home.

They named her Lassie, and true to their word, they organized an all-out campaign and went door-to-door to sell our neighbors on the "limited number" of adorable soon-to-be puppies. Sure enough, they found homes for all the future pups.

The delivery happened inside a cardboard replica of a McDonald's restaurant in which the kids played. When Lassie rejected two of her pups and wouldn't feed them, tears fell. When the pups died, the kids held a heartfelt little funeral in the backyard. They were learning about the cycle of life in a way that hadn't previously touched their worlds. The real jewel of this story was the way they continued to care for Lassie. As the years passed she remained their devoted charge.

This experience showed my wife and me the superior merit of having kids take part in decision making. Because they were part of the decision, they accepted the responsibility and rose to meet its demands, owning both the process and the outcome.

BRING ME SOLUTIONS, NOT PROBLEMS

Most people would be surprised how much you can discuss with a four-year-old. As a result, as my kids got older they routinely came to me with problems and questions: "What should I do, Dad?" they asked. Eyeing them, I was mindful not to "protect" them from the experience of figuring it out themselves, as my father had done with me. It's not that I didn't have the impulse. It's easy to be duped into thinking for kids. But it's far more valuable to let them wrestle with quandaries themselves. Issuing a contemplative "Hmmm," I would simply ask the child, "What do you think needs to be done? You're closer to the situation." I listened, and if I agreed with the answer, I said so. If I didn't, I'd say, "How about this?" and offer an additional possibility to consider. But I never imposed a solution.

It's easy to be duped into thinking for kids, but far more valuable to let them wrestle with quandaries themselves.

Although I didn't recognize it at the time, I was training them to approach me with solutions, not problems. Instilling it as a habit took varying degrees of reinforcement, and I always responded with the stock response, "Next time you have a problem along these lines, think about this and this and that. Before coming to me, you need to have thought through your various options, the effects of each, and which choice you believe is your best choice. Do you think you can do that?" "Yes," they offered back.

It was highly effective. Once, my fifteen-year-old son, a budding musician at the time, came to me wondering whether he should pursue a career in music, as he had been presented with an opportunity to join a rock band and go on tour. His own band was becoming successful and playing regularly in the local music scene.

The kid wasn't even old enough to drive! You can imagine the images that flashed through my mind: sex, drugs, and rock 'n' roll meet the underage, impressionable young rocker. But I kept my cool, inquiring, "What do you think? Have you thought it through?" He answered, "Yeah, I'd love to play professionally, but I don't want to leave school. I need my education for later in life." So I nonchalantly said, "OK," and then did silent cartwheels.

Not only did I inwardly applaud his decision, I could see that the thinking process that led to it was maturing. He'd come to me with his solution all worked out. To this day I wonder what I'd have done had he said, "I've thought it through and I really want to go, Dad." We probably would have discussed it with his mother and found a way to make it work—as in the whole family going on tour! I wouldn't have wanted his life's regret to be "I could have been a rock star, but my dad killed my dream." Nor would we have sent him into that world without a chaperone.

> *My* children knew the drill well: generate options and think things through.

From deciding whether to pursue football recruitment offers or go for a prime post at the White House, my children went through the same drill—generating options and thinking them through, time and again. For instance, when my daughter Lisa was a senior at the University of Maryland, a notice was posted on a bulletin board for an unpaid internship at the White House. She called me up and said, "Dad, there's an internship at the White House." I said, "What do you think about it?" She said, "It's mine. I'm going to go get it." Lisa applied, and by golly, she got it, and began working for then Vice President George H. W. Bush.

Not quite a year later she came home one weekend requesting a "chat" with me. "Dad, I don't want you to be disappointed. I know you're happy with what I'm doing in D.C., but I'm going to leave the White House. I've thought it through and, while I love my job, I work seven days a week and don't have any time for myself. I want to have a personal life, a social life, so I'm going to go work someplace else." She took a breath and went on to tell me where. She had worked it all out. She'd identified the problem, weighed her options, and crafted a solution. There was nothing for me to say but "Well done!"

OUT OF THE NEST AND LEARNING TO FLY

My oldest wanted to work for me and my response shocked him. "I'd like you to go into the world and make your own way."

By the time my kids went to college, my companies were well established and known to everyone in the family. My wife and I opened our first McDonald's restaurant before our third child was born. By the time our firstborn was college-bound, we had six restaurants, which in time became fourteen. As teens, all three kids had worked at one location or another. When my oldest son was approaching college graduation, he asked if he could come back to work for me. He said it with an expectance that took me aback. My response shocked him.

"No, actually, you can't," I answered. "I'd like you to go into the world and make your own way. Once you've done this, then we can talk about the prospect again."

A bit dejected and understandably nervous, he moved to Washington, D.C. Son of a gun if he didn't become quite a successful real estate developer. Years later he took me out for lunch and said, "Dad, I'd like to come back and work for you."

"Aren't you doing fairly well in Washington?" I asked.

"I am, Dad, but I really am interested in the family business and have been for years. I know what you've built, and I know what to expect when I come back."

There was only one response. "Sure, let's do it!" I replied.

His sister took a different route post-college, yet it led to the same destination. She willingly went off to develop her skills and, after leaving the White House, joined the worldwide educational and performing organization Up with People, in time becoming its vice president. Later, she joined the Dallas Center for the Performing Arts Foundation as vice president of public affairs. She was responsible for implementing an aggressive campaign to raise $250 million to construct a new facility with five performance venues. She grew her confidence and eventually returned home, capable and self-made, as a wholly refined and polished gem.

> The gift of a lifetime is to give kids knowledge of their own worth.

What looked like pushing them mercilessly out of the nest was actually endowing them with wings and introducing them to the gift of a lifetime: knowledge of their own worth. They learned to run their own businesses and develop the work relationships needed for that. They got involved in their local communities, relying neither on their mother's network nor mine, but extending their own outreach and honing their own social skills. Sure, they suffered a few bruises and scraped knees, but they rallied the character goods within themselves and went on to thrive.

To return to the family business they needed a résumé that they and our other employees could respect. My children would never feel they were back in the family business because they couldn't make it on their own.

Appointing them to such-and-such position because they were Mommy and Daddy's little boy or girl would have sold them short, and likewise shortchanged the respected employees who'd been with us for decades.

Each of my children did return and prove an asset to the company, building it beyond my singular vision. What began as purely a McDonald's venture has grown to include a real estate rental company, a hotel, a development corporation, and a multiplex cinema and drafthouse offering full food and beverage service, all shepherded by my children and me. When they approached me and made a presentation about expanding that last concept, they ticked off every single facet of the opportunity. I had little to add to their presentation, save for a few sage nods and grunts. I couldn't help but remember the young father who'd implored them to bring him solutions, not problems. They'd steadily done so, and on this day they did so in a way that surpassed anything I might have envisioned. Maybe I could relax a bit, I thought, and go wet a fishing line.

The gift I gave my children was first teaching them to solve problems for themselves, then nudging them beyond the confines of the nest to discover the heights to which they could soar. They had the wings, yet needed the encouragement to stretch. Once aloft, there was no greater victory—and certainly no grander view.

"There are two lasting bequests we can give our children. One is roots, the other wings."

Hodding Carter III, U.S. Assistant Secretary of State

WHO IS NICK NERANGIS?

(photos by) Lauri M. Bridgeforth, Full Frame Photography

above: Nick as a "Hoggette" with grandchildren
right: Nick with *(wife)* Kathy, *(children)* Lisa,
Nick Jr., and Steve

Nicholas "Nick" Nerangis earned his success the old-fashioned way—through hard work, long hours, great business sense, extensive community involvement, and caring for others.

Nerangis's success is evidenced by his company, Nerangis Management Corporation, which provides services to fourteen restaurants, a hotel, a cinema, a shopping center, and a properties company, all of which share Nerangis family ownership. His most recent venture—with his children—is the wildly successful Alamo Drafthouse, a restaurant/cinema palace in Winchester, Virginia.

Nerangis graduated in 1963 from the U.S. Naval Academy, majoring in electrical engineering and minoring in nuclear science. In 2004 he received a B.A. from Shenandoah University in acting, his lifelong passion. He has appeared professionally in dozens of film, television, and stage productions.

As owners of fourteen McDonald's restaurants, Nerangis and his wife, Kathy, were instrumental in the development of the Ronald McDonald Houses, which provide housing and other services to the families of hospitalized children. The Nerangises have received several national awards for their dedication to community service, including awards from Every Child by Two and the Center for Disease Control for their development of an international immunization program that has helped more than 30 million children.

In his spare time, Nerangis is a "Hogette," one of a group of Washington Redskins super fans who dress up in flowered dresses, pig snouts, and garden hats, and together have helped to raise more than 100 million for children's charities.

Nerangis is the father of three children and has six grandchildren.

TEACHING A CHILD TO "FISH"

If I Were Your Daddy ... I'd equip you to be financially self-sufficient. When you are challenged, I'd provide coaching and unconditional love. But I'd never weaken you by stepping in, rescuing, or lessening your responsibility.

TIM JOHNSON

Entrepreneur & Real Estate Investor

My father taught me something very important about money. As I was growing up in Calgary, Alberta, Dad had a small business changing the advertising on the city buses. It was tough dirty work, but if we wanted money, we'd go and work side by side with him. I learned early that money is always tied to some form of work.

When I was sixteen my dad died suddenly. I had four sisters, so I quit school and moved out to relieve the burden at home. I found an hourly wage job and managed to go to university only because I could work my way through. Then during the summer of 1982, all the work dried up, and the job I had was cancelled. I had no money, no food, no job, and no one to turn to. So I went down to Hire-A-Student, hoping they would find me another hourly wage job.

But they said, "Listen. There's a line out the door for that stuff. But we have a few contracts we need people to bid on."

"How does that work?" I asked.

"Well," the woman said, "here's a guy who wants his backyard sodded, and no one will bid on it."

Being a pretty resourceful kid, I said, "OK, I'll take it."

So I went to this guy's house and said, "I'm here to bid on the job." I measured length times width in feet, and divided by three. I contacted the sod company, found out the cost per square yard, and gave the owner my bid. I got the job.

So I ordered the sod and hired an experienced guy to help. We did all the prep work; then this big truck showed up and started unloading the sod—reams and reams and reams of sod. And I wondered what the heck was going on. When I saw the homeowner walking out, I knew he was wondering too. So I quickly asked my hired guy, "To get square yards, it's length times width divided by three, right?"

And he said, no, *you divide by nine.* And that's when I realized I'd ordered exactly three times more sod than we needed. By the time the owner walked over and asked, "What's all this sod for?" I was ready.

"We're doing several jobs in the area," I said, "and I thought it would be easier if we just unloaded it all here. It'll be gone in two days." That evening I went knocking on doors cold-calling. I drummed up other jobs in the area, and two days later that sod was gone.

Because I was up against the wall, I stumbled across an incredible lesson that has served me well throughout my life; the power of contract work (entrepreneurship). That summer I made three or four times more than I would have made working by the hour. Because I had no one to turn to, I became resourceful and figured it out myself. And at the end of the day this is true for all of us; we all have to make our own way.

> *At* the end of the day, we all have to make our own way.

HOW NOT TO WRECK YOUR KIDS BY GIVING THEM EVERYTHING

Having kids was always a high priority for Dawn and me. We filled our home and our lives with five great kids, three girls and then two boys. I was fortunate to have been successful in my business dealings, so I had the freedom to spend lots of time with my kids to experience and influence their childhoods. It's been proven that the lessons and behaviors children learn between conception and puberty, good or bad, are the lessons they carry through life.

Some of our strongest values, the lessons we wanted to pass forward to our kids, concerned the value of work and personal effort. We both agreed early that money had to be tied to work, so our kids' allowance was kept at a minimum and was always tied to doing chores. We knew eventually their wants lists would grow, and become a natural motivator for wanting to earn additional income. Among some of our friends we've seen what happens to kids when money isn't tied to personal effort. When kids are just given whatever they want because their parents can afford it, it's pretty much a disaster. The wisdom we gained from watching all this? If you want to ruin your kids, give them everything.

If you want to ruin your kids, give them everything.

Since we live on an acreage in rural Canada, it was easy to find chores for our kids, but when the three girls—Juli, Laura, and Alana—got into their teens, a new plan was needed. They were sixteen, fifteen, and fourteen and they were all looking for more—more money, more time, more of everything—and most likely that would be with minimum-wage summer jobs. This meant Mom and Dad would ultimately be driving them around, and they'd get paid very little.

So around Easter we had a family meeting and presented them with this dilemma. I told them about my college sod-contracting success; how—I earned far more than any hourly job would have paid. Then I said, "What do you think about doing contract work?"

"What kind of contract work?" they asked.

"Well, what skill do you have that you can offer someone else for money?" They came up with a few ideas like baby sitting, dog walking, and swimming lessons, but we kept guiding them back to something they could do *together* as a group—like landscaping, painting, or window washing. Certainly the team approach would make transportation easier. But more importantly, I told them, "If you work together as a team you'll be much stronger and earn far more than you could individually." Having all played team sports, the girls got this concept. They settled on exterior painting, and we formed a contracting company called 3 Sisters Painting™.

LEARNING TO "FISH"

Although my kids were primarily interested in getting "more," I saw 3 Sisters Painting as a vehicle to teach them self-sufficiency and financial responsibility. So I happily accepted my role as coach and business mentor. My goal wasn't to equip them for a summer, but for a lifetime. Whether or not they made careers of contract work wasn't the point; learning how to use their own skills and initiative to solve problems and become financially self-sufficient—anywhere,

Teach them to use their own skills and initiative to solve problems and become financially self-sufficient.

any time—was. An old proverb says, "Give a man a fish and you feed him for a day. Teach a man to fish and you feed him for a lifetime." I wanted to teach my girls to "fish."

"It's all about relationships," I began as I centered them on how to work with people successfully. "Relationship," I said, "has four components:

1. Always show up on time. 2. Do what you say you're going to do. 3. Finish what you start. If you bid on a job and you get it, once you start, no matter what happens, you have to finish it. *4. Always say please and thank you."*

First we had to market our services, so we worked through the basics of creating ads, and the hard skill of cold-calling. Sure enough, the work started coming in, and kept coming. They learned to play when it rained, and to keep moving their business forward. For the first year I did most of the estimating, teaching the oldest, Juli, as I went. They learned how to get pricing for paint and supplies, and rent scaffolding. We worked through drafting contracting agreements; they learned to pitch the estimate and the contract with me standing by their side. They learned that rejection is part of business, and life, and not to take it personally.

Kids have to make their own mistakes in order to learn.

Teaching three teenage girls to paint a house brought me lots of lessons in patience. They began slowly, but picked up speed as they learned. They made mistakes, but making mistakes was how they improved, and this led to a profound lesson for me. I realized my girls learned nothing when I was telling them something. When I found myself saying "I *told* you how to do this," they would look at me like I was from outer space. It was far more effective to just give them the paintbrush and let them make mistakes. I discovered that kids simply have to make their own mistakes in order to learn.

The next part was really fun, because when the job was finished, the girls got paid. They learned to pay for their supplies, rental equipment, advertising and then pay themselves. We tracked and reviewed the job and they learned how to keep a set of books, an invaluable life skill no matter how they ended up earning their living.

With Mom and Dad's help, the girls assembled a thick portfolio of before-and-after photos and glowing referral letters, which they then used to pitch new jobs.

Somewhere in that first year they started getting very proficient, communicating, and working as a team. I was pretty impressed. They were far more inquisitive, and brighter, than I ever was. But the biggest "wow" for me was watching them move outside the realm of just showing up to work a nine-to-five job, then leaving, and never worrying about it again. Instead, they were arriving early, working hard, cleaning up, going the extra mile to make clients happy, and saying "thank you" at job's end. By taking care of the four aspects of relationship, they were transforming themselves from hourly wage workers into *successful* self-employed business owners.

So this is a sketch of the mind-set, planning, and skills my wife and I helped them with. We didn't just say, "OK, kids, time to be self-sufficient; figure it out." Instead we equipped them, step by step, with how to do it. And along the way, we all learned invaluable lessons.

FINISH WHAT YOU START AND CREATE VALUE

Most of the jobs were straightforward, but then there were the tough jobs. There was one owner who was one of those difficult people who is never happy. As the job went on and on, the girls' spirits sank. "It's a tough job," I agreed. "It's a tough owner, but it's not up to you to make this person happy. Your job is to do the best you can, and finish what you start." The girls rallied and worked incredibly hard. At job's end there was a huge sense of satisfaction because they had done everything they could, and the place looked great. From this experience they realized you can't please everybody; sometimes you miss high or low on the quote, but it's still important to finish and do what you said you would—one of the four aspects of relationship.

> *You* can't please everybody, but it's still important to finish and do what you said you would.

At some point the girls began to realize the difference between good work and bad. Sometimes they'd notice a spot up high that the previous painter had left—because he knew the owners wouldn't see it. "You always do your best," I told them, "but the value always hinges on your client's perception." They learned to point it out to the owner and do that extra bit, things that might make the job better but were not in the contract—for no charge. It added great value in their client's mind, creating happier clients and better referrals.

HOUSE RULES THAT ENCOURAGE SELF-SUFFICIENCY

After the first year, 3 Sisters Painting was a great success, and they had their spending money banked for the entire next year. Laura and Alana were still in high school, and Juli headed off to her first year at university. But we soon discovered that learning to earn and learning to budget were two different matters.

We soon discovered that learning to earn and learning to budget were two different matters.

We have three house rules designed to move the kids into self-sufficiency as they go to college and beyond: (1) they have to earn their own spending money, even in high school; (2) once in university, if they want to live at home during their four-month summer break, they have to be working full-time, and pay room and board of fifty dollars a week; (3) they can live at home only while they're still enrolled in school. Once they finish school, they have to leave the nest. And we didn't wait until they hit their teens to tell them these rules; they grew up knowing them.

As parents, there are many financial responsibilities which the girls know they can count on us for. While they're at college or graduate school, we'll pay their tuition, food, room and board. If they're on the honor roll, we'll also pay for their books. But as far as spending money goes, they've always had to earn it, and that never changes. This means they have to earn enough during the summer to last the entire school year. Currently that's about sixteen hundred dollars for the eight months at university, plus the cost of a cell phone and a little extra for Christmas. They also know that if they fail a course, they have to pay us back that tuition.

But by Thanksgiving that first year, some of the girls had spent most or all of their money. As we watched this happen, Dawn and I were in total agreement: we would not rescue them by lending them money. If they were unable to go out to a movie it was because of *their* actions, and had nothing to do with us. And yes, it was difficult watching them—especially over Christmas when they couldn't go out with their buddies—but we stuck to our guns.

We would not rescue them by lending them money.

So the next year I came up with an idea we termed "pay forward," to help them budget. At the end of the summer, they each gave us, from their earnings, the spending money needed for the entire year. On the first of every month we put the monthly budgeted amount (about two hundred dollars), into their bank accounts. We continued this until one by one they indicated they were ready to take over the budgeting themselves with newfound awareness.

LESSONS FROM ROCK BANDS

When you look at the careers of famous rock bands, you notice a pattern. First there's the meteoric rise to fame. Then there's infighting, and living without consequences. The next thing you know, nobody gets along, the band splits up, and they can't figure out what the heck happened to their fame and fortune. As we moved into our fourth summer of painting, a similar pattern began to unfold.

Sometimes on workdays the girls would sleep in. On rainy evenings they didn't want to make cold calls. They stopped caring about the details and the extras. If I caught it of course they'd do it, but they now had an attitude.

My first year with them was full-on, working side by side with them. The second year, not so much; the third year, even less. As we moved into the fourth year, they said, "We really don't need you showing up on the job anymore, Dad. We have it all figured out. This is our thing now; we know our stuff."

I could clearly see that their quick rise to the top was the result of following certain success protocols, like following the four aspects of relationships and creating extra value. And now they were starting to chintz on those protocols. They were arguing and fighting on the job and at home. Then partway through that summer there was an absolutely catastrophic blowup, after which they all announced, "We're done with 3 Sisters Painting. Next summer, we're all going our different ways." The phone kept ringing with new jobs, but they wouldn't work. They were done.

THERE IS NEVER, EVER A LESSON LEARNED
IF YOU RESCUE

By now, all the girls were at university and living away from home. In January, Juli was accepted into Teacher's College in Saskatoon, beginning in September—eight months away. She opted to remain in Saskatoon, pay rent there, and get two different hourly wage jobs. Then, near the end of January, she called us and said, "I don't have enough money to make rent; I need to borrow some money."

After giving it some thought we said, "Juli, you're twenty-one now, and we're not going to lend you money. You're mature, strong and capable, and you have to stand on your own two feet. You're great and bright and talented, and we know you can figure this out." She was shocked. She'd always thought she'd be able to borrow money from Mom and Dad if she had to.

> "*You're twenty-one: we're not going to lend you money. You have to stand on your own two feet.*"

This was a very tough time of soul searching for Dawn and me. First, if we're not on the same page, *if any one of our kids can actually divide us, it's over.* Second, we have a twenty-one-year-old daughter who's away from home and can't make rent. As parents we kept asking ourselves, "Should we help?" I kept wondering, did I miss something? Is there something I should have worked on a long time ago that's showing up now?

But we stood by our decision. We felt strongly that if we rescued her from this situation, we'd be weakening her—perhaps planting the idea, even subconsciously, that she wasn't self-sufficient. We knew this wasn't so, and we gave her the time, space, energy, and love to work through her problem without our jumping in to save her.

My goal when we began had been to teach self-reliance. That previous summer they collectively had said, "We have

> If we rescued her, we'd be weakening her—even subconsciously, that she wasn't self-sufficient.

it all figured out, Dad." I respectfully and lovingly reminded Juli of these words, and then I said, "It would appear that you don't have everything figured out, and you need to, because until you solve the issue you have today, life will keep giving you the same test over and over again until you pass. So the fact that you have a situation this early in your life is great, and we know you are powerful and smart and enormously talented. We have every faith you will figure it out

Although we said no to loaning our daughter money, we didn't cast her adrift—just the opposite. Daily by phone we kept telling her, "You're bright and resourceful. You can figure it out. We love you, and we believe in you." We gave her *loads* of emotional and mental support. We just wouldn't loan her money and thus plant the idea that the solution to any problem is to go and find someone to rescue you. There were lots of waterworks. But she dug deep, summoned her strength and resourcefulness, and guess what happened? She figured it out.

She got out her painting overalls. She made a trip home, picked up her painting stuff, returned to Saskatoon, and started making cold calls. She understood that relationship was about showing up on time, doing what you say, finishing what you start, and always saying please and thank you.

She started bidding on and winning contracts with the 3 Sisters Painting portfolio, which showed the track record of their success.

Juli began employing her sisters on the weekends and in the summer, whatever their school classes allowed. 3 Sisters Painting was back in business. Money started coming in, and Juli figured out how to start budgeting herself—again. But this time she was doing it 100 percent by herself. She assembled a set of books to reconcile the money and pay bills. She started paying forward on her own, and actually organized herself so she could spend the last three weeks of the summer out at the lake with us and her brother.

Once again I saw my own "aha" playing out. No matter how much you guide and teach them, kids—like adults—just have to make their own mistakes in order to learn. Being in dire straits was one of the best things that ever happened to Juli. If we had rescued her, she might never have discovered how truly powerful she really is, and the results could have been quite different. When we bail our kids out, we handicap instead of strengthen them; we deny them the opportunity to experience the life lesson of failure, which ultimately provides them with the tools they need to move forward.

> When we bail our kids out, we deny them the opportunity to experience the life lesson of failure.

All three sisters tell me this fifth year in the painting business is different. They have a tremendous level of respect for their clients, and for each other. They now understand how to create value by doing more than they're paid for. They're relying on each other, and I can hear the difference in their voices. As their coach and their dad, I'm overjoyed, because they're doing it on their own.

My kids now have the foundation to be successful at *any* business venture, should they ever want or need it. Juli plans to be a schoolteacher, but if there's ever a shortage of teaching positions, no problem—she's got a backup plan. And Juli's now teaching Laura and Alana the parts of the business they didn't understand or care about before. Big Sister has taken over my job as the teacher, and she's passing it on. I get to sit back, love them, admire their self-sufficiency, and watch them "fish."

THREE SISTERS AND A BOY

The summer their younger brother Levi was eleven, he entered the world of "more." Levi had been playing golf with my old set of golf clubs. He saw a new driver that he wanted, but the cost was somewhat prohibitive for him to buy on his own. "If you want that driver," I offered, "you need to earn half the money working for 3 Sisters Painting. If you do, I'll put up the other half."

Did Levi *need* a new driver? We didn't think so, but he definitely *wanted* one. There's a big difference between wants and needs, and it's always a judgment call whether something children say they "need" is *really* a need, or actually a "want." Do they need swimming lessons, golf lessons, or upgrades on golf clubs? Our position was that kids need swimming lessons, but they don't need new, top-of-the-line golf clubs. We're happy to provide basic sports equipment, but if they want top-end stuff, they have to contribute.

There is a big difference between wants and needs. It's always a judgment call whether something children say they "need" is really a need, or actually a "want."

So last summer, Levi started painting with his sisters, and saving money for his new driver. They changed the company name to "3 Sisters and a Boy," and my son started learning contract work from *three superb* teachers. If the girls hadn't been around, I would have just started the same education all over again with him.

Levi earned his deluxe driver. Now I'm around the golf course a lot, and I see that the way kids who are *given* golf clubs care for them is very different from the way Levi cares for his. He knows exactly how many hours he had to work to pay for his half of that driver, and respects that.

To develop self-sufficiency and financial responsibility, money has to be tied to work.

The story of 3 Sisters Painting is a case study in allowing my children to develop into self-sufficient and financially responsible young adults. It all goes back to the foundational wisdom: having money has to be tied to work. I wanted to teach my kids something that would empower them and endure, but the irony is that during this process, they taught *me* to be a warmer, more tender, more loving, more understanding, more patient man. At the end of the day, I'm left with the strong feeling that they taught me way more than I taught them. And for that, kids, I'm forever grateful.

To read a longer description of what Tim taught his kids, a step by step approach to teach contract work, go to
www.ifiwereyourdaddy.com/timjohnson

"The number one problem in today's generation and economy is the lack of financial literacy."

Alan Greenspan, American economist who served as chairman of the Federal Reserve System of the United States from 1987 to 2006.

WHO IS TIM JOHNSON?

Tim with (wife) Dawn, (children) Sam, Juli, Laura, Alana, and Levi

Highly successful real estate investor, engineer, and Ironman triathlete, Tim Johnson graduated from the University of Alberta, in 1984. While working at his first job, he began buying "fixer-upper" investment properties in his spare time. Within a few short years he had built a net worth and positive cash flow from his real estate portfolio that dwarfed his annual income.

With a new bride and a family on the way, Johnson left his cozy salaried job to become a full-time real estate investor. Soon realizing his approach to real estate investment was unique, he began offering insights and consulting to fledgling investors by co-creating R.E.I.N., the Real Estate Investment Network. In 2006 real estate values soared. Knowing this exponential spike was unsustainable, in less than a year Johnson sold his sizable real estate portfolio and bought up a large position in a junior oil sands company.

Johnson and his wife, Dawn, have raised five "great kids," Juli, Laura, Alana, Samuel, and Levi. In 1999 tragedy struck when six-year-old Sammy ventured out onto the thin ice of the pond at their home in Millarville, Alberta, fell through, and lost his life. The event shook the Johnson family to its core. In the year after Sammy's passing, Johnson poured his heart into his first book, *Searching for Sam: A Father's Quest for Meaning*. Today Johnson has come to terms with his son's passing, and has always been a tender, loving, and present father.

Although Johnson has successfully acquired significant wealth, he measures the richness of his life by the love he shares with Dawn and their children. The Johnsons live on a lake in British Columbia and give generously of their time and money to their community.

www.searchingforsam.com

LEAVING A LEGACY

If I Were Your Daddy ... I'd teach you how to create a bridge to the future and leave a legacy, not a disaster.

CHRISTOPHER "KIP" FORBES

Forbes Vice Chairman
& Art Collector

Malcolm Forbes was my father. Sadly, we didn't realize the importance of the lesson he was teaching us until after his passing. I am leaving this same lesson to my daughter in hopes that she in turn will pass the process along to her three children.

Most of us focus on the "living" part of life rather than planning for the time when we are gone. Yet it's all but guaranteed we will pass before our children, leaving them to face whatever lies in our wake. How our financial affairs are handled and redistributed to the next generation is incredibly important. Ensuring family harmony at such time is itself a priceless gift. Not having a plan can devastate a family, and we won't be there to personally explain our thinking, change our wishes, or help our children transition into the responsibilities they need to assume.

For my father, it was paramount that the whole family know and discuss the contents of his will long before his death. Malcolm wanted us to have our acts together so we could not only manage our financial affairs, but continue and even expand the Forbes family contributions to the world. When that fateful day occurred (my father had a heart attack quite unexpectedly), our family, though shocked and saddened, responded like a well-oiled machine. Everyone knew what to expect. There were no surprises and, correspondingly, no strife. We simply moved forward with our affairs.

My gift is this: like my father's, my will and testament will be completely transparent to my wife, daughter, and son-in-law while I'm still alive. They will know what to expect. The picture I hold is one of an intact family proceeding without breach, interruption, or delay when my time comes. I've taken the opportunity to directly address my legacy matters now so as to leave a smooth transition of financial matters in my wake.

I've known members of families who were perfectly close during their parents' lifetimes, only to be broken apart by surprises when the will was read or the siblings had to divide the possessions. The discord may have little to do with the amount inherited or monetary value of the possessions, but with long-harbored feelings of favoritism, entitlement, slight—the list goes on. Add the emotional impact of a parent's death, and the tension only compounds. My father didn't gain his wisdom on legacy matters from quiet reflection. He and my mother Roberta both lived through difficult experiences that convinced them there was a better way. Based on what he observed, Malcolm went into action to ensure a positive evolution of the Forbes clan.

> *Close families can be broken apart by surprises with the will and in dividing the possessions.*

When my grandfather, Malcolm's father, B.C. Forbes, founded Forbes Inc., he prided himself on being fair in all his decisions. As such, he left equal amounts to each of his four surviving children. On the surface, this sounds like an equitable thing to do, but in reality it's a recipe that can seriously encumber a family business. No matter how close the siblings, when it comes to business somebody has to be in charge; someone has to have a voting majority to make the decisions and keep the family business running smoothly. For many years we watched the discord play out between my father and two of his brothers over my grandfather's poor (in hindsight) decision. On my mother's side, hard feelings lasted for years because there was no equitable system established for dividing personal property and family heirlooms.

OPEN DIALOGUE, CONSENSUS, AND SIMPLICITY

My mother and father, Roberta and Malcolm, learned from this, and so did we. They determinedly changed the process to make the time of inheritance and financial reconciliation into something positive and meaningful. No detail was left hidden or undecided. My parents planned ahead, gained their children's cooperation and consensus, and personally resolved rifts rather than chance later disputes. From the biggest to the smallest components, we knew what their wills contained, and openly discussed the contents during Sunday lunches together. This gave my father the opportunity to watch our reactions to disclosures, determine whether we were up to handling the responsibility, and make adjustments as he deemed sensible.

My father watched our reactions to disclosures, determined whether we were up to handling the responsibility, and made adjustments.

Even the method used to divvy up the chattels was decided upon in advance. It was neither complicated nor sophisticated and went like this: the "children," all of us adults by this time, gathered. No spouses were allowed, but they could tell their partners ahead of time which possessions they might like, thereby giving them a voice, but one delivered through us.

Each sibling made a list of five items that really meant something to us. It wasn't unusual to see a popular item on multiple lists, so we cut straws to different lengths, blindfolded each other, and agreed that whoever pulled the longest straw got the item. How's that for modern-day facilitation! After divvying up our "most wanted" items, we drew numbers out of a hat to determine the sequence in which we would pick from the remaining possessions (most of the house). The person who drew #1 chose his or her item first and so on through #5. Then we reversed the order and the person with #5 went first, and backwards through the sequence we went, with each sibling walking through the house and placing a color-coded sticker on the item of their choosing.

By day's end, everything in the house had someone's sticker affixed to it. We'd completely eliminated the "Oh, I want that …" scenario that had soured relations with at least one of my mother's sisters for years. Ours was actually a fun and bonding experience. At the time of my father's passing, my parents were divorced and living in separate homes, so distributing the physical contents of his house involved us five children only. We came together as informed adults, able to support each other, thanks to our father's groundwork.

We learned through my father's experiences with his family that the wake of a parent's life can be felt long after the mourning. Will it come as a stormy sea or gentle waves? The ideal will and testament creates a bridge for the family to move forward, harmoniously expanding the good into the next generation. My father succeeded in building a new passage.

PASSING THE TORCH

By her own initiative, my daughter drew up her first will as a teenager. It was an exercise I wholly supported. Creating a testamentary at such a young age was less about division of assets and more a heartfelt expression of the things and people she valued most. It was nonetheless an entry point for talking about life's fiscal matters—specifically, how to handle the details outright

With her first will, she learned how to handle details outright versus leaving them to chance.

versus leaving them to chance. It was a call to model what she saw the rest of the family doing. And thanks to my parents, her grandparents, what we were doing was an improvement over what their elders had done. A legacy isn't some staid "thing," some engraved silver platter that just gets handed down. Nor is a legacy the exclusive domain of families of means. It's people learning lessons and making changes year to year, generation to generation. In that way, legacies are alive and always subject to revision.

Now the mother of three, my daughter is carrying forth the Forbes family legacy. For those to whom much is given, much is expected. I expect her to be a good steward of our family's resources and to use them to promote widespread good. I have every confidence she will since we have discussed the subject openly so many times. We've given *each other* the gift of knowing. She knows what to expect when I die and what I expect as she lives. For my part, I get the gift of leaving this earth knowing that my legacy is in loving, prepared hands. Not only will the torch be passed but it will be held high. As it should be.

"*Everyone will leave loved ones behind when he or she dies.*
If you want to behave lovingly toward those you leave behind, please take the time now to plan so that, in the event of your death, your family and heirs will not become financially unstable at the precise moment they are most emotionally vulnerable.
I urge you to discuss your estate with your spouse or partner, with your children, and with anyone else who will be financially affected by your death."

From *The Road to Wealth* by Suzy Orman, financial advisor, best-selling business author, and television host.

WHO IS CHRISTOPHER FORBES?

"Kip" and his Grandson

"Kip" with (wife) Baroness Astrid von Heyl zu Herrnsheim, (daughter) Charlotte, (son in-law) Phillip, (grandchildren) Cornelius, Adelaide, and Max

Christopher "Kip" Forbes is the vice chairman of Forbes, a family business established by his grandfather in 1917. Forbes Inc. is one of the world's largest and most influential media companies, providing business information for top executives and affluent investors through diverse outlets. In addition to his familial business commitments, he serves on the board of Senesco Technologies, a biotech company in New Brunswick, N.J.

Forbes graduated with honors from Princeton University with a degree in art history. While still an undergraduate, he worked as a curator for the Forbes Magazine Collection. Throughout his life, he has organized many exhibitions and written several books, articles, and catalogs devoted to Victorian art and Fabergé.

His support to the art world has been substantial. In 2004, Forbes was elected the first chairman of the American Friends of the Louvre. He also serves as vice chairman of the board of advisors of the Princeton University Art Museum and sits on the boards of the American Jewelry Institute, the Newark Museum, the New York Academy of Art, the Prince of Wales Foundation, and the Watts Gallery. He's an honorary trustee of the New Jersey State Museum as well.

Forbes is a Knight of the Venerable Order of St. John of Jerusalem and was decorated with the rank of Chevalier of the Legion of Honor by the French Government in December 2003. Married to the former Baroness Astrid von Heyl zu Herrnsheim, he and his wife have one daughter and three grandchildren. They reside in New Jersey.

TOUGHER STUFF

COMMUNICATING EVEN WHEN IT'S TOUGH

If I Were Your Daddy ... I'd help you get in touch with your feelings and discuss issues openly. You'd learn that to communicae well with others, you must become honest with yourself, even in the toughest of times.

JOHN ASSARAF
Business-Building Expert
& Best-Selling Author

I got into a lot of trouble when I was young. I was not a "normal" kid: I would lie, cheat, and steal—things most kids don't do. Although there was an abundance of love in our house, my parents never found an effective way of dealing with me or relating to any of their kids, really. My mother was mostly loving, while my father was extremely strict. Neither had any ability to communicate how they felt, so when they were angry or frustrated with me or my siblings, their lack of skill in this area caused them to lash out. Discipline in our house meant a beating, either kicking us as we ran away or strapping us until our butts were red. I think my tush is still swollen from all the times I got the belt.

When I was twelve, I got a puppy. Whenever the puppy peed or pooped on the carpet, I hit him because I'd been taught that hitting was acceptable. One day when I raised my hand to *pet* my puppy, he cowered. Afraid of being beaten, he put his little head between his legs in submission, and in that heartbreaking moment I realized that what I was doing was wrong. I also saw that the way I'd been reprimanded wasn't right either. Then and there I promised myself I would never hit that puppy or any animal ever again. And I especially vowed I would never raise a hand to my own children in the future. My choice was made. When I became a parent, I would do it differently, by learning to communicate.

I strongly believe that parents who hit and scream do so because they don't know how to deal with their own emotions.

Despite this physical abuse, my brothers, sisters, and I knew our parents loved and cared for us. Sadly, their methods for getting us to listen were at a third-grade level, and their harsh discipline rose out of ignorance and desperation. With such limited communication skills, their actions and reactions likely seemed reasonable to them. But I strongly believe that parents who hit and scream do so not because of their children's behavior, but because they don't know how to deal with their own emotions. Hitting and screaming just vents their own frustrations and makes them feel better. But both are nothing more than cheap releases. Clearly my parents had no idea how to improve their children's behavior, so Dad resorted to spanking and kicking while Mom slapped and screamed. Neither response affected my behavior in any beneficial way *other than to teach me how not to be.*

After I was married and had children of my own, I vowed to parent differently. Because of the way I was raised, I wanted touch to show affection and communication to be thoughtful and constructive. This meant making sure there were no physical, verbal, or emotional barriers between my sons and me. My wife and I had two boys, born eighteen months apart. We held and hugged them every day. Every night we sang to them and read to them, tenderly stroking their faces and hair; this was the only touch they knew. I approached discipline, or rather behavior and learning, by questioning, sharing, and working things out, by verbally and honestly expressing emotions rather than letting them build to the point of bursting. Because of my upbringing, I knew it was critical for each family member to first learn how to process his or her own frustrations and feelings, whatever the cause. Then, through communication and dialogue, the family members needed to voice those feelings. My goal was to equip my sons with the ability to understand others by first understanding themselves, their thoughts and feelings. I did my best to teach by example. It was a good thing, because change visited our family in a big way, and it took every possible healthy reflex to navigate it.

UNITED ACROSS THE DIVORCE DIVIDE

Our sons were just two and a half and four when my wife and I found our marital difficulties too great to overcome and decided parting was best. So we sat down with them and tried to explain the changes that were about to occur.

"Mommy and Daddy wanted to have you and be together, but sometimes this happens to parents. We're going to have two separate homes now, but you'll see each of us regularly." We tried to normalize what was going on by explaining it to them and answering their questions. Together we talked through feelings, theirs and ours. At every step we told them what we were doing and described how we envisioned our family moving forward. And we kept asking, "How are you feeling about this?" "Do you understand what's going on?" "Is there anything you're uncomfortable with?"

My goal was to equip my sons with the ability to understand others by first understanding themselves.

As with other life-altering events, divorce requires superhuman communication at a time when emotions are raw and everything is just plain hard. The overarching question was *What had to happen in order for us to part ways in a loving, caring manner?* What was our divorce going to look like? What were the rules of engagement? What would our new relationship look like? What would the custody look like, so the children would not be affected?

Sometimes emotions ran high. There was resentment and anger and denial. There were financial issues that went on for years. I knew if I didn't keep doing my own work around resolving my own negative stuff, it would spill over to the kids—the last thing I wanted. So I pursued every possible outlet for self-support—therapy, prayer, meditation, reading illuminating books so my boys would have a whole, healed father. I'd been in this place of heightened self-study before, and now dove in again. From the time I was nineteen I'd sought sources, both inner and outer, of enlightenment. Back then, this seeking had literally saved my life, given the rebellious path I had been hurtling down. My goal was always to continue to become a better human being.

As my boys got older, I shared some of my personal processing with them, revealing select truths without dimming the positive light I shone on their mother. Children become that which they experience. Every day, good or bad, parents are megaphones of real-life education for their children; how we navigate our life challenges is how they'll navigate theirs. If I had held on to my anger, it would have taught them to hang on to anger. Even if we reframe our feelings with more neutral words, kids soak up our actions and inner beliefs as the definitive "Here's how it's done." Without conscious intervention, we create in them the very demons we're battling ourselves.

How we navigate our life challenges is how they'll navigate theirs.

Most people think children are unaware and try to keep them safe from unpleasant things, in order to create family harmony. But it's quite the opposite. Children are energy sensitive; they pick up anger, stress, and anxiety. They know when something's wrong even if their parents try to hide it from them, pretending everything is OK. But this charged silence can make them uneasy or insecure. Discussing these inner feelings at an early age validates a child's knowingness, the part inside that feels uneasy. When we can validate their internal sensors in this way, it is a gift, and one that's so easy to give—far easier than forcing them to rediscover and learn to trust it as an adult.

Having made an initial and workable peace with ourselves and each other, my wife and I consciously set ground rules about the kids, revising them as needed. Ultimately I knew it didn't matter who was right in any decision or dispute. At the end of the day, our kids would remember and care about one thing: was I there or not? I chose to be there and made sure it was as a positive presence. For the first couple of years I saw the kids every day no matter what, even if only for small stretches of time. On the days I had full custody, I cleared my calendar so I could really be present. I dropped them off and picked them up at school, took them to the park, and truly engaged as a father. By my daily actions, I showed them that a divorce from their mother wasn't a divorce from them.

At the end of the day, our kids will remember one thing: were we there or not?

When their mother and I began dating others, we expanded the rules to cover at what point we would introduce the children to our romantic interests, and when it was appropriate to have someone stay over. We didn't want them to go through the trauma of dealing with multiple dating partners. When a relationship became a monogamous committed union, we both had to agree the boys could safely and comfortably be introduced to this person. At that point we both helped them process and understand how this third person was going to affect their lives. Even though we were going through a lot ourselves, we did our best to create a stable environment for our children.

Nine years later we are both remarried and everyone gets along. Our kids are happily adjusted, having been in touch with their feelings and able to discuss them right from the beginning. Because their mom and I kept the communication going between us and with them, our kids did the same and still do. Talking things out is a regular, daily thing. And our pattern of good communication when the boys were little set us up for good communication later.

THEY HEAR EVEN IF THEY'RE NOT LISTENING

As my boys entered their teenaged years, I talked with them about every possible topic, and I mean every topic. The more taboo, the better. "This is what's out there. What you choose is up to you," I said. "Here's what to watch out for, what your feelings mean, what to expect. Here are some books to read and research to look through." Nothing was off limits: better to get straight facts from dad than half-truths from friends.

When my oldest son turned thirteen we talked about girls, parties, drugs, and what independence meant. Within myself, I had to face the fact that he was growing up, and his younger brother was right on his heels. I knew this meant that I too had to evolve. Not so long ago they'd been little tykes with far simpler and safer interests. Being up front with myself about how I was feeling about their budding adolescence, I had to ask, who do I have to be to allow them to develop? Can I be OK with that? Is this about my needs or theirs? It's about both, of course, but for me, the children's development took precedence.

Nothing was off limits: better to get straight facts from dad than half-truths from friends.

There's only one way to have great communication with kids and that's to seize every opportunity. You can't wait for them to bring up something any more than you can expect them to choose to watch a movie with you Saturday night instead of hanging out with their friends. Communication isn't about scheduling some big summit around the dining room table. I have found that daily interaction is by far the most effective teaching tool: the drip, drip, drip of giving children the means to identify, process, and express their feelings and be heard. It gives them the gifts of power and control.

"What'd you do today?" "What went well?" "What was not so good today?" These words constantly signal our interest in them, what they're doing, and, most important, how they're feeling about things. My sons grew up engaging in such dialogue. Their mother and I always made it safe to share, with no judgment or correction.

They also consistently heard words of support and praise, not so much about their accomplishments but about who they are *intrinsically*. At the end of every day, for instance, the last thing they heard from me is how fantastic they are. When I tucked them in at night, in person or by phone, I whispered, "I love you with all my heart and soul." And then, "You're a genius and you use your wisdom daily." I've been telling them that for something approaching five thousand nights now. My teenage sons now mock my practice and groan, "We know what you're going to tell us, Dad. We know we're geniuses." But still I keep saying it. What we do and say to our kids becomes what they do to others and say to themselves, just as I learned with my puppy. It took five thousand nightly whispers, but I got through to them: They're geniuses and they know it. Every night I whisper, "You're a genius and you use your wisdom daily."

I see the results of this showing up in the way they behave with other children and when they're at their friends' houses. I see it showing up in their school grades and the fact that they are both two grades ahead of their age. I see it showing up in their ability to communicate—with adults, babies, even with animals. I see it in every facet of their lives. They have developed into well-nurtured boys who understand love, compassion, and empathy.

There's only one way to have great communication with kids: daily interactions that drip, drip, drip.

In the end, the challenges faced during a divorce and subsequent remarriages brought to the fore and developed our family's communication skills. Today when I look at my sons, I see two young men who are in touch with themselves and, by marvelous extension, wholly and authentically in touch with others.

I saw this so clearly one afternoon when my friend Michael dropped by with his toddler son. Unasked, my sons (then about ten and eleven) took the little guy by the hand and led him upstairs to their room. After some exuberant chatter and video game noise, there was silence. Curious, Michael and I went upstairs to check on them. One of my sons had the child on his lap and was reading to him (just as his mother and I had done with him). The other son was sitting next to the child, stroking his hair (just as we'd done to him). We stood in the doorway in awe. Nobody had asked them to do this. They'd taken it upon themselves to include him, play with him, and give him love. I realized that not only had I taught them to communicate and to give love, I'd taught them to parent.

> *Every night I whisper, "You're a genius and you use your wisdom daily."*

My efforts to break the cycle of abuse, along with their mother's and my conscious commitment to communication, had opened the door to this moment and a lifetime more.

My sons know love and how to express it. And they do so generously, as if it's the most natural thing in the world. As it should be.

"*The way we communicate with others and with ourselves ultimately determines the quality of our lives.*"

Anthony Robbins, best-selling author, motivational speaker, and advisor to many world leaders, sports professionals, corporate executives, and celebrities.

WHO IS JOHN ASSARAF?

John with (wife) Maria, (children) Keenan and Noah

Whatever John Assaraf touches turns to gold. Assaraf is the force behind not one but four multimillion-dollar companies, including RE/MAX of Indiana, whose associates sell more than $5 billion a year, earning more than $120 million in commissions. His internet start-up, Bamboo.com, generated over $30 million within ten months, before merging with Ipix to become the world's largest provider of online virtual tours.

For Assaraf, a rocky childhood led to an even rougher adolescence, forcing him to decide between jail or worse, the morgue, and changing his habits. Assaraf chose change. That transformation inspired his book *Having It All,* which made both the *New York Times* and *Washington Post* best-seller lists. His second book, *The Answer,* landed on those same two lists within sixty days of its release.

Assaraf's success also earned him a featured place in the film *The Secret,* and made him a regular guest on such TV shows as *Larry King Live, The Ellen DeGeneres Show,* and *Anderson Cooper 360.*

Through his company OnCoach, Assaraf supports small-business owners and entrepreneurs in achieving their goals. His work is informed by his twin passions for quantum physics and brain research.

Assaraf lives in southern California with his wife, Maria. He enjoys cooking, exercise, and traveling and is "Dad" to two sons, Keenan and Noah.

www.johnassaraf.com, www.onecoach.com

BE THE EXAMPLE, CHANGE THE ENVIRONMENT

If I Were Your Daddy ... I'd teach you values by my actions, be a model for you to follow, and even be willing to make some big changes to get results. My love may seem tough, but there will be plenty of it.

ED TILLINGHAST

Arbonne International,
Executive National Vice President

As our golf cart lumbered up a big hill in La Jolla, California, I turned to my golfing buddy and said, "It doesn't really matter what your bloodline is. If you want to be a father, sperm has nothing to do with it. It's a matter of choice, of integrity, and a matter of being there." I was thirty-five years old. Just ten months earlier I had been a carefree bachelor. Suddenly I was married. I had a wife and found myself father to a boy almost as big as me!

When I first met Sandra we'd had a whirlwind romance. Very quickly, I knew she was the love of my life. Marriage plans followed, but I hadn't yet met her thirteen-year-old son, John. Would I like him? Would he accept me? My first thought was a logical one. If he and I didn't get along, how could I possibly marry her? Then I thought, that doesn't make any sense at all. No matter what we come up against, I'll go through it with her. After all, I reasoned, when you have your own child, you don't know how it's going to turn out either. You're just committed. Being a stepdad is no different.

While Sandra and I were dating, John had been away at a special camp that helped tougher-type boys stay on the straight and narrow path. I knew this, and it was a serious consideration that becoming his father might not be that easy. When we finally met just a few months before the wedding it was a funny scene, like two dogs sniffing and checking each other out. There was no denying it: I had an important new role. I realized that my vows would have to be to her and to him, and that's the pledge I made: "I'm here whether you like me or not, John. I'm going to be the best father figure I can possibly be." My eyes were open, and I expected to be hurled into fatherhood quickly—trial by fire. But instead, what I experienced could only be described as trial by flamethrower.

I made it a rule: ten "well done" compliments to every "no."

I was the "new guy," his mother's husband. But I definitely had to step into the parental role of providing some kind of structure right away, and this was rough. I realized I would have to earn his respect, and to do this I made it a rule to give him ten-to-one love to discipline: ten "well done" compliments or "attaboys" to every "no" or constructive criticism. This did a couple of things. First, because I acknowledged so many positive things about him as he was, it made him more willing to accept my authority when I exerted it. He realized I wasn't trying to control him. Second, my ten-to-one policy made him more forgiving of my mistakes as a new dad; he considered my good points like I considered his. I was just acutely aware that if it seemed that all I was doing was flexing my authority, constantly telling him what he had done wrong or disciplining him, he would lose respect for me and he would feel like a failure as well.

I soon came face-to-face with something in me left over from my only experience of parenting: the way my own father did it. It's amazing to notice how we're programmed from our childhood. I didn't even know I had been programmed to be a certain kind of father, because I hadn't yet been a father. But it came out very quickly. Whenever John got into trouble the consequence would be a restriction; he couldn't go outside. He loved to wrestle. He was very physical and to this day he's very tough.

So, if he'd misbehaved, and he was on restriction, confined to the house, he'd say, "Hey, Ted, let's wrestle," which was his way of bonding. And my first thought was, no, you've been bad, so I'm not going to wrestle. It was almost like I was going to withhold love from him, knowing full well that wrestling was his way of bonding.

I was careful not to withhold my love whenever I disciplined.

Then I thought, Wait a minute. Where is this coming from? He's on restriction. He can't go outside the house, but this has nothing to do with my love for him. He's not on restriction from wrestling or from love. I realized I had been programmed to withhold love and approval while disciplining because that's what my dad had done. When I was a kid, I was in trouble at least half the time. My father thought if he showed me or any of my brothers and sisters love, he was condoning that bad behavior. Here I was, twenty years later, repeating the same pattern! I quickly caught myself. Okay, I reasoned, he's on restriction but I love him, and I can show him that I love him. This was a big eye-opener for me. With that new awareness I got to go and wrestle and get beat up—and he loved it.

From that moment on I was careful not to withhold my love whenever I disciplined. When John got into trouble it didn't mean I loved him any less, and I made sure I showed it.

The next thing I had to quickly realize was that no one was going to tell John whom to hang out with, where to go, or what to do. His mother had tried with no success, and he certainly wasn't about to start listening to the rookie newcomer. And truthfully I understood. When I was that age, if my parents had told me not to hang out with somebody, and I didn't agree, I sure wouldn't have changed. I'd have hung out with whomever I pleased.

John had his own mind and a strong will too. But his crowd was much rougher than mine had been. In addition he was a tough and intensely loyal person, which was both the good news and the bad. He wasn't in a gang exactly, but you wouldn't have known it by looking at him and his friends. Gang clothes, threatening and hard ganglike behaviors were both acceptable and the norm. I could see that the path he was on was going nowhere fast.

But I had to believe in him more than he believed in himself. Once I told him how smart I thought he was and how successful he was going to be. "I don't know why you say that, Ted," he argued. "I don't do well in school, and I'll probably end up dead or in jail."

"I don't believe that, John," I said. Although inside I shared his concerns, I had to keep my focus on

I had to believe in him more than he believed in himself.

finding and seeing the good I saw in him. "You are brighter than all your friends, and the school system is failing you." And it was all true.

But it was also clear he was not going to be reached with a typical authoritarian "fatherly" approach. If I were to help him grow up and not end up in prison, it meant I had to give him something entirely different from external control and boundaries. I realized he needed a tool—a mind-set to check his own behaviors. Neither his mother nor I could control where he went or what he did, but he certainly could.

A MIND-SET TO LIVE YOUR LIFE BY

Like most thirteen- to seventeen-year-old boys, John wanted to be a real man. At this age it becomes very important, and for boys without a father present to model it for them as they grow, it can be a real mystery trying to figure it out on their own. At this point, the best I could offer was to try to influence John's decision-making process. The kind of life we live is a direct result of the decisions we make, both good and bad. It is simple cause and effect. I didn't lecture him that this or that was a bad decision. Learning from decisions is a necessary part of life. At times, we all make less than stellar decisions. So what? It was rather about trying to help John avoid making life-changing negative decisions. I felt he was smart, and deep inside he knew what a good decision was.

Since boys this age are trying to figure out what a real man is, I said, "John, a real man makes his own decisions. A real man stands on his own values and moral codes, no matter what his friends are doing." My words were clear, but I knew inside that just telling him would not be enough.

Years later, John told me that it wasn't what I said that had made the biggest impression. It was what I did. "You walked your talk," he said. Day to day he saw me living by my values and standing my own ground for what I believed. This was especially impactful because John hadn't seen that modeled by the men of his past. He needed to see somebody who didn't just talk the talk; he needed to see them walk the talk. At the time this was an aspect of the situation I didn't even realize.

He needed to see someone who didn't just talk the talk, but walk the talk.

For example, John never saw me drink alcohol. Once, he asked me about it, so I told him. "When I was twenty I made a decision to not drink alcohol anymore. It's not that I had a drinking problem, but I was putting myself through engineering school and it was very important that I do well. I learned quickly that drinking was just a waste because it affected your whole night, and the next day. Also, I didn't like feeling that I needed something to make me more courageous or to have a good time. I wanted to be all those things on my own. I just decided I didn't want to drink. I just made the decision." John was listening intently, so I paused. After a moment I continued, "About a year later, some friends asked me to join their fraternity. 'Sounds great,' I said, 'but I don't drink, you know?' 'Don't worry about it,' they replied. So I joined. But although they had said it was OK, they must have made a mental note to test me on it. For a while they did this by repeatedly trying, in really creative ways, to get me to drink. But I held my ground, and after a while, they got it. Then it became something they admired. It was like, 'This is Ted. He doesn't drink.' But I knew that what they were really admiring was that I stood for something I believed in. I was OK with their decisions to drink, and it had nothing to do with my decision!"

Then, looking him directly in the eyes, I said, "John, I had my own values, and while I wasn't going to impose them on somebody else, I wasn't going to let anybody else impose their values on me either."

I think my message got through, because after that he began to make better decisions. It wasn't that he made a dramatic or immediate shift; it was as if I gave him permission to think for himself, and this slowly began to impact his life. He seemed to embrace that being a real man meant "I have my own values. I make my own choices."

John didn't need lectures. He needed to relate to a man's challenges and successes to learn how to become a man. My experiences made something abstract—values, morals, standing up to peer pressure—understandable and tangible. Since my behavior was congruent with my values, I backed up my words and became credible in his eyes, which earned his respect.

CHANGE THE ENVIRONMENT TO GET RESULTS

While my stepson was making progress, he was still hanging out with his friends who were headed down a bad path. By then, gangs were actively trying to enroll them. Sandra and I realized we had to do something extreme to keep John safe. After doing some research we learned that for kids in this situation it's almost impossible to permanently make a change and adopt a new mind-set if the environment remains the same. So we made a very hard decision: we mortgaged our house and sent an unwilling John to a school in another state that worked with challenged youth. We didn't feel we had much choice; it was critical that we interrupt the direction of his life and remove him from this dangerous environment.

Although John didn't realize it at the time, changing his environment was a tremendous parental gift. It was both the toughest thing and the smartest thing I did. When half measures aren't enough and the kids can't find their own way out, it's up to parents to step in and radically alter their surroundings. Tough love. I had to be the father he needed.

When John came home eight months later we changed his normal academic environment by enrolling him in a small school that offered a progressive, tailored, home-schooling-like program. John thrived and excelled in this new atmosphere. It turned out that he had off-the-charts retention when he cared about the subject and could work on his own. On his SATs he earned the highest scores in his graduating class. And as I predicted, he outgrew all his friends.

It's almost impossible to permanently make a change if the environment remains the same.

So how does the story end, you might be wondering? Well, John never joined a gang. He finished school and became an elite, highly specialized personal strength and conditioning coach, built a thriving business, and married a beautiful wife. Two gorgeous little girls followed. A happy and successful man, he has achieved a lot of peace in his life.

We see each other five or six times a week. We hang out, play tennis, and work out together. My reward for all that tough stuff back then is the amazing relationship we have now. It's just unbelievable. I'm still a father figure to him, but I'm also a friend. If I did nothing else in my life, being a stepdad would be the most rewarding thing I've ever done and will do.

I gave John values to live his own life by, an example of a man to model, and an environment that supported his growth. And he gave me much more. He made me a dad.

"In all situations, it is my response that decides whether a crisis is escalated or de-escalated, and a person is humanized or de-humanized. If we treat people as they are, we make them worse. If we treat people as they ought to be, we help them become what they are capable of becoming."

Johann Wolfgang von Goethe (1749 –1832), regarded as one of Germany's most distinguished writers, with expertise in poetry, drama, literature, theology, philosophy, and science.

WHO IS TED TILLINGHAST?

Ted with (children) Audrey and John, (grandchildren) Emma and Cammy, and (wife) Sandra

Ted Tillinghast is an engineer who has engineered a new, full life for himself and his family. A graduate of San Diego State University with a B.S. in mechanical engineering, he spent twenty-five years working in product design and engineering before joining his wife, Sandra, in her successful network marketing business.

An immensely creative engineer, Tillinghast acquired eleven U.S. patents and numerous European patents, and has founded and become president of Golden Mean Engineering, where he developed products ranging from fashionable eyewear to a rocket for launching life preservers. In addition, he joined *Fortune* 100 companies Hewlett-Packard and Kodak in a joint venture to produce an industrial-sized inkjet printer.

To achieve this success, Tillinghast worked almost endless hours, which he described as "fulfilling, creative, but very stressful." Simultaneously, he saw Sandra succeeding and growing at Arbonne as she became one of the company's first leaders. He observed that she was able to set her own work schedule, take vacations paid for entirely by her company, and receive compensation exponential to the extent she worked. The choice to join his wife's business became obvious.

As a husband-wife team, the Tillinghasts have risen to the highest level in the billion-dollar-revenue company. They are frequently among its top ten income earners—and they regularly vacation together. Tillinghast has become a stepfather to Sandra's son John, a role he calls his proudest accomplishment.

Besides his work, Tillinghast's passions are flying (he holds an instrument rating), sailing, surfing, biking, tennis, and golf. He paints and is currently working on a novel.

www.sandratillinghast.com

FOLLOWING THROUGH

If I Were Your Daddy ... you'd learn that all your actions have consequences. I'd love you enough to enforce your agreements—so you'd learn to keep your word and be accountable and responsible, to others and to yourself.

KIM JOBST, D.M.

Integrated Medicine Specialist
& Medical Homeopath

"Dad, I really don't want to go," said my oldest son, Merlin. "My friend and I will be fine staying here at home alone. We'll feed and walk the dogs, and look after the house. I have that big gig coming up right after you get back, and I really need to practice."

Merlin is a rock guitarist—a very gifted one—and shortly after we were to return, Merlin had his first solo gig booked in a popular local café. We were all excited.

"Merlin," I said, "I know you're almost fifteen and really want to do this. But your mother and I really want you to come with us on the family trip. I have serious concerns about leaving you alone. Looking after yourself, the dogs, and our home is a big responsibility. You have to get your own meals and do your own laundry. This is our space, and you have to keep it clean, put out the rubbish, sort out the mail, and take care of it all on a daily basis."

"No problem, Dad," he reassured me confidently. "I can do all that."

I knew what he really wanted was to set his own schedule. He had always been strong willed, and he longed for this first chance of having a brief freedom from parental oversight.

I was not happy about this plan; I was not convinced he would follow through. So I said, "Merlin, here is the deal. If I agree to this, and you stay here alone, you have to follow through with what you've agreed to do. When we return, if you have not kept your word—not kept the agreement we are making now—then you will be grounded for two weeks. Do you understand?" He said he did. "And do you agree to this?"

"I do, Dad," he said, with all the assurance of youth. "When you get back, I promise the house will be in better shape than you left it."

So I reluctantly agreed. "Practice hard," I said as we parted. "We're all looking forward to watching you perform!"

So my wife, Belinda, and I went to Ireland with our three other kids—Theo, Hugo, and Natasha—to visit a family and learn how they were home-schooling their children. As it turned out, the journey presented a multitude of challenges, and by the end of the trip we were all looking forward to getting home.

When we walked into our house, I was devastated. It was a total mess. There was moldy food in the refrigerator, and dirty dishes were everywhere. Specific things he had promised to do had not been done. It was clear that Merlin had showed a complete disregard for the agreement we had made. To say that I was incredibly upset would be a total understatement.

For me, it was clear that this moment would be a defining one in my relationship with my son. I knew if I could not somehow reach him as an evolving man and human being, we would struggle for a very long time. The idea of using other people's things, then leaving them in a worse state than when one found them, was completely unacceptable to me. But more than that, Merlin and I had made an agreement—an agreement that he had signed on to. He had made a commitment and given me his word, and then totally betrayed my trust.

Belinda saw the situation differently. "Don't make such a fuss about it" was the position she took. That's what the mothers of firstborn sons do. As a firstborn son myself, I know.

Now, Merlin has always had a very intense relationship with his mother, and at times that relationship has been challenging for us as a couple. All sensitive children know when there's a divide between their parents over an issue … and how to take advantage of it. Merlin is extremely bright and especially skilled at widening that divide, then stepping into it. So in this moment, he was hoping he could work his magic. He hoped his mother would take his side and forgive him—that we wouldn't follow through with the promised consequences, that we'd let it slide.

But as the father, I felt I needed to take a very strong stand. I said, "Merlin, you broke your promise—you're grounded for two weeks." "But that means I can't do the gig!" he said in utter disbelief. "You can't do that, Dad!"

"That was our deal," I replied. "You agreed to it, and you know it. And if you break that grounding, I'll ground you for a month."

I might just as well have started World War III. The other children were upset because they'd really been looking forward to seeing their older brother do his first proper gig. And for Belinda, the position I had taken was *way* too harsh. In front of all our children, she said that what I was doing was wholly and completely wrong and indefensible. Until then, whenever Belinda and I had disagreed about important decisions, we had always remained unified in front of the children. This moment changed that—it was difficult for everyone involved.

EVERYONE HAD A JOB

In this sort of situation, everyone has a job to do. For Merlin, that job was to be "crucified" and "resurrected"—to die as a child and be born into a new life as a young man, with a new level of understanding. To do that job he had to really test the boundaries. And Merlin did his job perfectly. As I fully anticipated, he broke the two-week grounding, so I had to follow through again and he was grounded for a month.

Belinda also did her job perfectly. Her job as the mother, as the feminine energy and influence, was to bend and flex, to love and forgive. And sometimes this feminine energy is required to help resolve or repair a situation.

But I had a job too. This situation was about my son becoming a man, and a boy learns those boundaries from his father. Masculine energy sets firm lines of accountability, and a line had to be drawn in the sand.

Masculine energy sets firm lines of accountability.

If drawing that line had cost my relationship with my wife, it would've been worth it, because without limits a child has no structure—he forms little sense of right and wrong, of integrity, or of keeping one's word. From my perspective, we would have been teaching him that he didn't ever need to keep his word—to himself or anybody else—ever again.

I knew this went beyond Merlin and me—there was much more on the line. All the children had seen what happened, and I knew, at a deep level, if I didn't stand by my decision, my entire authority within the household to uphold consequences would be compromised. I knew with every cell of my body that I *had* to do it. But I also knew that this decision wouldn't be understood and accepted by anyone else—not for a long time.

BOURGEONING INDEPENDENCE AND THE CONFUSION OF A TEEN

This incident wasn't a one-time event. Merlin was pushing limits all around him, especially at school. He'd been at a private school, but he increasingly hung out at the corners of the schoolyard—either keeping himself apart, or hanging out with the kind of undesirable crowd that could lead him down a decidedly precarious path. Throughout this time he was very unhappy, and Belinda and I were deeply concerned. But we weren't sure how to fix things. It was no surprise when Merlin virtually engineered that he would have to leave that school, by getting into trouble with the administration. His choice was to attend one of the most challenging state comprehensive schools in the region—one with very low standards and a lot of unrest. It was local, and when I first saw it I felt physically sick. "Are you sure about this?" I asked him. "As your father and someone who loves you, I don't want you to be there." But he was adamant about his choice, so I had to watch this extraordinary child struggling to become a young man in that dreadful environment. He was miserable there too, often crying in the mornings before leaving. But he defiantly showed me and he stuck it out. I believe that he was finding his limits, testing his boundaries—putting himself under incredible duress—just to find where he belonged.

THE NEED FOR RIPENING

From my own father I had learned about ripening—the fact that sometimes things just take time. I was born in Zimbabwe, and when I was three years old my father and I planted a peach tree together. The first year, that tree produced three peaches.

I was beside myself with wanting to try one of those peaches, but my father would say, "We need to wait until they're ripe." One day they were looking wonderful. They had begun to get color, and it was more than I could bear not to try one of those peaches. I picked one and took a bite, only to discover it was stony hard and far from ripe. I tried to put it back. You can just imagine a three-year-old trying to put a peach back on the tree!

When Dad got home he saw that a peach was missing, and knew that only I could have taken it. So he took me to the peach tree, knelt down, put me on his knee, and talked to me about timing and ripening. I can remember the sound of his voice—everything about it. As he talked, I felt in my body the utter mystery that some things can't be put back, no matter how much you try—and that some things need time to ripen and cannot be forced or sped up, no matter how much you want it to. I had really, really learned something—in my body, in my cells.

RIPENING TAKES TIME

Some crises can be resolved quickly; some after a few months; and some, maybe never. In this case, it took three *years* before Merlin and I were able to really talk about the incident. "I thought I would be upset with you for a long time—perhaps my whole life—for grounding me that time," he said. "But, I've come to understand why you did it, and why you had to hold your ground. And have you noticed, I've never violated your trust again, have I, Dad?"

"*I* thought I could get away with it and persuade you to change your mind."

"Yes, I have noticed," I replied. Then I asked him a big question: "Merlin, what would you have done if you had been me?" He said, "Looking back on it from here your decision probably did need to be that harsh, because you're right, I thought I could get away with it, and persuade you through Mum to change your mind. I couldn't understand why you were so upset. I didn't really understand then that my actions had consequences, and that I was responsible for them. Now I do: it's about keeping your word, Dad—not for anyone else but for me—knowing I can trust myself."

I was speechless. At that moment I could not have asked for more. My son had validated my decision of several years before—an incredibly hard one for me to maintain. He had realized what it cost me as his father to take such a strong stand against the wishes of his mother, and he saw that he and his lesson were important enough for me to pay that price. The years of strain between us melted. I saw then that the fruit was ripe, and we began to talk more freely than ever before.

"Dad," he said, "I realize that the principle of keeping your word was important enough for you to go through something that challenging." He continued, "When something like this happens, it's important to understand the principle, and not just the actions. I can see now that the whole point of raising kids well is for them to not just know what, but also to know *why* things are important."

Merlin went on, "That whole episode was the beginning of my becoming aware of something very important: when your parent cares enough about a moral or principle or value to take away something you hold dearly, what they're trying to teach you rises above the thing they're taking away." When he finished, I was almost in tears. He had realized that there is love in the limits, and he had wholly received it.

Later, Merlin addressed his mother: "Mum, Dad was right. The problem is that you don't always follow through with consequences, and if you're going to make an ultimatum of some sort, it's absolutely vital that you follow through, no matter what it costs you." In that moment she was able to hear him. Her "little" boy needed boundaries, boundaries that were hard for her to enforce as the nurturing mother she is.

If you're going to make an ultimatum it's absolutely vital you follow through.

Like fruit on a tree, human learning takes time to ripen, and you can't rush it. When the parent who stands for principle follows his or her moral guidance, even when unpopular, and when the positive results of that decision can finally be seen, a whole new level of respect and intimacy results. It is so amazing to now be able to discuss the incident as a couple, and as a family, and to experience the maturity in Merlin to express it all.

HARVESTING THE RIPENED FRUIT

Merlin went on to graduate from a two-year program at a music and performing arts college, gaining an unconditional place to read for a music degree at the Academy for Contemporary Music linked to Surrey University. He achieved three out of three distinctions in his college finals, one of only two people in the region to do so, attaining a very distinguished position. I've come to realize that the defining event, that month of grounding, started a whole sequence of maturing. His entire behavior, the whole axis of responsibility in his life, is different now. Recently he commented again on the importance of missing that first solo gig. "Dad, it's not just what you did, which is still painful, it's *why you did it*. I've come to so value the importance of keeping my word that I won't give it unless it's really important to me, and I'm able to keep it. I feel completely different as a result of that. Thank you for allowing me to get this very difficult lesson so early." This was an extraordinarily mature comment from a young man, one who was now quite different from the teenager who had hung out at the fringes, looking for the boundaries.

Merlin has just returned from a big five-day music festival where he was surrounded by drugs and petty crime, and God knows what else. But at age eighteen he's now his own person. He knows his own values, and his actions are no longer motivated by the need to feel acceptance and approval from others. Merlin likes and approves of *himself.* And I've even noticed that when he's in that environment, people turn to *him* for guidance and support.

From this new found integrity, his creativity could flow unabated.

All this became totally clear when we went to see the regional finals of "the O2 Battle of the Bands" for unsigned groups. Incredibly, at only seventeen, Merlin managed to reach the last sixteen of sixteen thousand bands that entered. As I watched him perform, and basked in his stage presence and mastery, I could see that this event had come about because my son had found a core of integrity and stability. From this newfound integrity—first with himself and then towards others—his creativity could flow unabated, and everybody around him wanted a bit of that. Looking around at the concert, I could see that he's a real leader now. By finding those boundaries, *Merlin had found himself.* My greatest gift to him, as his dad, was to stand by my word, to make those first few lines clear, certain, and still—and give him boundaries that could be trusted.

"I can give you a six-word formula for success: 'Think things through— then follow through.'"

Sir Walter Scott (1771–1832), prolific Scottish historical novelist and poet, whose famous works are considered great classics in literature.

WHO IS DR. KIM JOBST, D.M.?

Kim with (wife) Belinda, (children) Merlin, Theo, Hugo, and Natasha

Dr. Kim A. Jobst is a healer—a physician dedicated to holistic healthcare — so much so that he was personally selected as one of the first Foundation Fellows for the Prince of Wales's Foundation for Integrative Health.

A trained MD from Oxford University, with specialties in internal medicine and in neurodegeneration and dementia, Jobst's practice is based on the understanding that all illness has a meaning, unique to each person. In exploring this meaning with patients, Jobst employs conventional medical tests to support diagnosis and treatment, alongside such methods as homoeopathy, nutrition, energy medicine, traditional Chinese acupuncture and Jungian psychotherapy.

Jobst has served as a visiting professor in health care and integrative medicine at Oxford Brookes University, and is sought after to advise organizations around the world, such as NURA Life Sciences in Seattle, The NeuroResearch Group in Dallas, Clarus Transphase Scientific in California, and the Soukya Holistic Health and Healing Centre in India. Jobst directs his own consulting company, Functional Shift Consulting Ltd., and maintains a clinical practice for select patients in London and Hereford.

Jobst is editor in chief of the most prestigious publication in the field of integrative medicine. He cofounded the National Care Farm Initiative, which promotes the therapeutic use of farming practices to "provide health, social or educational care services for one or a range of vulnerable groups of people."

Jobst fell for a beautiful nurse-midwife, Belinda, and as husband and wife, they are raising four children.

HANDLING DIFFICULTIES

If I Were Your Daddy ... I'd give you a strategy for responding to life's challenging moments with truthfulness and grace.

In loving memory, Sara (1962-1983)

JACK ELIAS
Clinical Therapist & Educator

As every parent knows, parenting is a journey of unimaginable growth, its untold highs and rewards matched by just as many struggles and demands. We, as parents, happily share the joys, telling anyone who'll listen of our offspring's latest ventures. However, we seldom talk about our stressful moments and darkest feelings outside the family, and often not even within it.

By avoiding our perceived parental failings in this way, we often cut ourselves off from potential sources of perspective and support. I believe this is why so many parents go for years feeling they've done a poor job of raising their kids. We've all made mistakes, but creative opportunities exist in even the worst situation.

The reality is that every human being, at some time, buckles under fatigue, stress, or impatience. Parents, operating as we do in a crucible of pressures, know this all too well. So it's little wonder that we sometimes

301

respond to our children in ways that fall far short of our parenting ideals. Yet these are great teaching moments. *How* we handle the difficulties of parenting, and even our "failures" themselves, is indispensable to our children's growth and discovery. Even at our lowest points, we're still their role models.

I'm grateful that early in my parenting I discovered how to respond to emotionally trying times in a way that proved effective for all involved. Although jolting at the time, an incident one night with my toddler son showed me how much my lack of self-awareness could drive my actions in a direction I would quickly regret. This profound "aha" experience forever changed my parenting and led to the development of our family's stress strategy. Instead of caving in to feelings of being overwhelmed, and then resorting to harsh words or impulsive acts, we developed a practice to connect with what was really going on inside us. Rather than resisting our raw truths, we learned how to go deep into that darkness to find and draw out the insight needed to respond constructively and kindly.

Even at our lowest points, we're still their role models.

I was thirty-nine at the time, a married father of three: seven-year-old Sara, four-year-old Karen, and two-year-old John. Working independently as a real estate agent and insurance salesman gave me the flexibility to be involved in my family's home life. Some might say that by forsaking the full-time role of a driven breadwinner I missed opportunities to accumulate material wealth during that period. They're probably right. Not only did I partially assume homemaking responsibilities, before and after the birth of each child I would "retire" for a lengthy stretch. During each "retirement" cycle I willingly went into debt and then rebuilt our finances a few months later. It was worth it. I was often the one who woke the children in the morning, made them breakfast, helped them dress and brush their teeth, and sent them off to school or playdates. At day's end, I loved tucking my children into bed.

One night, I had some important real estate calls I anticipated making as soon as I had put two-year-old John to bed. I assumed that bedtime would unfold as it usually did: I would call him to bed and he would instantly jump under the covers, falling asleep before I had even finished reading one of his favorite stories.

On this particular night, John didn't come when I called. In fact, he didn't come after I called several times. After I carried him into his bedroom, he didn't stay there. After I got him to stay in the bedroom, he wouldn't stay in bed. My call list waiting, I began getting uptight. My thoughts and voice became increasingly strident and stressed. Anger rose as I struggled against what to me was my son's obvious intention to be difficult. I was thinking things like "Show him who's boss!" "Don't let him get away with this!" "You're the dad! Don't let him push you around!" As John's refusal to cooperate continued unabated, my irritation escalated to all-out rage. Then came insistent thoughts that made a beating seem quite justifiable: "Don't let this manipulative little #$% screw with you. Hit him!" With self-righteous intensity, I wanted obedience *now!*

The heat of anger was pulsing through my body, urging me to act, urging me to strike out. Thankfully, I didn't. I didn't even move. I just stood there in the middle of his bedroom, breathing and watching my little son hop about—first onto the bed, then onto the floor, then onto a chair.

At the time I had sixteen years of Zen meditation under my belt. There are many ways to meditate, but the hallmark of Zen meditation is to sit in a precise upright position and hold the posture regardless of irritation or pain. Having developed this habit of holding still, I experienced my inner turmoil that night as if trying to keep my balance in an earthquake. I literally swayed in place as raging urges inside pushed and prodded me to hit my son. I thought the terrible thoughts, feeling the energy of my own rage. Without those years of training, without the meditative habit of observing and not reacting, I might well have forced my will upon John. That didn't

I thought the terrible thoughts, feeling the energy of my own rage.

happen. Instead, right in the midst of this emotional storm, a new thought emerged, one that would later form a cornerstone of my parenting.

INSPIRED THOUGHTS

"How would this be different if you had a million dollars in the bank?" The question seemed to arise out of nowhere. It dumbfounded me. What did a fantasy about a million dollars have to do with getting my son to bed? Still, I went with it: "I don't know. How *would* this situation be different if I had a million dollars in the bank?"

"*How* would this be different if you had a million dollars in the bank?"

I tried it on. Mentally, I began repeating, "I have a million dollars in the bank, I have a million dollars in the bank …" I sat while John continued hopping about the room. I closed my eyes and focused as I kept repeating, "I have a million dollars in the bank …" I visualized moving through my day—walking out to the front lawn to pick up the morning paper, thinking, "I have a million dollars in the bank." Waving to my neighbor: "I have a million dollars in the bank." Eating my breakfast: "I have a million dollars in the bank." Meeting with clients: "I have a million dollars in the bank." Shopping for groceries: "I have a million dollars in the bank."

After doing this for a few minutes, I opened my eyes and looked over at John. Miraculously, he'd transformed from a malicious so-and-so trying to "get" me, into an angelic being with no agenda whatsoever and, at two years of age, with no concept of time—bedtime or *any* other. The little guy was nestled gently under the covers now, absorbed in the pages of his book. He had no thoughts about his father, and certainly no intention of thwarting my evening's work agenda.

Clarity suddenly dawned. I realized that the whole "logical" argument for blaming my son for my work pressure and subsequent rage, even to justify striking him, was a cover for my own deep-rooted fear—fear that

I wasn't smart enough or strong enough or good enough to support my family. My emotions themselves, but also their intensity, were actually *telling me a story about me.* My initial vision of getting John to bed lickety-split was driven by my desire to place those prospecting calls because *I was afraid* of what might happen if I didn't.

I knew I had been feeling stressed, but now I saw the depth of those feelings. My stress arose from my fear about my worth and capacity as a human being and provider. All that fear and stress was masquerading as understandable and justifiable, given the circumstances. Now I saw that this stress was fear in disguise, a decoy covering up the real issues. In an instant it had mushroomed into such violent visions and impulses that I'd almost perpetrated them onto my child, just so I wouldn't have to face my own fear and self-condemnation.

The source of my fear was lack. I was astonished!

I felt relief, gratitude ... and shame. Connecting the dots, I recognized the statement "I have a million dollars in the bank" for what it was—my saving grace. And it was perfectly on target, hitting the exact source of my fear: *lack.* I was astonished!

Then I realized something more: being honest with myself rather than running away from these disturbing feelings had unraveled their source—in this case, my fear and self-doubt. By allowing the storm of feelings to move within while I remained still and didn't act on them, I was able to see what was really going on. Who could have guessed that thinking a thought about *money* would be the antidote to my anger and confusion?

I continued to watch myself. Even as I was softening inside, my heart opening, I felt another pulse of energy rise up within me—angry energy. It coursed through my body like a raging fist, pounding madly. As it passed my face, I heard a defiant voice within me shout, "No!" To this day, I'm convinced that this fist of anger wanted to knock me out of my state of clarity right back into the delusion I had just emerged from. This dark part of me didn't want to face the truth that I felt small and afraid. It wanted to keep projecting my problems outward and onto the world. It wanted to keep blaming other people, including an innocent two-year-old. That part of me wanted to maintain my blameless self-image at any cost.

The experience of this fist of rage left me marveling at the revelation I'd just been given. It demonstrated how the mind can spin full circle—from insanity to sanity and back again—if it doesn't remain on alert. The fist represented long-held habits—my familiar way of being—that would have re-engaged almost immediately if given the chance. My ego wanted to preserve its place and stature by seeing my problems as being "out there" versus "in here."

The jig was up. There could be no more blaming and justifying. No more believing that my children were driving me crazy or getting in my way. No more claiming stress as an excuse to act out. I saw the naked truth: I was avoiding my fear and self-doubt. Acting on my angry emotions would have been an ineffective escape from these underlying issues. *My son's behavior was not the cause of my anger.*

John went to sleep that night, but I woke up. From my near miss at doing harm, a family strategy was born. When one of us is about to react in anger, we can pause, hold still, and truthfully assess the matter. Doing this as a regular practice allows for a kinder, genuine response.

PAUSE, BE TRUTHFUL, ALLOW (PTA)

Now, PTA became my tried-and-true means of parenting—of living from a place of grace.

We can call this strategy PTA (not to be confused with the abbreviation for the Parent Teacher Association in U.S. schools): **Pause, Be Truthful, Allow.** Although I would occasionally experience resistance to doing this, it became my tried-and-true means of parenting—of living from a place of grace. And I passed it on to my kids as a strategy useful for them too.

Pause first: Immediate, outward action can seem entirely justified when the source of the problem appears to be outside you. But this is an illusion. The whole scene and how you perceive it is colored by what's churning inside you. **Be Truthful:** Stop and ask, *How would I feel right now if I had everything I need and want?* If you stay with it and imagine you have everything you wish for, right in this moment, your answer will begin to reveal the truth and shape a more appropriate and resourceful response to the situation. **Allow:** By acknowledging your feelings rather than resisting or judging them, you open the door for inspired thought to come in and assist. It's a way to welcome whatever's being triggered emotionally within instead of trying to make it go away or assigning its cause to something "out there." And so enters the clarity—what I call grace—often from seemingly out of nowhere.

When you are emotionally honest, it gives children permission to do the same.

After years of practicing PTA in our family, I can attest that the depth and value of the insight that comes is *directly proportional* to the degree to which I am willing to be honest with myself. When I am emotionally honest at this level, it gives my children permission to do the same: to look within for perspective instead of pinning the blame on someone else.

At first I practiced PTA with my children by stopping myself from hasty reactions. As my children grew—as I grew—we openly discussed this approach as something each of us could employ in the midst of stress or turmoil. The kids had long since imprinted the technique, having seen their parents model it for them time and again. Now, they had a conscious blueprint to follow when outside stressors threatened to override their cool.

The bedtime experience with little John those many years ago transformed my parenting. It gave me not only a valuable tool I could use, but one I could pass along to my children and to future generations as well. With this experience came the conviction that any time we feel a strong emotion, we need to pay attention. At that point we can choose to disregard the fear-filled messages running through our head, and instead Pause, Be

Truthful, and Allow ourself to see what's really going on. *How would I feel right now if I had absolutely everything I need?* Holding still—just sitting with this question and allowing truth and inspiration to dawn—offers untold potential for growth.

One of the priceless rewards of parenting is the mirror children hold up for us. Looking into that mirror, I see clearly now that John didn't miraculously transform that night. I did.

"Your mind knows only some things. Your inner voice, your instinct, knows everything. If you listen to what you know instinctively, it will always lead you down the right path."

Henry Winkler, actor, director, and philanthropist; co-author of more than twelve children's books.

WHO IS JACK ELIAS?

Jack with (wife) Ceci Miller, (children and grandchildren) Karen, Amiya, Andrew, Melia, Matthew, John, Aloka, Trillion, and Andrew.

Jack Elias is a master—a master of simple, yet powerful, techniques for achieving one's highest personal and professional goals. A clinical hypnotherapist, he has been in private practice since 1988, the year he founded the Institute for Therapeutic Learning in Seattle, which trains and certifies clinicians in Transpersonal Hypnotherapy and Neuro-Linguistic Programming.

Elias's approach is a unique synthesis of Eastern and Western perspectives on the nature of consciousness and communication, the result of more than four decades' study of Eastern meditation, philosophy, and psychology. Among his teachers, he counts such masters as Shunryo Suzuki Roshi and Ch^gyam Trugpa Rinpoche.

Seeking to further share his insight, Elias wrote *Finding True Magic: Transpersonal Hypnosis and Hypnotherapy/NLP,* an internationally recognized guide that provides an innovative, holistic approach to mind/body healing and creative manifestation. The book is directed at professional therapists, clinicians, and medical practitioners, as well as general readers. His experiential workshops are offered to healing professionals for credit and certification.

Elias served as primary caregiver to his eldest child, Sara, who passed away at age fifteen after a five-year illness. He lives in Seattle with his wife, Ceci Miller. He is father of four and stepfather of one, as well as a grandfather many times over.

www.findingtruemagic.com

HOW TO IMMUNIZE A CHILD AGAINST NEGATIVITY

If I Were Your Daddy ... I'd teach you how to immunize yourself against the hurtful things other people say. I'd teach you how to "dress" yourself from the inside, and validate yourself in order to live a full and happy life.

ℬROTHER ISHMAEL TETTEH

West African Child Educator & Author

Up until several months ago I had thirty-four children. Then my wife brought in three more, so now it is thirty-seven. Some of them are grown, and some of them are still in school and in our home. Only two are my biological children. So many children are in such need, and I am driven to try and help every child to have an education, as much as I can afford. In Ghana, where I come from, if the parents do not pay the school fees, the school sends the child home, and then the child roams in the streets. Sometimes you look into those eyes and just see the potential. So I step in, or my wife steps in, and we'll say, "Let's help." She is fond of doing that. She will say, "This is just for a year or two so they get some stability, so the parents can get back on their feet." Eventually the child just becomes our child.

Some of these children would be described as abandoned in courts because they have to fend for themselves. They probably sleep rough in front of their house or on the outside porch, and for the girls this means they are always in danger. They have to find food, maybe find something to sell on the street so they can eat, and that is why they don't go to school. They lose all sense of their own value, and become fearful and angry. I find them, or my wife finds them, and we say, "Come and eat" or "Come and stay for a while." The months turn into years, and I just adopt them. And I take them through many programs to help them recover their sense of value.

You, dear reader, may not be confronted with the extreme conditions in your children that I see daily in my country, where there is severe poverty. But from my experience working in many Western countries, most children at some point are confronted with unkind, cruel, or even dangerous individuals, whose words can leave emotional scars. Guns and violence are now common in public schools, and bullying has terrified or even caused children who have totally lost their sense of value to take their own lifes. Yet it can be avoided if we strengthen our children with tools. When you equip children correctly, you're immunizing them for those moments when you are not around, so no unaware or unkind human being can ever destroy their sense of self-worth or their joy. In the Etherean Mission, an organization I founded in Ghana in 1975, we have created many tools in games to help children everywhere. Here are some of the easiest and most powerful tools I've taught my children and thousands of others, so you can teach your own children to withstand the forces they'll encounter.

When you equip children correctly, you're immunizing them for those moments when you are not around.

TEACHING THE INNER DRESS CODE

Young people spend a lot of time on their external appearance. They are trying to find themselves, and they do this by copying the images of others. They are very focused on dressing according to current style to gain external approval, which may eventually lead to them losing the truth of who and what they are inside.

So as a father I say, "Find who and what you are inside, and dress that. Just think of how much time you spend thinking about clothes and accessories, looking for the money to buy them, shopping and choosing, and then actually dressing your physical body. Of course it is good to dress decently and appear nice so you feel good, perhaps important, because you want to be happy. But it is more important to 'dress what you are' and be nice from within. Remember that feeling important, along with all positive feelings like joy, wisdom, and intelligence, comes from within, so it is far better to find who and what you are within you, *and dress that*." And here's a few ways we dress the within.

THE MOST ESSENTIAL WARDROBE ITEM: SELF-ESTEEM

"Would you ever get dressed without pants or a dress?" I ask a group of children, and they all respond "no." I tell them, "Feeling good about yourself is like putting on a pair or pants or a dress—it is essential, and you are not dressed until you have done it."

Children universally need a sense of their own worth, so I help them build self-esteem.

Children universally need a sense of their own worth, so I help them build self-esteem. I tell them to first make a list of all the good qualities they know about themselves. For each quality they must then list several *examples* of how they have expressed that good quality. For instance, if they feel they are "thoughtful of others," they write down the times they were thoughtful that day: "I shared a snack with my sister," "I was kind to the new student at school," and so on. They record their acts of goodness or notice their strong qualities daily, so they have reason to feel good about themselves.

It becomes the proof that those good qualities really *are* them, and in this way they see their worth.

But it doesn't stop there. Next we have them read at least ten good things about themselves from their own list, *before leaving home* in the morning. Then I tell them to look into the mirror once a day and tell the wonderful person they see looking back about the good person he or she is. For instance, looking in the mirror at himself, Kojo would say, "Kojo, you are a very kind person, and you demonstrated this when you paid for the bus ticket for that child, and also when you shared your food with that boy who had none." By doing this these children are nurturing themselves, and they see there are many reasons to love themselves. And when children do this every morning and evening, they no longer need others telling them, or not telling them, how good they are or that they are OK, because they can see it so clearly.

EMPOWERING A CHILD WITH LOVE

Part of getting dressed is putting on outer clothing to provide protection from the sun, wind, or cold. I tell the children they must do the same with their inner wardrobe. "We must all be able to protect our inner selves from the hurtful or thoughtless words and labels of others, just like having a jacket would protect your outer self, only it's even more important."

Children grow up feeling "less than," so healing from negative labels is universally required.

At some point, children everywhere have negative labels imposed upon them. Some grow up subjected to labels like "slow" or "lazy" because they did not do well in some subject at school, or they're different from other children. Others, including many of the children I've worked with and adopted, have heard very damaging labels such as they're a "bad boy" or "bad girl" or "ugly" or "stupid." Often their backgrounds are so horrible that they have retreated into fear and anger.

Regardless of the degree of harshness, over time these negative words and labels are all disempowering. They cause internal damage and confusion, and children grow up feeling "less than," inadequate, and that they are not good enough. So in my work with children for over three decades, including children in many Western cultures, healing from negative labels is universally required. Here is one way I've helped my children heal and stay protected from the harmful words of others. This has worked even in the most extreme of cases.

STEP 1: FACING THE NEGATIVES

Allow the child to tell you the negative labels he or she has been subjected to that make them feel not good enough. Encourage them also to tell you about all the negative things they hear that make them angry, and (this part is very important) also ask them what they feel like doing when they are feeling angry. Some will say, "I feel like killing somebody," "I feel like hitting," "I feel like crying," "I feel like running," and so on. It is so important to listen to them, and not to judge them. They must feel safe telling these things. Asking questions in a dialogue and listening carefully to the answers will help you understand their thought process. A child's thought process will be different from yours, and only if you understand it, can you help.

To raise peaceful children, allow them to safely express their feelings and release them.

They'll tell you that every negative emotion has a physical representation, which they have actually suppressed. And that suppression builds internal confusion, which will eventually create a wall. But you won't see the wall; you will just see an angry child. If we want to raise peaceful children, allowing them to safely express these feelings and let those feelings out of their body is absolutely necessary.

STEP 2: GROWING FROM NIGHT-AND-DAY THINKING INTO SPECTRUM OR RAINBOW THINKING

We talk with the children and help them realize that their parents, aunties, uncles, teachers, and any other adults, whoever may have said these things, actually still love them, *and the things they say don't matter.* You cannot tell a child this; it *must* be conveyed in a one-on-one dialogue so each child can discover this truth for himself or herself. For instance, I would ask that eight-year-old-girl: "Who bought you the nice dress you're wearing? Oh, Mommy bought it for you. Does Mommy love you?" "Yes." "What does Mommy do that lets you know she loves you? Oh, she did this, she did that." In this way you help that child realize for herself the many good things her parents or others have done.

Children think in black and white—in their mind a thing either is or it is not. They are either good or bad, "Mommy loves me or she does not." Since children perceive life this way, when a parent's, adult's, or even friend's behavior changes they think at one moment he or she loves them, then the next moment he or she doesn't, and it is confusing. But with this kind of dialogue, where we help them consider the ways love was shown to them, we help them grow from night-and-day thinking into spectrum or rainbow thinking. This way they know it's not just about the bad things someone said about them in that moment. Now they can realize that *sometimes people just don't know how to do better.* People may love you, but they don't always know how to tell you. And with this, children can realize that a negative thing said about them *is actually not about them.* And that is exactly the truth statement we give them; *"It is not about me."* We use this phrase to begin immunizing children against internalizing this kind of negativity, and we teach it through a game.

> "It is not about me" immunizes children against internalizing negativity.

STEP 3: THE IMMUNIZATION GAME, "IT IS NOT ABOUT ME"

Once the preliminary steps are handled, we can begin the Immunization Game, and help them identify these negative words. In a group we begin to reinforce the truth *"It is not about me."* During the game there are actions involved: Tap left foot and say "**It**." Tap right foot and say "**Is**." Slap left thigh with left hand and say "**Not**." Slap right thigh with right hand and say "**About**." Both hands tap head: "**Me**." So when the facilitator presents them with a negative label, like "you are stupid," they respond with feet, hands, and voice, "**It—is—not—about—me**," and they are acting it out too. We do this again and again, slowly increasing the speed, which makes it fun for them. Over time it becomes part of their conscious-subconscious awareness.

Acting and singing it is the claiming process, and once a child has this, no one can take it away.

Acting and singing it out is the claiming process, and once children have this, it is theirs. No one can take it from them.

HAVE A SECRET SIGN THAT MEANS "IT IS NOT ABOUT ME"

Children love secrets, so this next part works very well. Once a child is able to say "It is not about me," when a relative or a school bully or any one else is imposing negative labels upon them when angry, if they stand there and say "It's not about me" *out loud,* that person will get even angrier, perhaps violent. So we teach them to say it in their head and have a secret sign. This secret sign is the Immunization. It could be as simple as a child putting his left hand behind his head or crossing the fingers of her right hand. The moment negative labels are thrown at the child, like bad boy, bad girl, or stupid child, the child will now say silently in his or her mind, *"It is not about me"* and do his or her secret sign, and that is all. This process activates the secret energy in the child's subconscious, and the child knows these negative words are not about him or her. We tell children, "Any time someone is imposing on you negative labels which you do not like, you simply do your secret sign."

Tell children "Any time someone is imposing negative labels just do your secret sign."

Once a child has her secret sign, you can no longer trick her into anger while she is going through the program. That sign is really the immunization.

CHILDREN TEACHING CHILDREN

Every parent really wants happy, confident, creative, responsible children with drives for excellence, but very few know how to create that. A parent cannot teach or give what they themselves were not taught or given by their own parents. We provide programs in schools and churches to ensure that every child who comes can find stability, balance, and self-worth. In Africa the program is run by my Etherean Mission. In the United States it is administered by Conscious Humanity Inc. Once children have gone through this program, they often know more than their parents do. These very empowered children then become the best teachers, so with our support, many who are ten to twelve years old have become facilitators, teaching the games to other children.

The Immunization Game has been taught to thousands of children in schools and churches, and I have seen it work over and over again. Children are teaching other children how to "dress" their inner selves. Now before these children leave the house every day, they are dressed from the inside out—they are feeling good about themselves, as well as being protected, "immunized," from any hurtful, damaging labels that might be said to them by others.

LOOKING IN THE MIRROR: ASSESSMENT HOUR

In our home, my own children love their big extended family, and they all call themselves brothers and sisters. Over the years we have created a Family Purpose Statement, which is always being added to. We do this by asking each person these questions: "What must our family be known for that will make you proud? What must *each person* in the family be that will make you proud?" These are the principles we want to live our life from, and everyone thinks about what that might be, and then we summarize the responses to form the Family Purpose Statement. I recommend that all families create a Family Purpose Statement and use it as their reference to healthy, whole living.

I recommend that all families create a Family Purpose Statement for healthy, whole living.

When we all come together at holiday time or for a special event, we have a family "assessment hour." During this time we read our Family Purpose Statement, and ask if we are living up to the ideals of that statement. One by one, we support each other, observe who is most living up to it, and then share ideas that person could use. We don't criticize or condemn. We just say, "I know you want this and that; here's another way of doing it." It is very enlightening, and at that time my children can all tell me that they believe *I* am doing wrong! And then we have fun and we joke, and sometimes we dance. I have an eight-bedroom house, but often during a holiday when all of them come home, we are overly full, so people sleep on the couch. But we are so happy, and I enjoy it always.

About thirty of my children are now fully out of school and on their own. Some have become dentists, pharmacists, biochemists, and so on. Many have become mothers, and now there are some grandchildren in our house in the process of becoming medical doctors. Presently my wife and I have about seven children we are still raising, plus our own two. My daughter will be entering into university this year, and my son is still attending the high school. When I travel I make time to call them and do their homework with them over the phone. I am very close to my children.

With my work and in my home, my goal is to create a whole generation of healed children who are free from fear and anger, and in touch with their sense of uniqueness. By 2026, I should have at least 10 percent of children on the planet able to access these games, using them in their life, and changing— finding comfort within themselves. We're giving them tools to handle life so they are strong within.

I do not train children to cower from challenges; life has mountains and valleys and you must have the tools to handle both.

Life is a passionate adventure, and in every adventure you challenge yourself to achieve the impossible. I do not train children to cower from life's challenges; life has mountains and valleys, and presents you with pain and pleasure. You must have the tools to handle both, float above them, and choose what you want when you want. I cannot change the environment, but I can help children "dress" within and cultivate inner strength so they can handle any situation they meet in life. I believe world peace is possible, and I am working on it, one child at a time.

"*To establish true self-esteem we must concentrate on our successes and forget about the failures and the negatives in our lives.*"

Denis Waitley, American author, speaker, and high performance expert, who has sold over 10 million audio programs in fourteen languages.

WHO IS BROTHER ISHMAEL TETTEH?

Brother Ishmael with (wife) Joan Tetteh (pictured). They have raised thirty-seven children, including (two biological children) Nii Kommey and Naa Dei Komley Tetteh

With all his being, Brother Ishmael Tetteh believes in world peace, "a world based on the identification and free expression of each person's creative potential." And he is trying to achieve it one child at a time.

Tetteh is the founder and leader of the Etherean Mission in Ghana, with programs that include hospital care, HIV/AIDS relief, and education for children. The Etherean Mission is represented in the United States by Conscious Humanity Inc., a nonprofit base for Tetteh's work.

A native of Ghana who now calls himself a "universal citizen," Tetteh began showing healing gifts at the age of five, when his touch and prayer restored the health of a young cousin. He went on to develop tools for cleansing the mind of fear, anger, grief, and depression, and healing many physical diseases. His work has been compared to that of Mother Teresa in India.

While running the Etherean Mission, Tetteh built a successful computer company. He has published twenty-two books and developed more than a hundred workshops, CDs, and other tools for self-healing and creativity. He has participated in a number of radio and television discussions, in Africa, Europe, and North America, on religion, healing, and world peace.

Tetteh has two biological children—as well as thirty-five others—and he and his wife keep sheltering, feeding, clothing, educating, and mentally restoring the lost, discarded, and abused children they encounter. Much of Tetteh's ongoing work with children is made possible through donations from caring adults worldwide.

www.conscioushumanity.com

REACHING HIGHER

LOVE, BE PRESENT, AND SERVE

If I Were Your Daddy ... with unconditional love I'd help you to be present with others, know that God loves you, and go forth into life as a servant leader.

JONATHAN RECKFORD
Habitat for Humanity CEO

Sometimes when I'm wrestling with an issue or reading the newspaper, I become oblivious to what is going on around me. I think every parent knows what I'm talking about. A number of years ago, my youngest child, Lily, caught me in one of those moments. I was absorbed in solving a problem, and I was home but not home. Lily wanted all of me there because this was supposed to be our time together. So she placed her delicate little hand on my chin and pulled my face toward hers so our eyes met.

Even at that young age, Lily understood that the first step to creating a bond is establishing eye contact and gentle touch. In this way she silently but effectively let me know I was not connected to her or truly present. It was a great reminder and I readily admitted, "I'm sorry, honey; I was in a zone." There was a second important message in my apology: "I may be your dad, but I'm imperfect, and it's okay if you aren't perfect either, but we should still try and do our best."

My ability to focus is one of my strengths, but it can also be a challenge. I learned early from one of my mentors the value of being present to those around you, especially those you care about. But holding myself to this ideal poses another challenge: it requires accepting that while I *want* to be this amazing dad and be present for my kids, I may fall short. For those days when "I should do and be more" thoughts start throbbing, I try to extend some grace to myself in the process.

Back when I was in college I had to write an essay about my personal hero for a leadership class. After some thought, I realized that my hero was a composite of three persons: my dad and two women who shaped my character and life's direction. Their influences were enormous, affecting not only my life but the lives of my children.

LEARNING FROM OUR HEROS

I was one of five children with very different personalities and gifts. My parents always accepted the uniqueness in each of us, delighting in our individuality. I always felt loved for who I was rather than what I did. My father, Kenneth Reckford, taught classics at the University of North Carolina, and his focus was on being interested rather than interesting. His combination of faith, personal humility, and passion for learning was foundational for me. He was always more focused on what I was learning than on my grades or performance. He encouraged me to be internally driven rather than achieving for the purpose of pleasing others.

Be internally driven rather than achieving for the purpose of pleasing others.

One of my dad's early gifts to me was to invite *his* mentor, John Conway, to be my godfather. John taught history at the University of Massachusetts, and his wife, Jill, was president of Smith College. When I was about ten I began visiting them regularly, and I treasured these times. They took me seriously, and I always left inspired to read and learn. One evening I was particularly moved when I recognized in Jill the rare ability to be completely present with others. I later learned that after she finished dinner that night, at least four hours of work awaited her as she tackled her job's endless challenges. But she never allowed her workload to infringe upon her time with me. For many years I observed that no matter where she was, she was totally present to the moment and its circumstances and, in particular, to the people in her company. It was more than superb eye contact; she invested her full heart in whoever was near. Jill is my second hero and she continues to be someone whose advice I seek out for major life decisions. Her ability to stay in the present moment is a value I have tried to emulate in my own life, especially as a father, with varying degrees of success.

My third hero is my grandmother, Millicent Fenwick. A congresswoman from New Jersey from 1974 to 1982 and a champion of civil rights, she was a formidable character, totally focused on global issues. Legendary news anchor Walter Cronkite once dubbed her "the conscience of Congress." She was an unusual mix of beauty and brain, grit and grace. As a young woman she'd modeled for *Harper's Bazaar* and went on to author *Vogue's Book of Etiquette,* a million-copy bestseller about manners.

When visiting Grandma's house, in order to graduate to the "grown-up table," my siblings and I were expected to sit up straight, hold our forks properly, and discuss starvation issues affecting sub-Saharan Africa! It was fascinating and terrifying. Virtually every time we saw her she quoted Micah 6:8:

> "He has showed you, O man, what is good.
>
> And what does the Lord require of you?
>
> To act justly and to love mercy and to walk humbly
> with your God."

Then she would grill us about how we planned to be "useful," her term for doing good in the world. She was anything but a warm, fuzzy grandmother type, and I was more than a bit in awe of her.

When I became a father, the combined influence of these three heroes, as different as they were from each other, greatly influenced my own parenting. My conscious goal was to emulate and pass on my dad's unconditional love, humility, and love of learning, my godmother Jill's wisdom and ability to be wholly present, and my grandmother's passionate charge to become servant leaders. My quest as a father has been to sort out how.

Parenting is, by definition, a humbling vocation, and I have hesitated in writing about it because of the risk of making it sound as if we've "arrived" or have it all together. Balancing the needs of each family member is a constant challenge. Yes, there are the good days when it works. But then we have plenty of "extra grace required" days, with tired parents and children who don't get along. It's an ever-changing drama, day to day, sometimes minute to minute. I like the roller-coaster analogy from the movie *Parenthood:* we parents are challenged to enjoy the thrill ride, with all the highs and lows and twists and turns. So if you're a parent struggling right now, I just want to encourage you.

CREATING WHOLE QUALITY TIME

In my job with Habitat for Humanity I feel called to do the work and privileged to serve. But my role requires a great deal more travel than any previous job I've held. I have three wonderful children whose ages range from elementary school to high school, and they frequently remind me I'm away too much. Between the travel, workload, and public appearances, a schedule nobody likes, it's a struggle. My wife, Ashley, and I compensate, in part, by creating rituals and routines that allow everyone to maximize our time together. It's about creating "whole quality time" during which I give myself permission to put aside everything but the kids.

I travel a lot, and we compensate with rituals and routines that maximize our time together.

According to Woody Allen, 80 percent of success is showing up, but I beg to differ. There's a big difference between just showing up and really being there, and everyone can feel it. Ashley deserves huge credit; she chose to give up a successful legal career to stay home with our children. While we try to share the parenting and home management load, she bears the brunt of the relentless schedule of doctors, orthodontists, music lessons, sports practices, play dates, and school projects. Without her leadership our life wouldn't work.

When I'm physically away, I call home every evening without fail and send text messages and e-mail photos. Technology is certainly no substitute for physical presence, but it does keep us connected. My children receive nightly affirmations that they're in my thoughts regardless of the physical distance separating us. However when I am home, being present means taking a page from an old-fashioned family playbook. We play card and board games, talk, and have fun.

CONNECTING OVER FAMILY DINNERS

It is also our goal to eat dinner together as a family as often as possible. It's a simple event of great value in helping us connect. But while it remains our goal, as the children get older it's become increasingly difficult. Around the table we share the normal end-of-day chitchat, while Dad tries to elicit highs and lows from everyone's day. We sometimes use a deck of cards called *Food for Talk*, featuring open-ended questions that have sparked some good conversations, questions like, "If you knew you had only one year to live, what, if anything, would you do differently?" And, "If you could be anyone, for the rest of your life or just today, who would you like to be and why?" For a while we substituted a manners book (what can I say—I'm Millicent's grandson!); we also use seasonal devotions, especially during Lent or Advent. By engaging in dialogue beyond the ordinary "How was your day and please pass the salt" fare, we create opportunities for connecting more deeply. Some days we never sit down at all. Other days the kids would rather tease each other and joke and laugh than engage in more positive dialogue, and when that happens we don't force it.

For family dinners, we ask open-ended questions to spark some good conversations.

Dinnertime segues quickly into homework and then bedtime. Tucking the kids in bed and praying with each child individually is my most treasured time of the day. But this too is becoming more fragmented as they get older and stay up later. I still get to read aloud to Lily, and often her big sister, Grace, reads aloud to me. They start their prayers by giving thanks for something nice from the day, asking God for help with a challenge, or both. Then we read a few Bible verses together before it's lights out. And every night, and every morning when I drive the kids to school, I make sure to tell them that, no matter what, God loves them and so do I. Whatever else happens in their lives, I hope they will always know that.

On some weekends, I carve out alone time with each child, a "dad date" when the child gets to choose what we do and where we go. This has included games, water parks, bowling, ice cream, bookstores, and lots of sports, especially with my son, Alexander. No matter how emotionally present a parent is, every child needs concentrated physical time alone with us, time to feel that he or she is the most important person in our universe. Once we're date-bound, I have to stifle my impulse to jump in and force bonding. I've learned it doesn't work that way. I've noticed too that as the kids get older, being present often means just being available. They want to be listened to when they've got something to say and accepted when they don't, with no lecturing. My teenage son, for instance, loosens and opens up after a few rounds of basketball. Nailing lay-ups and dribbling past my defense seems to release whatever's pent up inside him. Knowing this, I deliberately spend time in an environment that's comfortable for him—on his court, so to speak—instead of expecting him to come into my realm.

> *I* carve out alone time with each child, a "dad date" time to feel he or she is the most important person in our universe.

In our family we all enjoy board games and card games. I find that playing games creates space for us to have fun together, and we learn strategies about how to win and lose with grace. As the kids get older the games get more advanced, but win or lose we try to model good sportsmanship. And

Points of connection multiply and anchor a child's sense of well-being.

every now and then we even get to hear one sibling congratulate another for playing well or winning the game.

One thing I've learned for certain is that being present is a constant, and time together from yesterday or last week does not matter today. At no fixed point can you declare victory. Family dinners, meaningful conversation, and game nights may seem minor in themselves, but these points of connection multiply and anchor a child's sense of well-being. Inspirational scriptures and bedtime prayers serve as ballast. A family with a strong keel has more to offer the world, so my motive for being wholly present—in mind if not always body—isn't just about us. I want to set a course from which my children will sail forth and give of themselves, meeting the world with open hearts.

INSPIRING HEART

Thanks to my grandmother's influence and hammering home of the "give back to others" message, I believe contributing socially is central to leading a rich, fulfilling life. God has blessed us with gifts and we're called to be a blessing to others. I know that in my own life I've felt the most fulfilled when involved in some project that has made a difference to another person or community.

I don't ever want my children to feel guilty for all they have, but I do want them to be grateful and to realize how much they have to give. So when we talk about "doing good," I share stories about people I've met or give examples from church or school—people whose challenges offer real-life opportunities for us to do something of value. While traveling I often send them stories about how kids in other countries live. But there's a fine line. While I want to educate and inspire, I don't want to overwhelm them with the insatiable needs of the world. "Making a difference" needs to be something within their vision and reach. Whenever I visit a new country I bring back small dolls for the girls. It began as a whim and has become a tradition, and it gives us a way to talk about the customs and cultures of those countries and how families there live.

I want them to be compassionate and feel a heartfelt urge to respond as they can to the needs of others, and nothing beats direct, personal experience for making the plights of others more real. With that in mind, when I accepted the Habitat for Humanity position, I took the kids for a tour around the impoverished areas of Minneapolis–St. Paul, Minnesota, our home base at the time. My youngest was five and she was shocked that not everyone had a decent house to live in. This experience allowed her to catch, at her level, the Habitat vision. After that she more easily accepted my time away for work. "Can I help too, Daddy?" she asked. "Of course," was my response. She's now a relentless fund-raiser for saving the rainforest and for our local children's hospital.

I remember my dad explaining why he and my mother give so much of their modest income away ... my goal is to do the same.

All of our children have participated in our church service camps, giving them hands-on opportunities to help. Through World Vision we sponsor kids in Africa and Asia the same genders and ages as our own. We post their return letters and photos on the fridge, a regular and personal reminder of how much of the world lives. My son is now old enough to accompany me on short trips. It allows us to spend time together, but it also helps him understand my work a little better. This year, we'll help build a home for and with some AIDS orphans in Zambia. Alexander will learn infinitely more through direct experience than I could ever explain, and we'll build heartbreaking and heartwarming memories to share as well. As a family, we also visited a Habitat community in Costa Rica.

I remember vividly my dad explaining why he and my mother chose to give so much of their modest income away. It's my goal to do the same. By introducing the concepts of compassion and generosity in the safe context of family, service feels normal and natural, an extension of who my children are, so they'll be more likely to continue it when they're on their own.

But service doesn't have to be a grand outreach to parts unknown. One of my favorite stories involves my son, Alexander. It was his first day of kindergarten. Another boy, obviously terrified at the prospect of the unknown, was clinging to his mother's legs and crying. Suddenly, without prompting, Alexander stepped forward and said, "Don't worry; I'll be your friend." He then took the boy's hand and led him into the classroom. This pure and simple act of kindness, this shining example of servant leadership, left me speechless. I was so proud of him.

If I were to rewrite my hero essay today, each of my children's names, including Alexander's, would be alongside Dad's, Jill's, and Grandma's. All of six years old at the time, my son embodied what we were striving to teach. He arrived at school that September day whole and present, and his open heart immediately registered the other boy's pain and moved Alexander forward in service. Feeling God's love for him, he had love to share and passed that love along to another. And he did it all without expecting a note of fanfare. As a dad with a quest of teaching my kids those exact values, what a great validation it was to know that whatever we were doing, it was working.

There's more ... Jonathan Reckford describes the "80-20 rule" he uses to correct his children's behavior. Go to

www.ifiwereyourdaddy.com/jonathanreckford

"*Man becomes great exactly in the degree in which he works for the welfare of his fellow-men.*"

Mahatma Ghandi, world leader whose leadership and nonviolent methods freed millions.

WHO IS JONATHAN RECKFORD?

Jonathan with (wife) Ashley, (children) Alexander, Grace, and Lily

From Wall Street to corporate suite to church ministry, Jonathan Reckford—now CEO of Habit for Humanity International—has demonstrated a rare combination of passion for serving those in need with the executive skills required to lead an efficient, effective international nonprofit organization.

A North Carolina native, Reckford earned an undergraduate degree in political science from the University of North Carolina at Chapel Hill, and an M.B.A., with a certificate in public and nonprofit management from Stanford's Graduate School of Business.

Reckford's book, *Creating a Habitat for Humanity: No Hands but Yours,* centers on Reckford's "life verse," Micah 6:8,

Former President Jimmy Carter, who served as honorary chair of Habitat's succession planning task force, said, "Jonathan Reckford is a wonderful choice to become Habitat for Humanity's new chief executive officer. His background in business will help Habitat navigate the economy and business climate, and his pastoral experiences will help him shepherd Habitat's ministry."

Besides leadership experience at such firms as Goldman Sachs and Best Buy, Reckford worked for the Olympic Organizing Committee, preparing for the 1988 Olympic Games in Seoul, Korea. With experience in competitive rowing, he was asked to coach the Korean national rowing team.

Reckford lives in Atlanta with his wife, Ashley, and their three children.

www.habitat.org

PRICELESS HEIRLOOMS
THAT NEVER RUST

If I Were Your Daddy ... I'd pass on two heirlooms of divine character that will make life easier. Both gifts will help you glide through life challenges and tough moments toward success.

BILLY SHORE

Share Our Strength CEO,
Anti-Hunger & Anti-Poverty
Child Advocate

When my daughter, Mollie, was a child, we spent most of our time together taking the dogs for a walk, going swimming, or seeing a movie. Psychologists have long understood that males generally approach all relationships this way, not just those with their children. From the time they are little boys, they organize relationships around activities. They play games together or band together to watch other men play sports. Women, however, from the time they are little girls, seek simply being together. And Mollie was a little girl.

As time passed I sensed a distance growing between us. The more I tried to fix it, the less connection I felt with her. If Mollie and I didn't have a specific activity scheduled, I would read in my study, work on other chores, or make phone calls. From my point of view I was maximizing my time and being productive. It made perfect sense to me, but not to my daughter. I had not yet learned what her mother already knew: Mollie was not so much interested in what I could give her, where I could take her, or even what we could do together. She just wanted to spend time with me, without any agenda except being together. Not only was I trying too hard, I was trying the wrong things. It took a memorable incident one warm summer night to teach me this lesson.

She wasn't interested in what I could give her, where I could take her, or what we could do together. She just wanted me.

For several days Molly had been diligently trying to build a "secret hideout" in our backyard. On this particular evening she had grown increasingly frustrated with her efforts. When the walls fell over for the last time with a loud crack, she burst into tears. Her sad little face spoke to me to a degree I could not ignore.

"You know what you need to make this work, Molls?" I offered.

"What?" she huffed, her tears still flowing.

"You need about sixty bricks."

"Great," she replied, "but I don't have sixty bricks."

"But we could get them."

"Where?" she said doubtfully.

"Home Depot," I said. "Get your shoes on and hop in the car. Real quick." Dad to the rescue! As I watched her tie her shoes in double time, I realized this was my shot at winning her over.

When we arrived at the store we grabbed a wheeled flat cart and headed to the brick department. Choosing from a greater selection of bricks than one could possibly imagine, we settled on the twenty-three-cents-a brick variety. Because it was already late and I wanted to get home, I started loading those bricks as quickly as I could, two-handed, two to four at a time. They were rough and heavy, and I wished I'd brought gloves.

"Oh please, let me do that, Dad, please!" Mollie begged.

What? I couldn't possibly imagine anything more unrealistic. She was little, the bricks were heavy, and she would have to use two hands just to pick up one of them. I knew if Mollie did it we'd be there forever. Glancing at my watch and taking a deep breath, I tried to keep my resistance in check.

"But, sweetie, they're very heavy," I said to discourage her.

"Please, Dad, I really want to," she begged again, moving quickly to the pile of bricks and hoisting one up with both hands. As I watched, she lugged it over to the cart and laid it next to the handful I'd already placed there.

I sighed inwardly. This was going to take all night.

Suddenly, as I watched Mollie walk back to the pile and carefully select another brick, I realized she wanted it to take all night. It might have been my agenda to do it fast and get back home, but it wasn't hers. I'd been traveling a lot, and I realized she was trying to make up for lost time. This little expedition wasn't about getting something finished at all. It was rare for the two of us to have time alone together, and Mollie wanted it to last.

With this new awareness, I took a deep breath and leaned back against one of the wood pallets in the store. It no longer mattered that it was late and past her bedtime. As I stood by and watched, Mollie worked steadily at loading the bricks. Sensing that the pressure was off, she relaxed and became chatty. As I listened, she talked about what she was going to build, about school and her girlfriends and her upcoming horseback riding lesson. When she finally finished loading the bricks we headed home, having connected in a new way.

> Kids don't always have to be steered in a particular direction; just being along for the ride with them is often enough.

This was a wake-up call for me. How had I missed the subtle indicators of what Mollie really needed? All she wanted was for me to be present with her, period. Kids don't always have to be steered in a particular direction; just being along for the ride with them is often enough. I realized then I had taken a wrong turn and was in need of a course correction. The way I had been interacting with Mollie wasn't in sync with her needs. My work-family time wasn't balanced. My daughter set me straight that night and righted me, all for just twenty-three cents a brick.

ADOPT A HUNDRED FOOT PERSPECTIVE

Webster describes balance as "mental and emotional steadiness." Because we are always learning and growing, steadiness may mean a willingness to shift priorities. Perhaps you too have fallen a bit out of balance and need to readjust, as I did with Mollie. But steadiness can also mean seeing the bigger picture and gaining a perspective that can help neutralize the intensity of a sticky moment.

My father, grandfather to my three kids—Zach, Mollie, and Nate—was a master at neutralizing sticky moments. He was one of the most balanced men I've ever known, and his calm, patient, and unruffled manner kept our whole family steady through many storms and challenges. In a difficult moment he would often say, "Catch your breath. Nothing is ever quite as it seems at the moment."

"*Catch your breath. Nothing is ever quite as it seems at the moment.*"

My dad said it often enough that it made a permanent imprint upon me. More than just a success mind-set, the ability to rise above a problem and see it from one hundred feet up made life easier and happier, no matter what transpired. That perspective was a golden nugget worthy of being called a family heirloom, and I passed it on to my kids throughout their childhood and teenage years.

There were plenty of occasions when this balancing perspective helped me immeasurably in the face of rejection, disappointment, or loss. When my children were in their teens, it was the same for them. It came in handy when Mollie wasn't invited to a party she wanted to go to and felt excluded. It got pressed into use when Zach didn't get on the hockey team he wanted to and was heartbroken. On both occasions this perspective allowed them to acknowledge how they really felt now, yet distinguish that from how the situation was going to look later. As a result, each recovered more quickly. The 100-foot viewpoint had the wonderful effect of redirecting that initial impulse to react out of pain and helped them to think in the long term.

On another occasion Zach got into trouble when he and his buddies covered a neighbor's house with toilet paper, and afterward had to go and clean up the mess. Embarrassed and ashamed, he had learned his lesson. Not wanting him to be scarred or traumatized by overemphasizing the experience, I reassured him, "Nothing is as important as it seems at the time, Zach. Don't forget, this too shall pass." So the heirloom was passed down. And I'm quite sure he'll pass it down to his kids as well.

Kids need tools to get through passages. If you give them ones that make sense, they'll hang on to them.

For a kid, a 100-foot perspective can be pretty comforting when you expect your dad to come down hard on you, when you're coming down hard on yourself, or when you're drowning in the intense feelings of the crisis of the moment. Kids need tools to get through passages, particularly in adolescence when it's difficult enough to navigate. If you give them tools that make sense, they'll hang on to them.

EVERY STORY HAS TWO SIDES

Another thing kids come face to face with as they grow up is gossip. They hear opinions and judgments about other people and things they've done; they hear about who's right and who's wrong. Without a better, wiser way of finding perspective, it's easy for them to simply accept what they hear. To combat this, we reminded our kids, "There are two sides to every story." For our family, this saying became another heirloom of sorts, and putting it into practice has been nothing less than profound.

When Zach and Mollie were young, for instance, close friends of ours went through a divorce. Their kids, like everyone else, took sides in gossip, mostly against the mother, and made it her fault. Zach and Mollie, playmates of the children, became very upset with her themselves and discovered firsthand how unpleasant it feels to criticize others. So I offered them an alternative: "We don't know the full story here. You don't live inside somebody else's life or house or marriage. You've heard only one side of the story, and you have to understand there are two sides to every story, like two sides to a coin." With this, they were more easily able to let go of their opinion, adopt a neutral position, and comfort their friends as well.

On another occasion we learned that a friend's son had been kicked out of school for a while. Everybody formed the opinion that he was a "bad kid." We later learned there were things going on in his home that no one knew about, and had made his life very difficult. Once again it was a case of hearing a small part of the bigger story, and not having all the facts. You've got to leave space for the possibility that things you can't see and don't know are affecting what's happening. You've got to ask yourself, "Is there something else going on here?"

That's come up with all my kids, even my youngest. Nate is only four, so things often happen that he doesn't understand. One day at school, another little boy didn't share a toy with him and his feelings were hurt. So I said, "Maybe there's something going on with that little boy that you and I don't know about and made him do that. So it's OK. It probably has nothing to do with you." My reassurance was just what he needed to let go of his hurt feelings quickly.

> When you're tolerant, when you suspend judgment, you become compassionate and kind with others, as well as yourself.

People are so diverse. Everyone has different strengths and weaknesses, and we all approach things so differently. That's why tolerance is so important in life. When you criticize, you attack differences like a prize fighter in a corner of the ring. When you're tolerant, you suspend judgment. Emotional swings are evened out because you haven't let an opinion which is not fact, sway you to a position left or right. Tolerance helps you get along better in the world, but it also helps you become a better friend, more compassionate and kind. Ultimately, you learn to be more forgiving of your own failings, sparing you disappointment and heartache. In this way being tolerant allows you to help yourself, and I've tried to pass that on to my kids.

Novelist Walker Percy once said that passing life's lessons on to our children is like two prisoners pushing notes between cell blocks. You never know if you're getting through, but you keep doing it anyway. Years later, I heard Zach counseling a friend, "So-and-so did this, but he's had a hard life. You can never know the whole story." It felt pretty good to know that some of those messages got through after all.

THE NATURE OF SUCCESS

There's an underlying theme these two family heirlooms have in common. They both are healthy responses to disappointment and defeat. Taking a 100 percent perspective and looking for the other side of the story are resourceful mindsets that when adopted lessen the sting, whether it's about yours or another's actions. Success is never a straight-line journey, a string of unbroken successes like a record-breaking winning streak on a PGA tour. I speak about this all the time to my own kids as well as to many college students. So many of them believe that to be successful you can never have a misstep, that you must carefully toe the line, not take any chances, and get your ticket punched in all the right places.

> *Success is not a straight-line journey, a string of unbroken successes.*

In fact it's the opposite. Most successful people have had all kinds of setbacks and defeats that helped them to become more successful in the long run. I let my kids and other young people know it will be no different for them. Sometimes they're going to miss the mark they've set for themselves, like I did with little Mollie, when I was a busy dad *doing* rather than *being*. At some point they'll be off base, headed in the wrong direction, or staring at less than ideal results. Whether it's at school or in athletics or on the job, sometimes you just mess up. The important thing is to understand it's OK; it doesn't mean the die is cast forever. You just pick yourself up and get back out there. And for these times, I hope my kids will consider it a gift that their dad taught them to always ask these two questions:

Is it possible it's not as bad as it seems?

Could it be that things are not as they appear to be?

Lifting ourselves up to that one hundred foot vantage point and suspending judgments about one another are *our family heirlooms,* though ones that all families can possess. These heirlooms make us better friends and more compassionate beings. They level the ups and downs, and leave us more mentally and emotionally steady as well. These are heirlooms of divine habits of character, a morality in action that can endure for generations and make the world a better place.

I say, always assume the best and let's pass these heirlooms on.

"The most important human endeavor is the striving for morality in our actions. Our inner balance, and even our very existence depends on it. Only morality in our actions can give beauty and dignity to our lives."

Albert Einstein, theoretical physicist, philosopher, who is widely regarded as the father of modern physics. He was awarded the 1921 Nobel Prize in Physics.

Billy with *(children)* Zach and Mollie

Billy with *(wife)* Rosemary and *(child)* Nate

Billy Shore is a world-changer. His organization Share Our Strength® has raised more than $265 million for more than a thousand anti-hunger, anti-poverty programs.

Shore founded Share Our Strength in 1984, while serving as a staffer for Senator Gary Hart. Since its small beginning in Ethiopian famine relief, the organization has grown to be the nation's most successful at reducing world poverty and hunger. Shore also chairs Community Wealth Ventures®, Inc., a for-profit subsidiary of Share Our Strength that advises foundations and nonprofit organizations on creating community wealth—wealth generated through profitable enterprise to promote social change.

Shore's move from politics to community service is documented in his first book, *Revolution of the Heart,* which also lays out his prescription for community change. His second book, *The Cathedral Within,* profiles a new breed of leaders who are improving community life across all sectors of society. His most recent book, *The Light of Conscience,* demonstrates how small acts of conscience can change the world.

US News & World Report called Shore one of "America's best leaders," the Caring Institute called him one of the "top ten caring people of 1995," and the James Beard Foundation named him "Humanitarian of the Year."

But most important—three children call Billy Shore "Daddy."

www.strength.org

YOUR SPIRITUAL ID
& THE GOLDEN RULE

If I Were Your Daddy ... you'd learn that you and everyone else are created in God's image and likeness. I'd help you learn to live the Golden Rule, not just in words but in actions.

$\mathcal{R}$ICK LIPSEY

Sports Illustrated Journalist
& Philanthropist

My basic premise for fathering is that I'm not my children's true father. Yes, of course I'm their human father. I get my oldest children, Claudia and Ricky, off to school each morning, and I coach their hockey and soccer teams. I take my toddler, Timmy, to the playground and swim class, and I make diaper and formula runs to Costco for the baby, Alexander. By all standards, I'm a fully involved dad.

But when I look at my four children and myself beyond the human framework, I see a spiritual vision that is radically different from what the human senses present. I see a marvelous relationship that transcends parent-child. This awareness affects everything I do, and especially how I interact with my kids.

Here's how I see our family tree. At the top is God. Below are my wife, our children, and I—all of us on the same line. We're really all children, and God is our one parent. In this same vein I believe that my fathering abilities and activities don't originate with me. It's really quite straightforward: I believe my primary job as a father is to love and listen to God, share God's thoughts and actions, and teach my children to do the same.

As a man and as a father, I'm always learning. Humility is something I strive for daily. I admit that sometimes I *forget* that my real job as my kids' dad is to listen to God and hear His will. But when that happens, the situation at hand quickly reminds me of my need to *stop and listen.* One summer we were at a country club with our oldest son, Ricky, who was three and a half at the time. Happily playing away in the baby pool with his pail and shovel, Ricky was oblivious of the sun glaring down on his skin. Concerned about sunburn, I tried to get him to put on his swimming shirt. However, involved as he was with toys and water, he wanted nothing to do with that shirt—or his dad.

> My primary job is to love and listen to God, and teach my children to do the same.

"Ricky," I said, "you need to put this on. You have to put this on!"

When Ricky continued to resist, I tried to wrestle the shirt over his head, which made Ricky cry, and he darted away. Ready to give chase, I caught myself. What was I doing? This simple interaction had become a contest of wills.

Sitting down, I reminded myself that Ricky was a child of God, made in God's image and likeness, and thus never separated from His care. As soon as I did that, everything changed—and radically. I began to feel calm, and I turned away to read something. Ricky kept playing in the pool. Lo and behold, a few minutes later Ricky silently came over and nonchalantly put on his shirt. That was that. When I had let go, Ricky had responded quite naturally to God's guidance. What was right for everyone was accomplished without a fuss.

THE GOLDEN RULE ON THE STREET

When I used to walk Claudia and Ricky to preschool, we had a ritual.

While navigating the noisy streets of Manhattan's Upper West Side, we would discuss how we were going to treat others that day and apply the Golden Rule. Often I would ask them, "What's the most important thing we need to do today?" and they would both answer, "Love our neighbors!"

I'd then ask, "How are you going to do that?"

The kids would rattle off some ideas: smile at a teacher, give a friend a high five, say hello to Ray (the preschool's custodian), and so on—all good ideas. I wanted Claudia and Ricky to know the Golden Rule wasn't just *words*. I wanted them to think about how to make it practical, how to live it.

Our daily route to school took us past a ventilation grate on the sidewalk where two homeless men often slept because of the warm air wafting up through the grate. Ricky wanted to know why the men were homeless and sleeping outside. "Well," I said, "I don't

The Golden Rule isn't just words; we have to make it practical. We have to live it.

know what caused them to live here, but I do know it's our job to try and see them as God sees them."

The kids and I often spoke with the men—whose names turned out to be Stan and Bernard—and we became friends. One morning while walking to school after Halloween, Ricky decided he wanted to live the Golden Rule by sharing some of his candy. Before leaving the house, Ricky stuffed his pockets full. As we approached the grate, Ricky bolted toward the men, and when I caught up he was talking and sharing his stash of candy with them. They had big smiles and were thanking Ricky profusely. Another day, Ricky wanted to give Stan a more personal gift, so he brought him a picture he'd made in art class. Stan and Bernard were very touched.

Most memorable was the morning Ricky didn't want to say hello to Stan, who was sleeping alone on the grate, curled up in a sleeping bag. When I asked Ricky why he wouldn't speak to Stan, Ricky just shrugged his shoulders. I didn't relent. I took Ricky's hand and walked him over to

Stan. I said, "Good morning, Stan. Ricky has something to say." I nudged Ricky and motioned for him to say hello, which Ricky sheepishly did. What happened next is a treasured memory. Stan awoke from his slumber, sat up, and reached into his pocket. He pulled out a one-dollar bill and handed it to Ricky. "Thanks a lot, Stan," said Ricky.

"Buy yourself some candy," Stan said.

I explained to Ricky how amazingly generous that gesture was. A man who had next to nothing had given away what might be his only dollar. In his own way, Ricky understood the magnitude of the love in Stan's gesture, because he skipped to school with as big a smile as he's ever had. Ricky had learned about the rewards of giving.

From this experience, we felt the power in giving that goes hand in hand with identifying everyone as our brother, and when this happens, Divine Love has touched everybody.

THE GOLDEN RULE AT SCHOOL

When Ricky was in kindergarten, we got a call from a teacher about a little incident between Ricky and his classmate, Sam. There had been some pushing and shoving. Nothing big—the teacher just wanted us to know what had happened. By the time Ricky got home, I'd given the incident some thought. There were two routes to pursue: I could look at the problem, lay blame, and then come up with a solution, or I could pray and listen for how to handle this. I decided to pray.

Rather than come up with my solution, I decided to pray and listen for how to handle this.

When Ricky learned that his teacher had called, his face went red, and he got quiet. I began our talk not by referring to the incident, but rather by asking a question. I said, "Ricky, do you remember the Golden Rule?" He replied that he did. I continued, "Is it just words, or should we actually live it?" "Live it," he mumbled. "If we live it, this means we always try to treat others the way we want to be treated ourselves. Can you think of some way to put that Golden Rule into action that will help heal the situation with Sam?" Ricky sat down on his bed to give it some serious thought.

Right then, I remembered a story Ricky and I had recently read in a church magazine. A boy from England had been bullied in school by a bigger boy who had decided to make this little kid his punching bag. When he and his mother prayed about the situation, it came to him that he needed to love the boy who was acting as the bully. To do that he made a list of things he liked about him, and wrote a letter telling him these things. After basically seeing the good in that boy, they ended up becoming friends.

I reminded Ricky of that story, which I remembered he'd really liked when we first read it. I suggested that Ricky do something like the boy in the magazine. With my help, Ricky started writing out a list, but he was writing begrudgingly. Soon, though, Ricky's list grew to include about eight things he liked about Sam. A little surprised, Ricky said, "Wow, Sam is actually a cool guy." Next, I suggested that Ricky write a letter to Sam in which he'd tell Sam that he was sorry for what had happened, and include the list of things he liked about him.

The next day Ricky hand-delivered the letter to Sam at school. Shortly after, the two had a playdate that turned out really well, and they became friends.

For my family, this experience was proof of the power of the Golden Rule and how putting it into action helps to resolve things quickly and permanently. The Golden Rule is one of our family's most important and reliable guiding values, and I try and mention it in some form with my children every single day. Something so valuable is worth saying a lot.

Something so valuable is worth saying a lot.

HELPING OTHERS ON THE PLANET

"Gratitude is much more than a verbal expression of thanks. Action expresses more gratitude than speech." This quotation from Mary Baker Eddy inspires me every day. To me, those words mean that we need to use and share not just the material things we own, but also the spiritual qualities and human abilities that we have. As a parent, I often ask my children to find actions in their daily lives that will express gratitude—actions such as saying hello to the doormen in our building, picking up litter on the sidewalk, and sending thank-you notes after getting presents.

Action expresses more gratitude than speech.

Some of the things we do as parents are difficult to gauge. We don't always know if concepts we share with children impact them, or if they take in the ideas. So I was thrilled in the spring of 2010 when my oldest child, Claudia, said she wanted to set up a food stand to raise money for those impacted by the enormous Gulf oil spill. Claudia, who was eight years old, had seen another young girl from our building running a food stand to raise funds to support the relief effort, and Claudia wanted to do the same thing. "I want to help," Claudia said.

Claudia told Ricky about the idea, and Ricky immediately wanted to join in. Both children, with my help, had run a food stand several times on the sidewalk outside of our apartment building. In those instances, the kids had kept the money. Now, they were eager to "make a lot of money," as Ricky said, "so we can make people happy."

The morning our stand was to open, we bought fruit, doughnuts, cookies, and bottled water. We set up a wooden table with a big poster. With my prodding, Claudia and Ricky spoke to pedestrians old and young, soliciting business and explaining their fundraising effort. Within a few hours, they'd sold almost everything. Claudia and Ricky wrote a letter and sent the profits to the Greater New Orleans Foundation to help people like fishermen and their families, whose lives or livelihood had been seriously impacted by the Gulf oil spill. I was thrilled to see the love of giving that my children were living.

HAVING A SPIRITUAL BREAKFAST: DEVELOPING AN ATTITUDE OF GRATITUDE

Every morning, just as my kids are waking up, I go into their rooms and we have a brief prayer time. Usually the kids are still in their beds and I lie down on the floor in their bedroom. I'll say, "Let's have our spiritual breakfast." It's like filling up your gas tank for the day. You wouldn't think of taking your car out without gas, so you wouldn't want to take your mind and heart out unless they are filled up full with good stuff to keep you going for the day. During this time—and again before we go to bed at night—we always share what

> "*Let's* have our spiritual breakfast." It's like filling up your gas tank for the day."

we're grateful for, because I want to nurture this awareness in the children. Whether you're religious or not, gratitude is vital for healthy, happy living. The only way to live it is to think about it and talk about it every day. So that's what we do.

Sometimes my kids will say, "Oh, I don't know what I'm grateful for," and I'll respond with some obvious examples: "Well, what about the ability to talk? What about your shoes? What about yourselves?" I admit that sometimes the prayer time can seem a little forced, but I'm pretty militaristic about doing the right things, like making your bed, brushing your teeth, and cleaning your room. Being strict doesn't bother me, and the more we

> *Build* an attitude of gratitude.

practice good routines and habits, the better off we'll be. There are few things more important than building an attitude of gratitude, and that is is precisely why prayer and gratitude begin and end our day.

I'd rather *do* than talk. Even though I'm a sports writer, I'd rather play a game than write about one. Kids are natural doers too. They're always asking what to do, how to do it, and can I do it? I try to answer the children's relentless queries, but at the end of the day, my goal is not to tell them what to do, as much as it is to provide them with thoughts and skills to do whatever is necessary. A friend and parent had a good description of my mind-set: "You don't want to prepare the path for kids. *You want to prepare them for the path.*" Often when a child asks me, "Dad, how do I do this?" I'll reply by saying, "Shepherd [God], show me how to go" (a favorite line from a cherished hymn by Mary Baker Eddy).

Don't prepare the path for the kids; prepare them for the path.

Based on my experience as their dad, I of course offer my best human intentions to my children when they need help. But I always try to first humbly listen to God. And then we go from there. I tell my kids that we each have to check in and be receptive, so that "Shepherd, show me how to go" becomes our first call, not our last. And as children of God, young and old, we will be shown the right way to go.

"*We have committed the Golden Rule to memory; let us now commit it to life.*"

Edwin Markham (1852-1940), American poet whom President Herbert Hoover named as one of the most important artists of his age.

WHO IS RICK LIPSEY?

Rick with (wife) Carrie, (children) Claudia, Ricky, Timmy, and Alexander

Rick Lipsey is a sports writer with a difference. A former captain and MVP of the golf team at Cornell, where he majored in English, Lipsey was the first person to work as a full-time golf teacher in the tiny Himalayan country of Bhutan, where he created the Bhutan Youth Golf Association (www.golfbhutan.com), whose mission is is to help young people "develop friendship, honesty, integrity, morality and self-motivation."

The immediate product of Lipsey's work in Bhutan is his book *Golfing on the Roof of the World,* which *Sports Illustrated* called "beautiful and often breathtaking . . . equal to its setting. . . [Lipsey] illuminates two subjects of eternal mystery and fascination: Golf and the Himalayas."

As a staff writer-reporter for golf with *Sports Illustrated* since 1993, Lipsey has also contributed to *Golf, Golf Illustrated, Golf Pro, The New York Times, The Wall Street Journal* and *The Christian Science Monitor.* In addition to his latest book, he has coauthored an instructional book, *In Every Kid There Lurks a Tiger,* with Rudy Duran, Tiger Woods's childhood teacher.

An only child raised by a single mother, Lipsey has been a practicing Christian Scientist for his entire life. He received the Andrew Heiskell Community Service Award from Time Warner in 2002, and he has received the volunteer of the year award from Achilles International, a track club for disabled people. Lipsey lives in New York City with his wife, Carrie, and their four children.

The Golden Rule is a guide—perhaps *the* guide—to human behavior that has transcended time, culture, and religion. It is the common ground "upon which the spiritual dignity of mankind stands," and thus an essential must to teach our children.

THE GOLDEN RULE

Do not do unto others all that which is not well for oneself.
Zoroaster, sixth century BC

Hurt not others with that which pains thyself.
Buddha, sixth century BC

Do not do unto others what you do not want others to do unto you.
Confucius, sixth century BC

May I do unto others as I would that they should do unto me.
Plato, fifth century BC

Do not to others that which if done to thee would cause thee pain.
Mahabharata, third century BC

Do not do unto others what thou wouldst not they
should do unto thee.
Rabbi Hillel, first century BC

Do unto others as you would have others do unto you.
Jesus, first century AD

None of you truly have the faith if you do not desire for your
brother that which you desire for yourself.
Muhammad, sixth century AD

Lay not on any soul a load which ye would not wish
to be laid upon you and desire not for anyone
the things you would not desire for yourself.
Bahá' Alláh, nineteenth century AD

(These versions of the Golden Rule are courtesy
of Marilyn Wilhelm, of Wilhelm Scholê International.)

SHOWING UP

If I Were Your Daddy ... I'd do my best to be involved and engaged with your life, and I'd hold you responsible and accountable for your words and actions.

ℛOLAND WARREN

National Fatherhood Initiative president

I literally *fell* into my most important lesson about fatherhood. It was winter, and as is common in New Jersey, it had been snowing, and the ground had a film of ice. My wife, Yvette, and I had been out for the day of errands with our newborn son. We returned home to an extremely slippery parking lot.

Yvette was nervous about the ice, so I told her I'd carry our little guy through the lot. These were the days before those secure travel carriers, and I don't mind admitting I was a little anxious about carrying him. I was still getting used to idea of being a father.

With Yvette's arms full of groceries, and mine with our tiny son, we cautiously began to make our way toward our apartment. I looked down at the tightly swaddled bundle in my arms, his round, chubby face peacefully asleep and peeking out from his wrapping.

I hadn't taken more than three or four steps when I hit a patch of black ice and was immediately airborne. I literally went up in the air with my feet completely out from under me—horizontal! As I was "falling" backward, time stood still. The only thing in my mind was, "Don't drop him, *I can't drop him!*" Decision made, I held on to him for dear life, and purposely took the *entire brunt* of the fall on my back, banging my head hard on the pavement as I went down.

INITIATION INTO FATHERHOOD

Lying there on the frozen ice-covered parking lot in pain from head to toe, I tried to sense if anything was broken. I panicked! My son! Did I break him? Was he breathing? I looked up to see his long eyelashes, perfect lips, angelic expression—all undisturbed. Snug in my arms, he was still fast asleep. In that split second, I had chosen his safety over mine.

What really turns a man into a father is to go from being self-centered to "other-centered."

Looking back, I realized the impact of that experience. Most men grow up thinking the world revolves around them, and I was no different. But what really turns a man into a father is being able to shift gears, and go from being self-centered to "other-centered." Not many experiences will do that for a man. I learned it early, while I was flat on my back. It reminded me of what I was supposed to be: "I'm a father now; I'm *supposed* to take the hits; I'm supposed to make sure my kids are OK; This is now my *job.*"

If you've ever been knocked off balance, you know it's a natural reflex to let go of whatever you might be holding. It was a miracle that day that through my decision to "not let go" I was able to hold onto our baby. But that's what fathers do, and this was my private initiation. My life was now about protecting and serving another, and showing up for my son.

LIKE FATHER, LIKE SON

My own father was a life-of-the-party kind of guy. As a teenager, he got my mother pregnant when she was sixteen, and they got married. Things went well initially, but eventually he was "out and about." When I was only five or six years old, he stopped being around our family in a big way. My mom left him when I was seven. Caring for four kids alone, all under the age of eight, changes a woman in a big way. Mom had to work all the time just to get the food on the table. The most consistent memory that I have of my dad—was his absence.

I remembered him as a whirlwind. When he came in, it was all fun and excitement, and this made it all the more difficult when he left. I knew he wasn't there, and that he was in and out. I picked that up even though I didn't understand it.

For a myriad of reasons, children will replicate the behavior of their parents, even when they hate it. Sure enough, as I became a teen, I would occasionally sneak out of the house at night while my mom slept. Just like dad, I was in and out, and sometimes I dated multiple girls simultaneously.

Children will replicate the behavior of their parents, even when they hate it.

When I was eighteen I met Yvette and fell in love. When she got pregnant, I remembered that my dad got my mother pregnant, and here I was repeating his life. I decided it had to stop here. I had to change—I *had* to do a better job as a man and a father than the model I knew.

Thankfully a couple of things created epiphany-like moments that told me, "You're going down the wrong path, Roland. You must change your ways and be a different guy." One of them was Yvette. She saw something in me, and began teaching me how to love. The other was my Christian faith, which helped me understand and embrace my responsibilities to my family. I just knew I had to be different.

LEARNING HOW TO BE INVOLVED AND ENGAGED

When a guy has a father who is not involved or engaged, he sometimes mirrors that behavior and becomes the same kind of father too. But by the grace of God and my desire and commitment to be different, I didn't repeat all my dad's life patterns any further.

Gratefully my wife came from a very different home environment. She's just a love machine, and she saw the good in me and taught me a lot about love. Her own father was loving and engaged, so she had *clear expectations* of me as a father. To meet her expectations, I needed to step up and be a certain kind of guy. I loved her and didn't want to let her down, so I made a commitment to do the very best I could. I watched how she interacted with her own healthy family, and I saw that I needed to become more other-centered and other-focused, like she was.

I had to teach them two things: take responsibility and be accountable for your actions.

Two and a half years later, when our second son was born, I had a better idea of what I needed to be as a man, husband, and father. I had real motivation. I didn't want my sons doing the kinds of things I'd done in my youth; I wanted them to go down a different road. And by now I had learned that being different and teaching my sons to be different meant living by godly principles: taking responsibility and being accountable for your actions. I became very focused on being involved and engaged with my sons,

It's hard to be what you don't see, so I believed that if my boys were going to grow up to be a certain kind of man, they had to see that kind of man modeled in front of them. Looking back, I guess it worked. I wasn't a perfect example, because we're not perfect people, but *even imperfect people can have a perfect effort.* From my standpoint, that was always the driver for me. I just focused on committing to *the effort,* because that's what I could control.

RESPECT 101: HOW TO TREAT GIRLS AND WOMEN

Today my boys are twenty-eight and twenty-five, but when they were little, one thing I was really focused on was how they treated girls. I did not want them behaving the way I had behaved with girls. I think one of the critically important things a father needs to model for his son is how to treat girls, and how to treat women.

A father needs to model for his son how to treat girls, and how to treat women.

My wife is a beautiful woman inside and out, and my boys are both pretty good-looking guys. My younger son, in particular, caught the girls' attention early. When he was in about third grade and probably eight, there was a little girl at school who liked him.

One day I was sitting in the dining room, and the phone rang. He went and answered, and I heard him say, very rudely, "I don't like you"—this, that, and the other—being very nasty to whoever was on the other end. He practically hung up on the caller.

So I went over and asked him, "Who was that?"

"It was this girl at school," he said distastefully. "She likes me, and I don't like her."

It just happened that I was there for this incident and saw the way he treated that little girl, and it was mean. I didn't want my boys to be like that, so I jumped on it right away.

"Well," I said, "I appreciate that you don't like this girl, but the way you spoke to her just now was inappropriate and rude. You're going to change that. Here's what you're going to do. You're going to call her back right now, and you're going to apologize. You're going to say, "Listen, I appreciate the fact that you like me and everything, but I'm too young to have a girlfriend at this age." It was very hard for him, but he had no choice, because I just stood there while he did it.

IT PAYS TO SWEAT THE SMALL STUFF

You might think that was a small thing, but from the time they were little I was very focused on how my boys treated girls. Whenever these little things came up that others might take a pass on, I didn't pass. I used them as teachable moments because I knew, even though it was a little thing and he was only in third grade, that one day he would be fifteen, and then sixteen, *and I wouldn't be there,* and I didn't want him to be that kind of guy.

The guys who become "dogs" with women, it starts when they are little boys—no one held them accountable

For a lot of the guys who end up becoming "dogs," or whatever term you want to use, it doesn't start when they're adults, or even teenagers. It starts when they are little boys, because no one models for them and holds them accountable for how they are supposed to behave and treat little girls. It's no surprise that when they are left out of control, they grow up not treating women very well. I didn't want a son like that. I wanted a son who was respectful, and not arrogant. I wanted a son who understood that a key part of *being* responsible was *acting responsibly,* and treating people with respect.

It was a small way to deliver such an important message, to an eight-year-old even, but it got through. It's interesting how these things run their circle, because recently he was doing some Internet dating and got a match with this one young lady. After their second date he came home and said, "You know, Dad, she's very nice, but there just isn't a spark there. I don't feel that attracted to her."

I said, "Okay, well, you don't have to keep contact with her. It's Internet dating, and she knows she's not going to match with everyone."

But he said, "No, no, no, I need to sit down with her and tell her. I want to make sure I leave this situation in a way that is respectful," and despite my reassurances, he really just went on and on about it.

To me, there's a direct link between how he handled this situation and how I made him handle the phone incident when he was little. Because I addressed it so unequivocally *then*—"It's OK that you don't like someone, but you still need to be respectful of her"—he's carried the lesson through his life. He was so concerned about this young woman that he went above and beyond what even I thought he needed to do.

Then, just recently, I hired a new woman at the office. During our interview she said, "By the way, I know your son." It turned out she went to high school with him, and she said, "I just wanted to tell you, your son is the nicest guy. He's so respectful and he treats girls so well ..." and she just went on and on about him being one of the "good" guys. He was a star athlete in football, got a scholarship to play Division One football in college, all that stuff, so he was in the demographic where someone behaving badly could have done a lot of damage to a lot of people. Instead, people loved him.

THEY'LL BEHAVE THE WAY YOU BEHAVE

Do I think all this wisdom about being respectful to girls came from that one talk? Probably not—but it *was* important. Making that call was a really hard thing for him to do, so he took it to heart in a big way. Still, many other things have contributed too. My sons watched how I treated their mother, just as I watched how my dad treated my mom, and I was very aware of this fact.

Obviously we're not talking perfection, but on average, to the best of our ability, their mother and I spoke to and treated each other very respectfully. If one of us got short or nasty, the boys would see us apologize shortly after, and when children see that, it just get imprinted: this is how you are supposed to behave and interact with a woman. I think our Christian faith has also been a key driver as well; it's the basis for our value to "always treat others the way you would like to be treated." That's our worldview, and it got reinforced all around our children.

THE "AC" EQUATION:
ACTIONS ALWAYS HAVE CONSEQUENCES

Something I told them repeatedly is what I called my AC equation—

that actions have consequences. Quite frankly, this is something I wish I'd learned much earlier in life myself. I told my sons consistently, "Although you may have 100 percent control of your actions, you have zero percent control over the consequences. But because you are totally responsible for your actions, once you act, the logical consequences *will* occur, so you have to pay keen attention to those consequences, and choose your actions carefully."

As a result, I constantly impressed upon the boys that taking responsibility for their actions, meant thinking those actions out *in advance*—evaluating what might happen as a result of whatever action, or nonaction, you decide to take. You might be in a situation where you hadn't studied the way you needed to and therefore didn't get the grade you wanted to. Or you may be in a situation as serious as having casual sex and getting your girlfriend pregnant. The reality is that your actions will always have consequences, and you're *always* responsible for them. There's no "get out of jail free" card in life. But the good news is you have 100 percent control over your actions. Every single day, moment to moment, you make decisions that you have total and complete control over.

There's no "get out of jail free" card in life.

That is just the culture of our house. Our boys just grew up knowing they were responsible for themselves and their behavior, and whenever they did something irresponsible, they were going to feel the consequences. I made it clear: I was going to hold them accountable. I would support my sons as they went through the consequences, but they still had to live with them.

BE TRUTHFUL AND RESPECTFUL

There is an old saying that goes, "Sticks and stones may break your bones but words will never hurt you." Well, this is one of the biggest fallacies in the world, because most people aren't damaged by sticks and stones; they're damaged by the hurtful words of others. That's why we held our children absolutely accountable in terms of their language and how they treated each other, and we made a big deal out of what they said to each other. We *did* sweat the small stuff: everything mattered. We required truth and had no tolerance for lies. So there were very few times where lying was a problem.

I can think of only one instance in our sons' entire youth when they ever hit each other. We saw other parents just go, "Oh, boys will be boys. They'll work it out." But no. We jumped all over that stuff, and always held them accountable for their behavior. Small stuff leads to big stuff, so we handled it early.

TAKING RESPONSIBILITY AROUND SEXUAL ACTIVITY

I made a big deal out of accountability around sexual activity. First we focused them on the consequences of having casual sex—which could easily involve getting a girl pregnant or contracting some kind of STD. Secondly, we discussed what sex is actually about: if you are engaging in casual sex, you are really actually using another person for your own sexual pleasure, ignoring the impact on that person. You have a responsibility to yourself, but also to the other person. Each of them told me that this perspective made sense and resonated with them, and we held them accountable for upholding that perspective.

We discussed what sex is actually really about.

Now, this is not a conversation you start having with your kids when they are sixteen. It must begin when they are younger, and it's directly linked back to the story of the phone call.

It's important to note that a lot of these values were anchored in our faith, and were in sync with the values of the people we socialized with. To the best of our abilities we modeled these values for our kids, so the message ran consistent.

The most important thing we did was create an environment in which we and our children could talk about values and consequences, and that's how my work with the National Fatherhood Initiative actually began. I started going into schools and talking to teens about their healthy choices, and the effects of those choices, drawing on my own experiences growing up.

CHARACTER IS EVERYTHING

"Character is more easily kept than restored" is a quote I heard a few years ago from the movie *The Internationals,* and it really resonated with me. I always had this notion that I needed to help my boys *develop* good character from the outset, rather than try and *repair* poor character or lack of character somewhere down the road. As fathers, we have the opportunity right from the beginning to help our kids develop a certain kind of character, because once it is in place, it "is more easily kept than restored."

NATIONAL FATHERHOOD INITIATIVE IN AMERICA

Today, as president of National Fatherhood Initiative, a nonprofit organization dedicated to helping dads embrace the responsibility of fatherhood, I spend my whole day talking about fatherhood. Sometimes I go back and revisit my own life, its issues, challenges, and triumphs. I just knew that if my own sons were going to be different, they had to see something different from me, and that's why I do what I do. I try to help guys understand this:

I just knew that if my own sons were going to be different, they had to see something different.

> Your kids have to make sense of your presence and they have to make sense of your absence. As a father, you have to understand that you are modeling for your kids in your presence, and you're also modeling for them in your absence. When you are absent, kids tell themselves a story to make sense of it. Unfortunately, sometimes this story can lead children in a harmful direction.

FATHERING CAN START FROM FLAT ON YOUR BACK

We've all had moments when we've made a mistake, and we know it. This is called "being human," and it's a condition that afflicts our children as well. *How* we handle our missteps, not the missteps themselves, is what makes us great.

When we fall down as fathers (or as mothers), we must focus on the getting up rather than dwell on the falling down. For me, getting up meant taking responsibility as a man and as a dad. That's what I asked of myself, because that's what was required. It's the job we signed on for when we had children. It's the toughest job in the world, but also the most amazing, fulfilling, and rewarding.

I took responsibility by becoming fully involved and engaged with my sons, and by making them responsible and accountable. The joyous result: the wonderful young men they have grown into. When we do a good job, it impacts future generations. After all, our kids will parent the way we parent; they will love the way we love.

> *When we fall down, we must focus on the getting up rather than dwell on the falling down.*

"Anyone can be a father, but you have to be a daddy too."

The words of Susie Buffett to her husband, billionaire Warren Buffett, from *The Snowball.*

WHO IS ROLAND WARREN?

Roland with (wife) Yvette, (children) Jamin and Justin

For thousands of people whose lives he has touched, Roland Warren means *fatherhood.* As president of National Fatherhood Initiative (NFI), he has led it to its position as one of the nation's major providers of skill-building resources for fathers, providing them to community-based organizations, schools, prisons, hospitals, businesses, churches, and military bases.

NFI, founded in 1994, has a mission of "improving the well-being of children by increasing the proportion of children that are raised with involved, responsible, and committed fathers." It employs its "3-E," for educating all Americans, equipping fathers and organizations, and engaging every sector of society to accomplished its mission.

Warren is a graduate of Princeton University, with an M.B.A. from the Wharton School at the University of Pennsylvania. His business experience helped him direct an award-winning public education campaign that brought NFI more than $500 million in donated media. Warren has also built strategic partnerships with businesses, governmental bodies, and nonprofit organizations, and he often represents NFI in local and national media outlets. Warren is married to Dr. Yvette Lopez-Warren and has two sons: Jamin, a journalist and Harvard University graduate, and Justin, a graduate of the University of North Carolina, who recently completed a master's program at Indiana University of Pennsylvania.

www.fatherhood.org

Dear Reader,

So now you know these dads the way I do.

Gathering their wisdom has made a remarkable difference in my parenting. I hope you'll write and tell me that reading it has done the same for you.

I invite you to share your parenting wins by visiting www.IfIWereYourDaddy.com/share

... and we'll post a lot of your messages on the website.

Growth and change don't happen overnight; habits like to linger.

My wish for you is that you're as kind and loving with yourself as you are with your child. If *"each of us is always doing the best our current awareness permits,"* as dad Paul Scheele tells us, why not be gentle with yourself as you walk this path?

There are certainly plenty of ideas here to learn from, and I've heard it said that one needs to see something seven times before it's remembered.

In my vision I see you referring back to these pages, year to year, as your child develops and his or her needs and demands change. Sticky-note and flag the pages that speak to you, share your favorite ideas with a friend, and remember:

Raising a child to be the best he or she can be is a grand journey, not a destination.

With Love and Hugs,

Julia Espey

The Wisdom of the Dads
REFERENCE GUIDE

Many of the take-away thoughts and personal experiences from each chapter are outlined for reference and available on the website as a **FREE** resource for you. Use this guide when you're looking for ideas about a particular family challenge, or to facilitate your book club discussions.

Go to **www.IfIWereYourDaddy.com/guide**
to download and print the complete guide.

Keep it handy, perhaps folded and placed near the back of the book.
Here's a sampling:

T. Harv Eker, Entrepreneur & Best-Selling Author
CHAPTER 2 - "TRUSTING THE COMPASS WITHIN"

Teach a child to access and trust her inner guidance

Henry David Abraham, M.D., Harvard Psychiatrist & Co-Recipient Nobel Peace Prize
CHAPTER 7 - "THE UNIQUE YOU"

Discover a child's purpose, talents, and gifts in life

www.IfIWereYourDaddy.com/guide

PERMISSIONS

WHO IS JULIA ESPEY?

Author Julia Espey is many things: a rocket scientist (literally), a business executive, a classical painter whose masterpieces have a loyal following, and a researcher in the area of conscious parenting—parenting aimed toward enlightened child development and life preparation. Julia's calling to be an author and speaker arose not from her professional pursuits but from the very personal experience of finding herself as a single mom with a young son. As he grew into a little boy, Julia was struck with the realization that she had to be both a mother and father to him—and she had no idea how to be a father!

So Julia turned to what she knew best from her years as a NASA researcher—research. She began asking dads to share their parenting wisdom. Her burning question for each of them was "What's the most important lesson—mind-set, idea, or value—that you taught your children?" This book comprises the answers she got from thirty-five highly successful men—committed fathers all.

Julia graduated from Georgia Tech in 1989 with honors in aerospace engineering. She spent the next decade working as a NASA flight test engineer, and contributed to the development of advanced space transportation. In 1995, she took early retirement from NASA and traveled the world, living in Bermuda for a time and eventually settling in New York City. There, Julia discovered that her right-brain gifts equaled those of her left, and she began devoting her energies to studying fine art full-time. Within seven years, she'd established herself as a serious classical painter with works that have been sold in prominent galleries and are on collectors' walls nationwide.

In 2004, Julia joined Arbonne International, an international health and wellness company, becoming a vice president after only eight months. In her first two years with the company, she built and trained a national sales organization with thousands of independent consultants and net yearly sales of over $1.5 million.

Now living in Minneapolis, Minnesota, Julia has remarried and is raising her son with husband, Lance. She is currently at work on the next book in the "If I Were Your™..." series, *If I Were Your Mommy, This Is What You'd Learn*, featuring successful women reflecting on their most impactful mothering moments and practices. Its release is slated for 2012.

www.juliaespey.com

WHO IS JACK CANFIELD?

As the beloved originator of the *Chicken Soup for the Soul®* series—with more than 125 million books sold worldwide—Jack Canfield is uniquely qualified to talk about success. His proven formula for achieving goals received global acclaim with his most recent national best seller, *The Success Principles™: How to Get from Where You Are to Where You Want to Be.*

Behind the empire *Time* magazine called the "publishing phenomenon of the decade," Jack is America's leading expert in creating peak performance for entrepreneurs, corporate leaders, managers, sales professionals, corporate employees, and educators. Over the last thirty years, Jack's compelling message, empowering energy, and personable coaching style have helped hundreds of thousands of individuals achieve their dreams.

Jack is the founder and chairman of the Canfield Training Group in Santa Barbara, California, which trains entrepreneurs, educators, corporate leaders, and motivated individuals how to accelerate the achievement of their personal and professional goals. He is also the founder of the Foundation for Self-Esteem, which provides self-esteem resources and trainings to social workers, welfare recipients, and human resource professionals. He wrote and produced the Goals Program, a video training program for California welfare recipients. To date, the program has helped 450,000 people get off welfare.

Jack has earned a bachelor's degree from Harvard and a master's degree in psychological education from the University of Massachusetts, and has received several honorary doctorates.

Jack holds the *Guinness Book* world record for having seven books simultaneously on the *New York Times* best-seller list. He also holds the *Guinness Book* world record for the largest book-signing ever—for *Chicken Soup for the Kid's Soul.* And he's the only author to have won both the ABBY (American Booksellers Book of the Year) Award and the Southern California Book Publicist Award in the same year—honoring him as both an outstanding writer and a consummate book marketer.

Jack has been a featured guest on more than a thousand radio and television programs worldwide, including *Oprah, Montel, Larry King Live, 20/20, Inside Edition, The Today Show, Fox and Friends,* and many others.

www.jackcanfield.com

IF I WERE YOUR DADDY

One of the greatest things about parenting in the twenty-first century is that you don't have to do it alone! Author Julia Espey collected some FREE resources from the dads that we have made available online. There's something for everyone to make parenting easier, all the ages and stages, so check it out:

Visit www.IfIWereYourDaddy.com/resources
to download these **FREE** resources.

5 Things Great Dads NEVER Do:

A video series. "... profound but simple. They've changed my parenting already!"
Jerry Conti, California

3 ESSENTIAL Things Moms Must Learn from Great Dads.

"Thanks for this eye-opener! I sent it to all my mommy friends."
Janet Little, New York City

GREAT Parenting Made Easy the *"If I Were Your Daddy"* Way

Your 365 day guide!

End struggles, get cooperation, teach kids about money ... practical tips delivered once a day.

RESOURCES

Access to Our Parenting Blog (GiftED Iam)

featuring a column from **Julia Espey** every issue. Be part of our community of like-minded parents and get your questions answered.

AND MORE …

Step-by-step ADHD survival guide: How Dr. Roy Martina handled ADHD SUCCESSFULLY with his son without medication!

E-book on creating positive beliefs in your children

10 biggest attitude changes I had while writing *"If I Were Your Daddy."* (Julia Reveals All!)

Teaching abundance to your kids in 6 easy steps (money, happiness, and health)

Visit www.IfIWereYourDaddy.com/resources
for these **FREE** gifts.

SPECIAL GIFT OFFER

When you gift this book to TWO others, we'll do this for you:

1. Send you an **immediate Thank-You Gift**—an exclusive audio interview and transcript from a self-made multimillionaire dad, Dr. John DeMartini, who overcame a severe learning disability to become physically, emotionally, and financially successful. He'll tell you EXACTLY how to equip your child to be financially smart, by disclosing exactly how his dad taught him this priceless lesson.

2. Enter you into the "**Family Angel Rewards Club**," where we give you first-chance opportunities, such as never-before-heard interviews, monthly chats with the dads and author Julia Espey, discounts on future purchases online, and exclusive reports on parenting issues … for an entire year!

How to claim your thank-you gifts: Using the honor system, register online, or mail us your *name, e-mail address,* and *address.* And then tell us *the names* of the two other people whose lives you've touched by gifting them this book.

Register Online:
www.IfIWereYourDaddy.com/familyangelclub

Or, by Mail:
Family Angel Rewards Club
P.O. Box 793, Lithia, FL 33547

*Consider that parents everywhere need our full support.
This book is the gift that doesn't get eaten up,
or left hanging in the back of a closet.*

For bulk orders of 10 or more, see our discount guide at
www.IfIWereYourDaddy.com/bulkpricing